Notes on
Spiritual Discourses
of Shrī Ātmānanda

Notes on Spiritual Discourses of Shrī Ātmānanda

TAKEN BY NITYA TṚIPTA

Volume 3 of 3

Notes 1122 to 1451

NON-DUALITY PRESS
& STILLNESS SPEAKS

2nd edition published December 2009 by NON-DUALITY PRESS
& STILLNESS SPEAKS

Non-Duality Press | PO Box 2228 | Salisbury | SP2 2GZ
United Kingdom

www.non-dualitypress.com
www.stillnessspeaks.com

ISBN: 978-0-9563091-4-3

CONTENTS
(of all 3 volumes)

Notes on discourses

3rd February 1956

1122. WHAT HAPPENS TO THE EGO AFTER VISUALIZATION?

Even on the first visualizing of the Truth, one is liberated. But the ego seems to function even after that. Yes, Truth was visualized in spite of all adverse samskāras. Therefore, now, with the additional strength and light of the Truth, you have to face the samskāras and subdue them.

This is done easily by clinging on to the Truth and repeating the experience of visualization, as often as possible. The mind, having relinquished all adherence to the ego, turns to Ātmā as its only support; the ego also, like a slave or a shadow, follows the foot-steps of the mind and continues to function as a mere pointer to the Ātmā.

1123. WHY DOES THE SAGE COME DOWN FROM THE ULTIMATE LEVEL TO THE LOWER ONE AND ACT ACCORDING TO THE LAWS AND CONVENTIONS OF THIS WORLD?

1. The question assumes that the Sage is a person. No. The Sage is impersonal, and as such can never act.
2. The ego is the product of time, space and causality, and these laws have been created solely for its traffic with the outside world. Therefore, as far as phenomenal activities are concerned, these laws are all quite in order. But concerning anything in the beyond, or concerning the world as a whole, these laws cannot apply. Therefore the question is illogical.
3. Swami Vivēkānanda answers this question this way: 'Illusion cannot arise except from illusion.' But this answer is not convincing at all levels. So a clearer answer is given below. This very same question was raised and answered also in the Upaniṣhads.

    jñānēnā 'jñāna-kāryasya samūlasya layō yadi
    kathaṁ tiṣṭhaty ayaṁ dēha iti śaṅkāvatō jaḍān
    *samādhātuṁ bāhya-dṛṣṭyā prārabdhaṁ vadati śrutiḥ

*ajñānijanakāryārthaṁ prārabdhaṁ vadati śrutiḥ
na tu dēhasya satyatva bōdhanāya vipaś citāṁ

[* marks alternative versions of the third line.]

Shrī Shankara, Viveka-cūḍāmaṇi, 462-3

It means: If the fire of knowledge has destroyed everything, how does the body of the Sage continue? The vast majority of people cannot understand the Sage in the true light. The question has arisen from the ignorant man's standpoint, attributing reality to objects perceived; and it boils down to time, space and causality. To satisfy such dull intellects in the gross plane, the shāstras put forward the argument of 'prārabdha' [remaining samskāras continuing to unfold, at the level of personality]. But it was never intended to establish the reality of the body. The apparent body of the Sage forms part of the world which he has transcended long ago.

1124. HOW TO DISPOSE OF SAMSKĀRAS AFTER VISUALIZATION?

The Truth has been visualized. But by that alone, you are not always cognizant of the Reality. When you are swayed by the former samskāras of your life, you forget the Truth. Then you can either look deep and destroy the world as nothing but consciousness or, conceding the existence of the world, you may know that you are its witness and unaffected by the witnessed. A time will come when the inner eye will be ever clear, showing you in your real nature even while engaged in activities.

1125. WHAT IS REASON AND HOW DOES IT WORK?

Reason is of two kinds: the lower and the higher.

Lower reason (mind) is a negative instrument. Its findings are sometimes negative and sometimes positive. The negative findings may be helpful in disproving the reality of the apparent world, and in bringing one nearer the Truth. But the positive discoveries of the lower reason emphasize duality and have always been an impediment in the progress towards Truth. It is too objective and speculative.

Higher reason is a positive instrument and its positive discoveries, being based upon the one real being within, are always true and changeless. When we say the higher reason 'destroys', it only means that it clearly exposes the falsity of appearance. Our samskāras themselves, when they become more sāttvic, begin to notice and question the vagaries of the lower reason.

It is then that the presence of a higher faculty becomes necessary, in order to enquire and come to an ultimate decision. The higher reason comes in to answer this urge. But at last, this higher reason turns out to be the Truth itself, which stands established as the permanent background.

15th February 1956

1126. HOW DID LOGIC COME TO BE INCORPORATED INTO VĒDĀNTA?

In very ancient days, the Upaniṣhads were the spoken words of universally accepted Sages. They were clear statements, most of them bold assertions regarding the ultimate Truth, as experienced by each of them.

In course of time, the blind and implicit faith of people disappeared; and different schools sprang up, questioning the assertions of Vēdānta, in the light of reason. It was then that Vēdānta began to use that supra-intellectual organon, called 'higher reason', to answer such questions and to establish the position of Vēdānta. This weapon is also logic, but of a purely sublime nature, making reference only to one's own real being.

24th February 1956

1127. HOW IS TRUTH RELATED TO THE WORLD?

Truth is the text; and the world, senses and mind are the commentaries thereof.

The commentaries always point to the Truth, which is only one, crisp and pointed. But the commentaries are laborious and voluminous, and they approach the Truth from different standpoints. Yet they prove the Truth, each in its own way.

25th February 1956

1128. WHAT AM I?

Am I the body, senses or mind? No. If I claim to be anything, that must be with me wherever I go. Doing, perceiving, thinking and feeling do not go with me wherever I go.

'Knowing' alone is always with me. So I am knowingness or Consciousness alone. I am that always, and I am free. I can only be that which remains over, when the object or active part is separated from the perceiver, perception or percept.

4th March 1956

1129. LIFE'S EXPERIENCES – AN ANALYSIS

Life's experiences as a whole can be easily classified into two major groups: (1) activity, and (2) absence of activity. The former comprehends the whole of waking and dream state experiences and the latter comprehends deep sleep experience alone. The former is surcharged with activity and the latter is one's own real nature. The former is activity and the latter is the Reality.

Then a legitimate question might naturally come up: 'Why then does this activity come in?'

Here, activity is used in the generic sense. But the question is itself a particular activity and, as such, it is not competent to question the inactivity, which is generic. An activity cannot exist divested of consciousness. Therefore activity is nothing but Consciousness. Thus, when minutely examined, even the question – as an activity – stands revealed as the Truth itself.

Therefore, activity as such has never been, and Consciousness was always shining in its *own* glory.

6th March 1956

1130. WHAT IS MY POSITION IN RELATION TO KNOWLEDGE?

I have two positions in relation to knowledge:

1. As pure knowledge, and
2. As the knowing knowledge or knower.

The knower is not affected by the known. The knower, divested of the known, is knowledge pure.

> prapañcam ēva durbōdhaṁ manyē tasyā 'nirūpaṇāt
> subōdhaṁ brahma satyatvād ātmatvāt svaprakāśanāt

Viṣhṇu-purāṇa [unverified]

28th March 1956

1131. IF CONSCIOUSNESS IS BEYOND OPPOSITES HOW CAN IT BE KNOWN?

How do you know the opposites? Certainly not through the opposites themselves. Can that principle which knows opposites have any opposite? *No*. That is Consciousness, pure.

Consciousness or Happiness is that which never ceases to be. Opposites are always limited by time, and so cease to be. Therefore Consciousness or Happiness is beyond all opposites.

The teacher and the disciple both stand depersonalized when the Truth is expounded by the teacher and understood by the disciple. When you say 'he talked', you emphasize the talking and miss the Truth. So also, when you say you understood, you emphasize the understanding and it becomes mental.

1132. Mr. P.B. asked: WHEN AM I REALLY LIVING?

Answer: I really live only during those moments when I identify myself with the ultimate Truth. At other moments, I was simply living dead.

1133. (P.B. again) WHEN DOES ONE VISUALIZE THE TRUTH?

Answer: When the when is not.

29th March 1956

1134. WHAT HAPPENS IN SAMĀDHI AND HOW TO DIRECT IT TO THE ULTIMATE TRUTH?

In seeking samādhi, you are trying to see the Truth through the absence of all activities, because you do not see the Truth during the activities. But Truth (your *svarūpa*) is not to be found in either the presence or the absence of activities which constitute the mental realm. Therefore, you must go beyond both, to get at the Truth.

The world ties you down by its presence here. The world ties you down by its absence or non-existence in samādhi. You must transcend both, in order to reach the Truth. It is beyond both activity and passivity. It is knowledge knowing everything and knowledge not knowing anything, at the same time. It is simultaneously active and passive; that is, you must transcend both to come to Truth.

You desire samādhi only for the happiness you suppose you derive from it, just as you desire an object for the pleasure you hope to derive from it. *Māṇḍūkya-kārikā* advises you to take away the desire from both and you will be in your own centre. But it does not suggest how that desire can be taken away. It can only be done by knowing that the happiness experienced in either case is not the outcome of either the samādhi or the object, but that it is your own real nature and therefore intrinsic in you.

All effort to achieve one's own real nature is meaningless; because it stands already achieved. So the desire for the fruit vanishes, and you stand in the Reality.

1135. WHY DOES THE GURU TEACH AND WHAT?

Because the disciples earnestly and sincerely ask questions. But when the Truth is being imparted, the Guru stands as Truth beyond the talk; and the disciple is also pulled up, in spite of him. The disciple may begin by listening to the talk, but he is soon taken beyond the talk. The talk is not itself the Reality, but the Reality is in the talk and is the goal of the talk.

The personal is taken up by the impersonal for discussion, and the language of the personal acts as the medium. But the personal –

including the medium – is given up, when the background is visualized.

The question presupposes that the disciple is imperfect and that the teacher is perfect. The teacher shows the disciple that he too is perfect, and there the teaching ends.

1136. WHAT IS THE JNYĀNA PATH TO TRUTH?

It consists of both the traditional path and the direct path. According to the traditional path, a jnyāna sādhaka, directed by a Jnyānin (*Kāraṇa-guru*), has to pass through four definite stages in regular order:

1. 'To know it.' — From the lips of the Guru.
2. 'To enjoy it',
3. 'To become it', and
4. 'To be it'.

By dint of personal effort.

This method is built upon the samskāra of duality, so that the teaching lasts even after 'being it.' This trace of duality has yet to be transcended, in order to get to the ultimate Truth.

But according to the direct path to the Truth, non-duality is emphasized at the very start, proving that there is nothing other than knowledge. The samskāra of duality immediately disappears. Thus, 'to know it' is 'to be it'; and so there is, practically, only one step to the ultimate Truth.

1137. WHAT IS LIBERATION TO A DEVOTEE?

According to the path of devotion to a personal God, there are four stages to liberation (*mukti*), in a regular order of progression.

1. *Sālōkya* (being in the same world as the deity),
2. *Sāmīpya* (being in close proximity with the deity),
3. *Sārūpya* (being of the same form and features as the deity),
4. *Sāyujya* (getting merged in the deity itself).

From the standpoint of Truth, the personal God – as well as the state of *sāyujya* – are only concepts of the devotee's mind. In *sāyujya*, that mind merges in its own concept. It is impossible for the individual mind to come out of that state at will; because the mind, being merged, is deprived of all initiative. Therefore, the state is more or less a well earned and indefinite rest, without any specific experience of misery. Even this state, in the relative realm, has its natural termination; and the devotee is inevitably born again as a man.

1138. WHAT IS THE SIGNIFICANCE OF THE THREE STATES?

1. *The waking state* represents diversity in all its nakedness. 'Realistic' (or materialistic) philosophy is based upon the apparent reality of this state.
2. *The dream state* (mental state) shows that it is all the manyness of the one. The idealistic philosophers base their philosophy upon the relatively greater reality of the mind, as compared with sense objects.
3. *The deep sleep state:* Truth alone is absolute non-duality. Vēdāntins depend upon the experience of deep sleep to expound ultimate Truth, the real nature of Man.

1139. WHAT IS THE REAL SĀDHANA?

The only sādhana that the higher jnyāna shāstras ask the earnest aspirant to undertake is: 'Listen, listen, listen, to the words of the Guru; and contemplate nothing.' This can also be: 'Say to yourself over and over again what the Guru has told you regarding the Truth, the arguments used, etc.' It is as good as listening to the Guru himself, over again.

1140. WHY DO ASPIRANTS ADOPT SUCH A VARIETY OF PATHS, ALL CALLED 'SPIRITUAL'?

It is only very few, among such practitioners, who earnestly desire ultimate liberation. Those few never fail to obtain a *Kāraṇa-guru*, at some stage of their spiritual search; and then they realize the Truth without any further difficulty.

The great majority desire the enjoyment of pleasures, according to their own tastes and temperaments. The most important among them are the *bhaktas*, *mystics*, *idealists*, *nihilists*, etc. They emphasize only certain aspects of the Reality and ignore the other aspects. Therefore, they experience only limited happiness, in varying degrees.

Bhaktas emphasize the *ānanda* aspect, subordinating existence and reason. *Mystics* emphasize the *sat* and *ānanda* aspects, subordinating reason. *Idealists* emphasis only the lower reason or intelligence, subordinating *sat* and *ānanda.* The *nihilists* (kṣhaṇika-vijnyāna-vādis) – standing as idealists and using intellect alone – go a bit further, but get stranded in nothingness or 'shūnya'.

But *jnyānins* – adopting *cit* as the higher reason, without subordinating either *sat* or *ānanda* – prove that *sat* and *ānanda* in their true nature are *cit* itself. The jnyānins thereby stand established in the ultimate Truth.

1141. FALLACY OF THE DEFINITION OF 'TIME' AS THE PLURALITY OF EXPERIENCES.

Question: Some Philosophers have tried to define time as the 'plurality of experiences, each complete in itself'. Can this be accepted?

Answer: No. There is a confusion of thought here. The word plurality itself presupposes time. So the definition begs the question itself.

14th July 1956

1142. WHAT IS REALIZATION?

Seeing things in the right perspective.

And how to achieve it?

Know yourself first.

15th July 1956

1143. WHAT IS THE SECRET OF RITES TO THE DEPARTED?

From the ultimate standpoint, the problem does not arise. At that level, there is neither the departed, nor any rites for them.

But on the phenomenal or dual level, there is relative significance and relative truth in such rites. The dual plane is dominated by the mind. The mind, by its very nature, cannot exist without a support, gross or subtle. Therefore, it is believed that the mind, immediately it leaves one body, takes possession of another.

Thus the yōgin's mind, by dint of exercise, takes possession of the body set as his ideal in meditation. The jnyāna-yōgin's mind does not take possession of a body as the ordinary yōgin does, but is merged and lost in the ātmic principle or the ultimate Truth.

The departed spirit or '*pitṛi*', as it is called in Hindu religion, is only a thought-form of the departed soul, possessed of all the samskāras it had when it was alive. The purpose of all rites and ceremonials directed to the *pitṛis* is only to destroy those samskāras and set the *pitṛi* relatively free. This can be done in two ways.

The first and the highest is to know by the knowledge of the ultimate Truth that the very concept of the '*pitṛi*' is an illusion. Thus, if the son of the departed one is a jīvan-mukta, his very thought and the strength of his conviction – that he is the ultimate Truth – relieves the thought-form called '*pitṛi*' of all the bondage of its samskāras.

The next process is the performance of elaborate ceremonials, like *Tila-havana*, by which one convinces oneself that the *pitṛis* have been amply propitiated, as enjoined by the shāstras [scriptures]. An intellectual satisfaction arises out of this conviction, which gives one some peace of mind. This method is the one adopted by the very great majority.

19th July 1956

1144. SOME STATEMENTS OF FERRIER AND SOCRATES EXAMINED

Ferrier, the French philosopher, has said: 'Apprehension of the perception of matter is the subject of metaphysics.' But I say: 'It is not the subject, but only the beginning of metaphysics.'

Socrates says: 'Don't go after the "beautiful", but go after "beauty", and you shall be free.' Higher religion also says: 'Don't be satisfied with being virtuous, but be virtue itself.' The statements are right, but how to achieve the goal is the problem. Both are silent on that point. The statements demand a separation of the material parts or appendages from the beautiful or virtuous. This is never possible unless one has transcended the mental plane oneself. Therefore the statements are not of much practical help to an aspirant and do not enable him to visualize the Truth. But after visualizing it with the help of the Guru, one may make use of these statements to get established in the Ultimate.

Divested of their material parts or appendages, beauty and virtue no longer stand separate, but stand as that which was the common background of both the beautiful and the virtuous.

1145. Efficacy of moral laws

All codes of ethics and morality, if strictly followed, make you come nearer to the Truth. All such laws demand, to some extent, the sacrifice of lower self. The ultimate goal of all such laws is certainly selflessness. But unfortunately, ethics and morality – being objective in the strict sense – cannot take one to absolute selflessness.

Absolute selflessness is Truth itself, the ultimate subject. It can be visualized only with the help of a Kāraṇa-guru. All thoughts of striving for and recognizing selflessness are in the mental realm. Pure selflessness dawns only when one transcends the mind and stands as Ātmā, the real Self.

1146. Why the siddhis or powers?

They are quite illusory, in relation to the ultimate Truth.

Truth is Truth, at all times and under all conditions and in all states. That which leads you to the Truth should also have some of its characteristics, such as permanence and self-luminosity.

Siddhis, acquired by dint of exercise, do not last for more than a limited number of years (usually twelve years). Even when one professes to possess them, one does so only in the waking state, which is only one third of one's whole life. One does not possess any of the siddhis in one's dream and deep sleep states. Therefore siddhis are impermanent, and depend upon the body and mind for their very existence – even during the limited time they seem to exist.

It is the exhibition of such siddhis (called miracles) that are often cited to prove the spiritual greatness of even founders of religions. Such and much greater and deeper siddhis are possessed, and sometimes exhibited, even by the commonplace yōgins of India. But such yōgins and their siddhis are shunned and detested by all Sages and all real aspirants to Truth. All men of real experience and all the higher shāstras, directing attention to the ultimate Truth, have declared unequivocally that siddhis or powers are the greatest obstacle to realization of Truth. Therefore avoid siddhis at all cost, if you aspire to the Truth.

vịta-saṁsargavat siddha-saṁsargaṁ mōha-varddhakam …

[Source of quotation uncertain]

Sages also possess infinite siddhis even without their knowing it; not as a result of exercise, but as a result of the knowledge of the ultimate Truth. But they use these powers with the greatest restraint; nor do their powers ever fade away from them like the yōgin's siddhis, by lapse of time or by constant use (even if they do so).

1147. EXAMINATION OF AN OBJECT BY THE SCIENTIST AND THE VĒDĀNTIN

A scientist examines an object to find out its material composition alone, and that too only in the waking state. His process is objective and involves the purely physical or mental effort.

But the vēdāntin examines an object to find out its svarūpa – that which does not change throughout all the three states which constitute the totality of man's experience. Here, dream has to be conceived in a sense more comprehensive than usual. Whatever is purely mental, or everything that is past, may be said to belong to the dream state. Evidently, the states are created in order to enable man to examine a thing subjectively or objectively, in the right perspective, and to discover the Truth behind it. The states are thus the key to the Reality, as expounded by Vēdānta.

A so called gross object is constituted of Consciousness, thought-form and grossness. Of these, the grossness disappears when the enquirer gives up the waking state; the thought-form disappears when he gives up the dream state (mental state); and in the deep sleep state, Consciousness alone remains over. But Consciousness was present in the other two states as well. Therefore, viewed from that standpoint, Consciousness is the substance of every object.

1148. WHAT IS THE GOAL OF EVERY QUESTION?

The usual question asked is: 'What is the truth of this object?' What is sought is the 'Truth', which can never be bound by any object. Truth being imperceptible to the senses, the perceptible object is made use of, to find the ultimate Truth.

The process adopted [in the direct method] is an attempt to eliminate the material parts from the particular object. When they are thus separated, the Truth – which was the background of all that was separated – shines by itself, being self-luminous.

Therefore, whether you search for Truth through the individual subject or through a particular object, it is the ultimate Truth that is experienced as the result. It is the right perspective alone that has to be obtained from a Kāraṇa-guru.

1149. CAUSALITY IS A MISNOMER

The thief comes in surreptitiously, whenever you ask a question applying the principle of causal relationship.

Causality is the product of the waking state. Nay, it is the waking state itself. It can never be successfully answered from the waking state, where alone the law of causality obtains. To answer the question, one must get beyond the waking state, to the dream or mental state. Then causality and the question both disappear, as mere illusion. One who raises such a question is pinned to the waking state.

It may pertinently be asked, is there not causality in the dream state? *No*. Certainly not. Because, what we call the dream state is a full-fledged waking state when it is experienced, and it is called a dream state only when it is past. Then causality, which appeared quite reasonable when the so called dream was in progress, becomes unreal. This amounts to admitting that causality is not real in the dream state.

There is no connection between objects themselves in the waking state. Causality is only an object, just like any other object; and the senses also are only objects, just like others. Therefore you cannot establish causal relationship, between any two objects of the waking state.

27th July 1956

1150. LIFE AND DEATH

Man is afraid of death. Who says this? Is it life? Or is it death?

Certainly death cannot say this. Because it is lifeless. Then will life say so? *No*. Because life can never be out of life, and so it can never comprehend death. Then can it be the dead inert matter (body) that says so? *No*. Because it is already dead, and it cannot speak.

There is none else present to say so. Therefore either it has never been said, or it can never be seriously said, by anyone. Hence death is not, or death is a myth.

1151. HOW IS THE DREAM STATE NEARER THE TRUTH THAN THE WAKING STATE?

The waking subject holds that sense perception is the highest test of Truth. From this position, it denounces dream objects as unreal, as they are not perceptible to the waking physical senses.

In the waking state – dominated as it is by the triad or tripuṭī – the perceiver, perception and the percept are so clearly distinct and separate that it is very difficult to find anything common between them.

But as far as the dream state is concerned, there is a great difference. As soon as the dream is past, one can see clearly that the subject and the object series – appearing in that state – are both creations of the same mind, and therefore one in essence. So there is this much of non-duality in dream. To that extent, the dream is nearer the Truth.

Therefore, the clear diversity of the waking state is first examined from the lesser diversity of the dream state, and the waking state is found to be nothing other than an idea.

28th July 1956

1152. (Miss T. asked) FROM WHAT STANDPOINT AND HOW AM I TO EXAMINE AN OBJECT?

Answer: For the time being, take it that you do it from the waking state. But you have heard the Truth from the Guru and know that you are not the body, senses or mind.

Examining gross objects from the waking state, you find, first of all, that objects are nothing but percepts. You can only compare the qualities of one object with those of another in the same state, or at the most refer to causality which is only another object obtaining in the waking state. This sort of comparison does not give you any satisfactory solution, about the Truth of percepts.

Thus puzzled by your vain efforts, you begin to think deeply about it. Immediately, but unknowingly, you change your own stand and become a psychological being (in the dream state). Sensual objects vanish; and so you find that gross objects, as such, are unreal. But instead, you find that the thought-forms or ideas are the Truth of all that you perceive.

This also does not satisfy you for long; because ideas also seem impermanent, as they keep on appearing and disappearing. Therefore you begin to examine ideas, in their turn. The moment you take to this, you again unknowingly change your stand to the deep sleep state, represented by awareness as the higher reason. Examining ideas accordingly, you find that they cannot exist without Consciousness and so are Consciousness itself, which is your real nature. Therefore every object is nothing but consciousness.

Causality as a law has the advantage of taking you from diversity to unity, but not beyond. Even that unity still remains only as an expanded object, and so it does not take you beyond the waking state. Causality depends upon precedence and succession, for its very existence. In other words, time is the parent of causality. But on closer examination, we find that time depends upon thought for its existence and thought depends upon time for its existence. Therefore they cancel out each other, and so time is not. Therefore causality is also not.

An honest examination of the Truth of any object is possible only when you take that object as representative of the state to which it belongs; and then you stand as the witness of that state.

The mind is the witness of gross objects. Therefore, you have to examine every gross object from the mental (dream) state. Then the grossness of the object (space-element) vanishes; and it appears as nothing more than an idea (thought-form), having existence only when the idea appears. It is a generalization of this experience that is expressed as the law that '*Objects do not exist when not known.*' This fact is the beginning of the vēdāntic perspective (viṣayaṅṅaḷkkˇ ajñāta sattayilla).

This is only a partial Truth. The idea has again to be examined from the still higher plane of Consciousness (deep sleep). Then you find that the object or the idea does not exist as such, even when known; but it is only pure Consciousness, through all the three states. This is the ultimate Truth, according to Advaita.

30th July 1956

1153. WHAT IS LIBERATION AND BONDAGE?

The certitude that you are that changeless, self-luminous principle is *liberation*; and the conviction that you are bound is *bondage*. It comes in accordance with the general saying that you become what you deeply think yourself to be.

> bhaviccapōlē bhaviccituṁ nirṇṇayaṁ
> [It's as one thinks that one becomes, essentially.]
>
> *Eṟuttacchan.*

The moment you hear the Truth from the lips of the Guru, you transcend your body, senses and mind, and visualize the ultimate Truth, your real nature. Nevertheless, you find yourself again at the feet of the physical Guru, the embodiment of ultimate Truth. But your lower samskāras return, and seem to possess you.

Since you had been instructed in the direct perception method, your realization of the Truth – on your first listening to the words of the Guru – was complete. Neither *asambhāvana* [incomprehension, sense of nothingness] nor *viparīta-bhāvana* [misconception, sense of difference] can haunt you ever again. Whenever your old samskāras of body, senses and mind seem to take possession of you, you have only to take a deep thought of your real nature as already visualized by you, in the light of the arguments then advanced or fresh arguments as they occur to you.

When you have done this over and over again, the old samskāras of the lower self will become emaciated and die. It is then that you may be said to have established yourself in your real nature; and the shadow of your old samskāras, if at all they appear, will do so only in obedience to your sweet pleasure.

1154. WHAT IS THE BEST WAY TO GET ESTABLISHED?

The best and the easiest method to attain that glorious goal of establishment in the Truth is to listen to the Guru over and over again.

But if such frequent personal contact with the Guru is not possible, the next best alternative is to take, as often as possible, a deep thought of the Truth as first visualized in the presence of the Guru. This brings you into the climate of the Truth every time, and you experience it afresh.

When the samskāras of your real nature become strong enough to subdue the old ones by their very presence, you have no further sādhana to do. Desires can no more tempt you away from the Truth, and questions can no more disturb you. Because you always rest all alone in your own glory; and even when your body, senses and mind are functioning, you know (without knowing) in your heart of hearts that your real centre is never shaken.

You can face the death of the body with as much ease and complacency as you used to witness a pleasant ceremony in life. You may give vent to your feelings and emotions as vehemently as any ignorant lady; but you will be able to stop your feelings surprisingly suddenly and engage yourself equally naturally in any other activity of life, like an adept actor on the stage. If ever your attention is drawn to your real nature – by any word or hint from the outside – the activities of the body, senses and mind all vanish like a dream, and you remain in Peace at the inmost core of your being.

1st August 1956

1155. WHO?

The question 'who' is the samskāra of the waking state. When closely examined, we find no 'who' even in the waking state perceptions. Examine the tripuṭī [the triad of doer, doing and deed, or knower, knowing and known].

> jñēya vastukkaḷ vērpeṭṭāl jñānam onna vaśiṣṭamāṁ,
> jñātṛ svarūpam atu tān; śūnyam allatorikkaluṁ
>
> [If objects that are to be known
> are clearly separated out,
> one knowing consciousness remains.
> That is the knower, in its own
> true nature, as it always is.
> It never can be emptiness.]

Bhāṣha Pancadashi, Pancakōsha-vivēka, 23
(Malayalam translation)

There is no agent 'who', behind the tripuṭī. The knower is knowledge itself. So activities go on without an agent. The agent comes in after the incident, as an impostor.

> ninav ill onnu ceyyuṁbōḷ
> tan ceyyunn enn oruttanuṁ
> vyaktam āṇ atināluṁ tān
> karttāv all enna vāstavaṁ
>
> At the time a thing is being done, there is no thought or feeling that one is doing it. This is further proof that one is not a doer.

Ātma-darshan, 9.4

It is admitted that there is seeing and that there is an object, but not a separate see-er. Nobody experiences a see-er, at any point of time. In this prakriyā, only duality is taken into account and not the triad. It is the impersonal principle in the seeing (Consciousness) that examines the object.

It is .... mind ....seeing.
It is .... principle consciousness ....mind.

Therefore it is the same impersonal principle that knows your body, senses and mind. The personal principle is not present in any activity.

The ego is a child born of no mother. The ego is a bachelor who dreams that he married the body and senses. You are always groaning under his weight.

2nd August 1956

1156. WAKING AND DREAM STATES DISTINGUISHED

When you perceive an object outside, you are in the waking state. When you find that your perception had been a dream, you have come out of that state. Thus when you see that grossness is a dream, you get out of the waking state.

1157. INDIVIDUALITY

Individuality is the impersonal principle, standing as the background of the changing body, senses and mind and also lighting them up.

But this word is grossly misunderstood and misapplied. It cannot be denied that individuality is changeless. A changing personality can never be the changeless individuality.

The urge for individuality comes from deep below. It comes from the changeless Ātmā behind. Ātmā is the only changeless reality; and individuality, if you want to use the term, is Ātmā itself.

3rd August 1956

1158. FROM DARKNESS TO LIGHT

There is no perception either in deep ignorance or in pure Consciousness, either in darkness or in dazzling light. In dim light alone, objects seem to appear. But do you really perceive the object? *No.*

1159. CONSCIOUSNESS ALONE, PERCEIVED OBJECTIVELY AS WELL AS SUBJECTIVELY

1. Light by itself is not perceptible to the naked eye. You perceive light only when it is temporarily obstructed by an object. This perception of light you wrongly call the object. This is a phe-

nomenon usually misunderstood; and the fallacy is, on the face of it, obvious.

Similarly, pure Consciousness is not perceivable, as is evident in deep sleep. But when it is confined or limited to a particular object, it seems to become perceptible. Even then, it is not the object but it is Consciousness alone that is perceived. Therefore, nobody has ever seen or perceived an object, but only light or Consciousness.

2. Take hold of an object. You find the object cannot appear without the help of Consciousness. Take hold of Consciousness that is in the object. This is possible only with the help of a Guru. Then you reach pure Consciousness objectively. Take hold of Consciousness in the senses or mind in the same manner and you reach pure Consciousness, your real nature, subjectively. Both being one, you stand in *advaita*.

If you achieve that degree of identification with the light of knowledge as you had with body in the waking state, there is nothing more to be achieved. Then the impersonal becomes stronger than the personal. The sādhaka [aspirant] who stands as the personal does the sādhana [spiritual work] of acting the part of the impersonal.

'*I know I am.*' In this, the 'am'-ness does not belong either to the senses or to the mind. This is intrinsic. This is the nature of self-luminosity.

7th August 1956

1160. MENTAL RECOGNITION OF TRUTH

The ordinary aspirant naturally desires to visualize and stand established in the ultimate Truth, and also to know and feel that he does so. But when he visualizes the Truth, he understands that it is never possible to know or feel it.

It will take time for the samskāra of that desire to leave him completely. Therefore, every time that samskāra comes up, he has only to direct his attention to the Truth visualized and the samskāra will vanish for the time being. When this is repeated, the samskāra will die a natural death.

If you say that you stand established in the Truth, you are wrong. It is also wrong to say that you have not established yourself in Truth. In either case it is mental recognition that is sought. Truth can never be recognized by the mind.

In the course of a discourse with Paṇḍit Panniśśēri Nāṇu Piḷḷa, Gurunāthan is said to have established by argument that everything that appears is mental and that *advaita* (Ātmā) is the ultimate Truth. At this point, the paṇḍit is reported to have interrupted: 'Then who is it that speaks?' Straightaway came the answer from Gurunāthan, 'Brahman.' The shrewd pandit knew he was cornered, and did not dare to ask any more questions. But what was the significance of that reply?

Speaking consists of two distinct parts or components in it: the material part composed of sound, words and meaning; and the other part, Consciousness, which is alive. The former depends upon the latter for its very existence; and so the latter, Consciousness or brahman, is the svarūpa [true nature] of speaking. Therefore, the reply directs you to emphasize that self-luminous principle in speaking, which alone makes speaking speaking.

1161. SEE THE IMPERSONAL IN AND BEHIND THE PERSONAL.

The personal can never know either the impersonal or even the personal. It is the impersonal, standing behind the personal, that enables it to know anything, even in the ordinary sense. Try to see that impersonal, even in the personal, and that will resolve all phenomenal problems. If the ego dies and still the speech continues, what speaks? Certainly the self-luminous Self, not the ego.

When you hear a sentence, what is it that connects the words which are already past? Only the Self. Therefore, see that Self through words, speech, act, etc. This exercise alone will in due course establish you in the ultimate Truth, the real Self.

1162. WHAT IS THE TEST OF PROGRESS?

1. If you feel pleasure in talking, discussing, singing or thinking about the ultimate Truth as often as possible, you may rest assured that you are progressing in the right direction.

2. If, when left alone or when retired to rest, the thought that spontaneously comes to your mind is about the ultimate Reality or your Guru, again you are well on the way of progress.
3. Usually, pleasure is enjoyed at the end of a thought. But if that pleasure begins to appear uncaused, even during the thought about the ultimate Truth, you are indeed fortunate and are in Truth already.

You go wrong when you bring in gender when speaking of the Truth. The words 'jīvan-mukta', 'Jnyānin' etc. are masculine. But you have no gender, as is clear from deep sleep. Not that you are neuter, but that you are beyond gender. Therefore, you are pure Jnyāna or Truth itself.

9th August 1956

1163. HOW TO NEGATE OBJECTS AND ARRIVE AT THE TRUTH?

The world of body, senses and mind and their corresponding objects may be viewed from two standpoints:

1. As being constituted of the presence and the absence of objects, gross or subtle; and
2. As being constituted of the ultimate subject and a variety of objects.

It has already been proved that one's real nature is pure Consciousness and Peace. Looking at the world from the first standpoint, the presence as well as the absence of objects have to be proved to be non-existent. This has to be done successively from all the three states, reducing the gross object first to a mentation and then the mentation to pure Consciousness. This process does not establish that the world is not, but rather that the world is nothing but your own real nature, Consciousness.

Viewing the world from the second standpoint, when everything objective (whether gross or subtle) is disposed of as unreal, that principle – the real Self – which disposed of everything else, remains over as the sole survivor. Even the mind being already disposed of, this survivor stands above in all its glory as pure Consciousness, the real Self.

1164. WHAT IS THE PROOF OF CONSCIOUSNESS?

That very question is the proof. That question is lit up by Consciousness.

The outer light, lighting up objects outside, and the inner light of Consciousness have something in common in their characteristics. Both are imperceptible to the sense organ or the mind. The existence of the outer light is affirmed by the fact that objects are manifested in its presence. Similarly, the light of Consciousness is proved by the fact that objects are lit up (or known) in its presence.

1165. HOW TO DISTINGUISH MONISM FROM ADVAITA?

There is a fundamental difference between the two.

Monism, meaning 'unity', is only a concept, with a definite trace of the mind in it. Its purpose is to destroy diversity, and not to find out the ultimate Truth.

Advaita or non-duality negates even the mind as unreal, and remains over as its background. This principle is therefore beyond the mind; and it is self-luminous, there being nothing else to light it up.

1166. WHAT IS ADVAITA (NON-DUALITY)?

Ātmā, the ultimate Truth established by Advaita, is the only thing that *is*. Everything else is only an appearance on it.

Truth is imperceptible, and the ordinary man knows only his perceptions. Advaita is a method of leading the ignorant man from the percept (object) to the ultimate Truth. Advaita refers to duality (or two). This 'two' is very often misunderstood to be the numerical two. But no, this 'two' stands for the basic 'two', viz. the subject and the object, or the perceiver and the perceived – the father of the many.

Your recognition of this basic two is otherwise called the basic error. Removal of this error and the re-establishment of the ultimate Truth is the purpose of Advaita (Non-duality).

> onnāyaninneyiha raṇṭennu kaṇṭaḷavil
> uṇṭāyoriṇṭal bata miṇṭāvatalla mama

paṇṭēkkaṇakkevaruvān nin kṛpāvalikaḷ
uṇṭākayeṅkal iha nārāyaṇāya namaḥ

[When what has always stood as one
is seen as two, there comes to me
a sad frustration and regret,
which can't be rightly spoken of.
To bring about the true, original
account, Lord may Your kindness
rain on me that worships You.]

Eṟuttacchan, Harināma-kīrttanam, 2

The quotation points to you – as Happiness, in the retreat into deep sleep every day. This process [of removing error] is easy enough. Infinite diversity can easily be reduced to the basic duality of subject and object. Applying the tests of Truth – namely changelessness and self-luminosity – to the subject and object, they are easily disposed of as mere appearance and unreal. But when the appearance is so disposed of, the common background which is pure Consciousness remains over and responds to all the tests of Truth. Therefore it is that Truth itself which appears as the diverse world.

The positive always has a taint of the mind in it. When the world is negated as unreal, it does not mean that the Truth is positive. Positive is also a relative term, within the realm of the mind. Truth is beyond both positive and negative, and is the background of both. But the term 'positive' is first utilized as a means to eliminate from you all that is negative. When everything negative is thus disposed of, what remains over as the supposed 'positive' no longer appears positive. Its relativity being lost, it stands in its own glory as the ultimate Truth. Therefore, the Ultimate is pointed to in a negative manner, as non-duality.

1167. WHAT IS LIFE?

In appearance, life is limited. But in reality, life is unlimited Truth. How? I know *I am*, and I say everything *is*. This is no inference, but the clearest of experience.

This 'am'-ness or 'is'-ness is the ultimate Truth, the source of all life. Because we see that even dead matter *is*. We are sure there is no life in dead matter. Therefore we see that 'am'-ness or 'is'-ness goes even beyond life and death, and lights up both.

It is from this 'is'-ness that all life flows.

1168. THERE IS NEITHER GIVING NOR TAKING IN LOVE.

'Love' means becoming one with the object of your love. When both are one, there is no one to give and no one to take. It is only in loose language or in degraded love that such transactions take place, where the personal identities are not lost.

Real love is advaita, and nothing else exists beside it. If love can be said to give anything, it is love alone and that in fullness, leaving no trace of itself behind to claim to have done so. In taking also, you surrender the whole of your personality to the object of your love. In either case the doer dies, leaving behind Love supreme.

1169. YOU MUST GIVE UP FREEDOM IN ORDER TO BE REALLY FREE.

Freedom is ignorantly attributed to body, senses and mind, though all the three are by nature bound. Most human endeavours are calculated to perform this miracle of freeing the ever-bound, and so they end in failure.

The urge for freedom is real and comes from beyond the mind. It is wrong to apply it to the mind, or to things lower still. What is needed is freedom from the traditional limiting agencies, namely time and space. Such freedom is the characteristic of Ātmā, the ultimate Reality, alone. This is one's own real nature, and it is from there that the urge comes.

Body, senses and mind being never-free, and the real 'I'-principle being ever-free, the only way to attain freedom is to identify oneself with that real Self within. This means surrender of attachment to body, senses and mind. In other words, you must give up the desire for the freedom of body, senses and mind, if you want to attain freedom of the Self.

1170. HOW TO UNDERSTAND THE TRUTH THROUGH LANGUAGE?

Ultimate Truth is beyond the mind and is imperceptible. Therefore Truth can only be pointed at from the phenomenal, with the help of certain words that have to be understood as *lakṣhaṇas* or pointers to the Truth. These words, however subtle in their concept, are still subject to certain limitations by time and space, imposed upon them by the mind.

Therefore, in understanding the ultimate through lakṣhaṇas, you have to relinquish with great care the material vesture imposed upon them by the mind, and then direct your attention to that which still remains over as the background of the lakṣhaṇas. That background is nothing but the 'is'-ness standing as the common background of all objects.

Sat, *cit* and *ānanda* are such lakṣhaṇas and have to be understood to mean nothing but this ultimate '*is*'. The ultimate 'is' takes one much nearer the Truth than any other word, because the 'is' has much less of the mind in it than the others, and it gives a much more correct import of the Truth. 'That which is' comes from the ultimate '*is*', and therefore the 'is' is nearer the Truth than that which is.

This is called *bhāga-tyāga-lakṣhaṇa* or *jagadahat-lakṣhaṇa*. [See note 353.]

11th August 1956

1171. 'WATER DOES NOT FLOW.' WHAT DOES IT MEAN?

No one can deny that one can make a statement only about something one has already known, and that the knower is distinct and separate from the known.

While examining any statement, brief or elaborate, it has to be taken as a single unit in itself and you are not entitled to split it into parts. If you do so, each part becomes a fresh statement which has to be considered independently and separately.

The question can be approached from different standpoints. Take for example an ordinary statement: 'I am walking.' Let us view it from different standpoints.

1. I must certainly have known the fact before the statement was made. Therefore as knower, I was behind the statement and separate from it (the known). Thus, in every statement of mine, I stand behind the statement knowing it – the statement always being the object and myself, though in it, not concerned with it in the least. 'Water does not flow' is only an illustration to prove this Truth. When I say 'I act', I am behind that statement knowing it. Again, when I say 'I think', or again when I say 'I know the thought', I am behind each of those statements, quite unconnected with the statements themselves.
2. When I say 'I am walking', I make you understand thereby that I am the walker. But just think, am I really the walker? *No*. If I am, I can be nothing else. But, the next moment, I seem to be the thinker or feeler. Therefore, I can be none of these. But it also cannot be denied that I was in the walking. Therefore it has to be understood, that I was in the walking, not as the walker but as myself, unconcerned with the activity, just as water *is* in 'flowing-ness' as well as in stagnancy.

1172. WHAT IS SLEEP?

According to grammar, the verb 'is' and its variants are considered verbs of incomplete predication and so do not denote any particular action. All other verbs always denote action. We usually say, 'I sleep.' What does it really mean? Sleep is used as a verb and must denote some action. But do I sleep? Is there any action in sleeping? *No*. Sleep is neither an action nor non-action. There is no ego in sleeping, and there can never be a sleeper. Therefore nobody sleeps, and sleep is *not*.

1173. WHAT IS THOUGHT?

Thought is an attempt at connecting the past and the present, by bringing the past to the present. But the past, being past, can never be brought to the present. Therefore thought is impossible. The past and the future depend upon the present for their very existence; and the present, on strict examination, disappears altogether. Therefore time is *not*.

Whatever is present is only Consciousness. Past was present once and so the same in content, viz. Consciousness. Every point of thinking is only Consciousness. What then are you going to connect and with what? Therefore thought is a misnomer.

1174. WHAT IS THE WORLD?

The Absolute, wrongly supposed to be time, space and causality, is the manifested world.

The three states exist here, not for nothing. Take them all together, as an integral whole and not separately. Between themselves, they explain each other. The waking and dream states also explain each other. Deep sleep explains the other two. So the three states are intended to enlighten you, about your real nature. A unanimous affirmation from all the three states, and particularly from the deep sleep state, is the only criterion for the reality of a thing.

1175. REALIZATION AND ESTABLISHMENT

When you listen to the Truth from the lips of the Guru you *realize* that very moment. When you allow that conviction to go deep into your very being and when you make it your own, you stand established in it.

13th August 1956

1176. LIMITATION OF ARGUMENTS TO GET AT THE TRUTH

Of course the Guru makes use of certain arguments to extricate the attention of the disciple from the obstacles, and to direct it to the Truth behind. Here the arguments do not work by themselves. They are supported by a mysterious something which emanates from the Guru and thus accompanies them. That is *love*. That is *light*. In its presence, the arguments penetrate so deep that they do not leave a trace of the obstacles behind.

Immediately, you visualize the Truth; and you are asked to cling on to that Truth already visualized. You are expected to cling on to the Truth spontaneously, without the help of any argument, if possible. In that attempt, if you find the obstacles still getting the better of you, of course you have to seek the help of arguments. In that case, it is always better to take recourse to fresh arguments of your own, so that you may avoid the possibility of ever becoming subservient to them. If fresh arguments do not come up, the only alternative is to adduce the old arguments themselves, keeping in mind that the arguments are there only for the purpose of removing stubborn obstacles which block the way to the Truth.

When one is thus established in the Truth, arguments are of no more service. Still you may see a Sage, well-established in the Truth, sometimes expatiating upon such arguments. It is a sweet recreation and a delight for him.

vidyayumāyi vinōdicciripporu vidyōtamānamātmānaṁ

Eṟuttacchan, Addhyātma-rāmāyaṇam

1177. GURU DISCIPLE RELATIONSHIP

The disciples, from their own standpoint, have a Guru. But the Guru, from his own standpoint, has no disciples. He is beyond duality and unity.

14th August 1956

1178. CAN A SAINT, THROUGH LOVE ALONE, REACH THE ULTIMATE TRUTH?

No. The devotee or the saint knows only objective or limited love. The saint might have risen to the state of universality. Still, it is only a concept and objective in character. He is entangled in his own creed. He begins to believe that his creed is the only means to 'salvation' – a term which he does not himself clearly understand. Therefore he tries to spread his creed as widely as possible.

An over-enthusiasm in this direction often makes fanatics of most of them. It is true that they start with love for their personal deity or their creed. But when fanaticism begins to set in, they begin to fall from the ladder of progress. Their egos get hardened and perverted, and they refuse to listen to reason. Their progress to the Truth is thus lamentably blocked. But an exceptional few among them, in whom an adherence to reason persists, succeed in getting a Kāraṇa-guru and attain liberation.

1179. THE FUNCTIONS OF THE HEAD AND THE HEART

The head and the heart are not water-tight compartments. They complement each other. It may be said that 'It is a harmonious blending of the head and the heart in the ultimate Truth that is called realization.' It may generally be said that one gets enlightened through the head, and gets established in the Truth through the heart. A thought, when it is deep, becomes feeling or in other words descends into the heart.

Deep knowledge or objectless knowledge is '*Love*'. Love always gives and never takes.

If only the giving is spontaneous and prompted by the heart alone, it is efficacious and divine. The slightest taint of the ego in the giving pollutes it to that extent.

If you follow the path of love, until love is its own fulfilment, you reach the highest. But an ignorant aspirant can never complete it unaided. The help of a Kāraṇa-guru is absolutely necessary, at least towards the end. The instance of Shrī Caitanya is an example of this.

1180. JNYĀNA SĀDHAKAS SOMETIMES THINK ALOUD. WHY?

When you follow the path of Advaita, you may, at an advanced stage, experience a spontaneous exuberance of knowledge or love overflowing from you freely. On such occasions, you may be found talking, even unasked, to those around you about the advaitic Truth. This may be said from your own standpoint to be simply 'thinking aloud', because you are not doing it with any intention to convince others or to convert them. Really, there is no doer or ego behind it. It is only your own real nature of advaita, not being able to contain itself within you, bubbling out through your mind and the vocal organ. This only shows that you are getting established, more and more firmly, in the advaitic Truth.

1181. SAGE, SAINT AND MYSTIC DISTINGUISHED

Sage, saint and mystic or yōgin follow three different paths.

He is the *Sage*, who starting as the seeker after the ultimate Truth, follows the jnyāna path under the guidance of a Kāraṇa-guru, and proceeds straight to his goal; examining his experiences in all the three states in the light of changelessness and self-luminosity, and disposing of all such as are found wanting. Thus transcending his own body, senses and mind (the personal), he visualizes his own real nature (the impersonal) and soon gets established in it.

The *saint* is one who follows the path of devotion to a personal god and develops an intense love (though personal) towards him. This love, in course of time, purifies the devotee's heart immensely and makes it sāttvic, though he still cannot transcend the limits of his own personality. His concept of God also develops, until it reaches omnipotence, omnipresence and omniscience. Here he is stranded, and has sometimes to wait for years to get help from a Kāraṇa-guru to take him beyond (as Shrī Caitanya did). If he is fortunate enough to keep his sense of reason alive, and if he succeeds in keeping himself away from the mire of fanaticism, he will be able to obtain a Kāraṇa-guru and will be liberated.

The *mystic* is a yōgin, who like the saint confines his examinations and his experiences to the waking state alone. The yōgin sets before himself a mental ideal of his own creation (a mere thought-form) and begins to concentrate his mind upon that ideal. During concentration, he gets into a state of blissful ignorance of everything else. It is a state almost akin to deep sleep, and he calls it 'samādhi'. This state is accompanied by a sense of happiness that captivates him; and he thus becomes engrossed and entangled in it. The concentration of mind releases the immense potentialities of the mind, in the form of powers or siddhis. These also, in turn, seduce and entangle him. Thus entangled in a vicious world of his own creation, the yōgin finds it extremely difficult even to aspire for a Kāraṇa-guru, and liberation is lost sight of. But there is a class of mystics who follow the path of rāja-yōga mixed with a course of jnyāna practices chalked out by a Kāraṇa-guru, of course in the cosmological way. They will certainly reach the ultimate Truth, though with some delay. All mystics and siddhas, other than this class of rāja-yōgins, have to be scrupulously avoided and detested as worse than lewd and licentious persons.

vița-saṁsargavat siddha-saṁsargaṁ mōha-varddhakam …

[Source of quotation uncertain]

1182. THE ORIGIN OF SAMĀDHI

The ordinary man perceives only objects and attributes reality to them alone. Though he would admit that there is also consciousness, he is incapable of believing that Consciousness can exist by itself. In order to give such persons an opportunity to perceive pure Consciousness without objects, samādhi was indented upon by Ācāryas of old. Even that samādhi was coloured, inasmuch as it was considered to be objectless.

But the same result, and much more, can easily be achieved by examining the deep sleep state in the right manner.

1183. WHAT IS ĀVARAṆA?

That by which you consider deep sleep to be a state of unconsciousness, while Consciousness reigns in all its purity there, is *āvaraṇa* [obscuring].

1184. REALITY IN THE WAKING STATE

Waking is reality to both the ignorant man and the Sage. But their concept of reality is fundamentally different. To the ignorant man, waking means waking to the gross world; but to the Sage, waking is waking to his own real nature.

1185. WHY DOES A JNYĀNIN TALK ABOUT STATES THAT ARE UNREAL?

A Jnyānin often talks about the three states or the personality, knowing full well that all of them are, as such, unreal. But it is not without a purpose. It is possible to show the Reality only through the so called 'unreal'. They are first examined in order to show that they are the known and that you are the knower. Next it is shown that the known is nothing but the knower itself – Pure Consciousness.

1186. G. asked: CAN IT BE SAID THAT THE ULTIMATE IS RESPONSIBLE FOR ALL ERRORS?

Answer: If there is error…

Error always has Truth as its background; and so error is strictly no error. Could there be an opposite of error?

15th August 1956

1187. SUBJECT AND OBJECT IN ACTIVITY

In every activity, there is only object and no subject.

Examine any activity. There seem to be two 'I's, functioning simultaneously: the ego or apparent 'I' as the doer, and the 'I'-principle or real 'I' as the knower. The former is ever-changing and the latter is never-changing. Therefore I am always the knower and never the doer. Thus there is no doer or subject, and there is only action without an actor.

The real 'I'-principle is present in all action. You believe that an actor or subject is indispensable for every action; therefore you conclude that the 'I'-principle is acting. Really, the 'I'-principle is not concerned with the acting at all. Thus you are no doer, enjoyer or perceiver, but only the knower.

At every step, the presence of Consciousness is absolutely necessary, in all thoughts, feelings and sensations. This Consciousness is unconcerned with the object or the activity.

For further corroboration, you may examine the deep sleep state. You had no thinking, feeling, or sensation in the deep sleep state. Therefore the 'I'-principle, as pure Consciousness, alone was there. So this is true of all the three states. Therefore the 'knower Consciousness' should rightly be called 'non-doer Consciousness'. Hence, if you say you are sleeping, it means you are not sleeping; and if you say you are doing, it means you are not doing.

16th August 1956

1188. Madam G: HOW TO GIVE UP BODY, SENSES AND MIND?

It is called 'renunciation'. Renunciation is of two kinds. The yōgin's and the jnyānin's.

1. The yōgin's renunciation consists of taking the mind away from body and senses. This takes one only to a blank state and not further.
2. The jnyānin's renunciation is *understanding* that he is the light or Consciousness on which the body, senses and mind appear, and that even that appearance does not exist when that light is withdrawn. Knowing this Truth, the jnyānin permits the innocent appearance to exist; and he literally *stands under*, in all his glory, as its background.

1189. KNOWLEDGE IN THE THREE STATES

Knowledge without quality is the content of deep sleep.

But in the other two states, quality is clearly perceived. And if the object is taken away from it, the suffix '-er' automatically drops away, leaving the knower as pure knowledge.

1190. WHAT IS MY RELATION TO THOUGHT OR FEELING?

1. You are thought or feeling, devoid of the characteristics of thought or feeling.
2. You are the knower of thought or feeling, when thought or feeling is there.
3. You are pure knowledge or Peace, when there is neither thought nor feeling.

17th August 1956

1191. HOW TO DISPOSE OF ANY OBJECT?

Whenever I want to dispose of any object, my stand is always in the background.

1192. HOW DOES *SAT-CIT-ĀNANDA* EXPRESS ITSELF IN EVERYDAY LIFE?

Every enquiry you make concerns some object that is believed to exist. In other words the enquiry starts with the 'is'-ness or the *sat* aspect of the Reality. But you don't stop there. Then you want to know it. Here the *cit* aspect comes in. When you know it, you immediately experience a satisfaction or peace which is the *ānanda* aspect of the Reality. Thus *sat-cit-ānanda* is experienced in every activity of life.

1193. WHAT IS THE SPIRITUAL SIGNIFICANCE OF THE LOGIC OF REINCARNATION OF SOULS?

People say they have had many lives, before the present one. But the truth is that you die with every thought or feeling. So you live many lives even in a short period of time. This is not noticed or perceived by the ordinary man. It is in order to draw his attention to this Truth that the illustration of the broader, and to him more conceivable, chain of life is brought in.

1194. HOW TO LOVE MY MASTER BETTER?

If one feels that he is not able to love his master as he desires, it really means that he still loves his master deeply, but that he is not yet satisfied with the love he gives him. That is all. This dissatisfaction with the depth of one's own love for the master is the nature of true love; and it will never disappear.

1195. PRAṆAVA-YŌGA

Of all paths of yōga, the Praṇava-yōga exercises [of meditation on the mantra 'aum'] take one nearer to the ultimate Truth. But still one has to listen to the Truth, direct from the lips of the Guru, in order to visualize it.

1196. HOW CAN DEEP SLEEP ALLEVIATE MY PAINS OF THE WAKING STATE?

Answer: You get cured of your pain and disease immediately you get into deep sleep; and you begin to suffer again when you come back to the waking state. But if you can bring something from deep sleep to bear upon the waking state, certainly the pain will be relieved in the waking state also.

30th August 1956

1197. WHAT IS 'MAN'?

In order to be a man, one has to indent upon Consciousness; in other words one must know it. Therefore, 'Man is Consciousness.'

Man has three distinct entities or spheres of life.

1. As a physical being,
2. As a mental being, and
3. As a knowing being.

1198. THE DIFFERENT PERSPECTIVES TOWARDS THE WORLD

1. The *scientist* identifies himself with the physical body, and so deals with objects and their relationship with each other.
2. The *yōgin* and the *mystic* identify themselves with the mind, as ideas or ideals which are only subtle objects, and visualize them accordingly.
3. The *vēdāntin* identifies himself with Consciousness, which is his own real nature, and sees everything as Consciousness.

1199. THE TRADITIONAL COURSE OF REALIZATION, INTERPRETED IN THE LIGHT OF THE DIRECT METHOD

The traditional course of realization is through *shruti*, *yukti* and *anubhava*. This may cosmologically be termed *shravaṇa*, *manana* and *nididhyāsana*. But in the light of the direct method they may be interpreted to mean:

1. *Shruti:* Listening to the words of the Guru, about Truth.

2. *Yukti:* Thinking, with the aid of intellect and reason, over the Truth so expounded.
3. *Anubhava:* Thinking profoundly, in the light of higher reason, about the Truth as one's own real nature – till the Truth descends deep into one's own being, as experience.

According to this method, the ultimate test of realization is whether the higher reason endorses your experience as true. If it does, realization is complete.

31st August 1956

1200. WHAT IS THE WORLD?

We experience only consciousness of objects, gross or subtle. Can you draw a line of demarcation between Consciousness and object, in that experience? *No.* Consciousness can well exist, all alone, without objects. But, objects can never exist without Consciousness. Therefore, all is Consciousness.

1st September 1956

> If one is deeply convinced of the unreasonableness of all questions, then it is very easy to get established in the Truth.
>
> A thing has never been born of itself and a thing has never been born of anything else…
>
> *Shrī Shankara*

If one has risen to the level of seeing that an object is nothing but Consciousness appearing in the form of the object, then in that level: 'To know is to be.' But in the waking state, one is in a much lower level, where tripuṭī functions and knowing is not taken right up to 'being'.

1201. THE HIGHER REASON AND ITS FUNCTION

The principle that impartially examines all the three states is called 'higher reason' or 'vēdāntic reason', and during that period it appears to be dynamic. When the examination is over, that principle seems to remain static.

But the truth is that it is changeless. Even when it seemed to be dynamic, it was also static. In other words, it is beyond 'static' and 'dynamic', though appearing as either even simultaneously. The function of this higher reason is either to annihilate the three states as such or to prove them to be nothing but Consciousness.

2nd September 1956

1202. THE TYPES AND THE ORDER OF DEVOTEES

According to the *Bhagavad-gītā*, there are four types of devotees or aspirants.

... ārtō jijñāsur arthā-'rthī jñānī ca bharata-'rṣabha ..

Bhagavad-gītā, 7.16

The lowest in the rung of the ladder is *arthā-'rthi* – the one who approaches the personal God for the attainment of worldly wealth and pleasures. When his efforts are crowned with success on some occasions, his attention is gradually attracted to the person of the God who has been so kind to him, and he desires to know more and more about that God.

During this period of transition, he begins to ignore with indifference his own pleasures as well as objects of pleasure. The devotee at this stage is called a *jijnyāsu* – one who yearns to know more about the Truth of God. He continues in this state for some time and his earnestness to realize God and the Truth increases by leaps and bounds.

The delay in the fulfilment of this desire makes him pine for it day and night. This state makes him what is called *ārta* – the 'miserable'. In this state, in most cases, the aspirant happens to meet a Kāraṇa-guru. Under instructions from him, the aspirant progresses very quickly.

At last he happens to listen to the ultimate Truth from the lips of the Guru. Immediately, he visualizes the Truth and becomes what is called a jnyānin in embryo. He continues his efforts for some time more to get established in the Truth already visualized. Thus in due course he becomes a *Jnyānin* at all levels. Such a *Jnyānin*, Lord Kṛiṣhṇa says, is His own *Ātmā*.

... jñānī tv ātmai 'va mē matam .

Bhagavad-gītā, 7.18

1203. How to face the ego's question?

It is the ego that puts all sorts of naughty questions. But alas, the ego dies immediately after every question, and does not remain even to listen to the answer.

'To whom, then, am I to address the answer?' asked Gurunāthan once. The ego has shown, by its own conduct, that the question is as frivolous and illusory as himself, and that no reasonable answer can be expected for such unreasonable questions. If an answer can be given, it is only to prove that the question itself is absurd.

If you want to understand anything said by another correctly, you must first correct your own stand in accordance with the level at which the topic is discussed. If the gross is discussed, you should take your stand in the subtle; and if the subtle is discussed, you should stand in knowledge to understand it.

4th September 1956

1204. Authorship and advertisement

Ancient Indian works of merit, particularly spiritual ones, were all *apauruṣhēya* (of undisclosed authorship), for example many of the Upaniṣhads.

Pauruṣhēya, the habit of advertizing the authorship in order to enhance the sale of the book, is a degenerate modern tendency of the inflated ego.

1205. Shrī Shankara as he appeared

Shrī Shankara has appeared in his life as a devotee, a yōgin, a mystic, and lastly as a vēdāntin. He appears in his true colours only in the commentary on the *Māṇḍūkya-kārikā* and in his last and independent prakaraṇa works.

The commentaries on the *Brahma-sūtra*, *Bhagavad-gītā*, *Dashō-paniṣhads* etc. were all theological in approach, intended only to crush the intelligentsia of the land, who were misguiding and polluting the spiritual life of the country. They could be fought and made to surrender only on their own ground of theology and the shāstras. Therefore Shrī Shankara, in the course of his work of destroying the wild and pernicious growths in the religious and spiritual life of India, made capital use of the existing systems of theology and shāstras.

After removing the weeds and preparing the ground, he sowed the seed of Advaita, in his own independent manner, and without relying on any external aids.

Some of the philosophers of the West as well as of the East did not understand what Shankara really stood for. Many of them took him to stand only for the waking state and the waking world. But his last, independent works clearly show that he stood for that permanent, self-luminous principle which is the background of the waking, dream and deep sleep states and their worlds.

1206. PERSPECTIVES CONTRADICTORY

Man moves indiscriminately between the sensuous, mental and conscious planes. An ignorant man holds that he is the body supporting the mind within, and that the mind supports the Ātmā still within. But the spiritual aspirant's position is exactly the opposite. He believes that Ātmā holds the mind and that the mind holds the body. A spiritual aspirant must fix his stand firmly before starting on an enquiry, to make sure that his findings are reasonable and correct. The following verse shows this stand quite clearly.

> arkkānalādi veḷivokke grahikkum oru
> kaṇṇinnu kaṇṇumanamākunna kaṇṇatinu
> kaṇṇāyirunna poruḷ tānennuṟaykkumaḷav
> ānandamentuhari nārāyaṇāya namaḥ

Eṟuttacchan, Harināma-kīrttanam, 4

1207. A NEW APPROACH TO EXPLAIN THE APHORISM 'THOU ART THAT.'

'Thou art that' consists of two parts, 'thou' and 'that', the meanings of which have to be clearly understood.

Explaining the meaning of 'thou', you are first told that you are not the body, senses or the mind. Leaving it there, the 'that' is taken up. You know you are there in deep sleep, without a body, senses or mind. That which you are in deep sleep is shown to you to be the meaning and goal of 'that'.

Thus you are quite naturally made to visualize – not merely to understand – what you really are. This is how the aphorism 'Thou art that' is to be understood. The following verses amply illustrate this Truth.

śraddhasva tāta śraddhasva nā 'tra mōhaṁ kuruṣva bhōḥ .
jñāna-svarupō bhagavān ātmā tvaṁ prakṛtēḥ paraḥ ..

[Be sure of it, be deeply sure
that you make no confusion here.
You are what knowledge truly is,
just that from which all guidance comes.
That is the self, just what you are,
beyond all nature's functioning.]

Aṣhṭāvakra-samhitā, 15.8

appanē kēḷkka, mōhikka vēṇṭā prakṛti-dūragan
ātmāvāṁ bhagavān bōdha-rūpan nī tanneyāṇ eṭō

Malayāḷam translation of above, by Shrī Ātmānanda

yadi dēhaṁ pṛthak-kṛtya citi viśrāmya tiṣṭhasi .
adhunai 'va sukhī śāntō bandha-muktō bhaviṣyasi ..

[If separating body out,
you stand at rest in consciousness,
then here and now you come to peace
and happiness, where you are free
from all restraining ties and bonds.]

Aṣhṭāvakra-samhitā, 1.4

1208. ALL INDIRECT PATHS TO THE TRUTH ULTIMATELY COME ROUND TO THE DIRECT PATH.

Innumerable paths have been adopted, from time immemorial, for the attainment of Truth; and Sages who came out that way had also been not few. The path adopted by the majority was cosmological.

Whatever sādhana one might adopt in the beginning, actual visualization is possible only through the direct method represented in the aphorism '*Prajnyānam asmi*' – '*I am consciousness.*'

This aphorism is taken up by the cosmological approaches only at the very last stage, after other aphorisms have been exhausted.

But the direct method is based upon the truth of this vital aphorism, and the aspirant assimilates it even at the initial stage of his sādhana. Therefore, his visualization is complete, the moment he listens to the Truth from the lips of the Guru.

13th September 1956

1209. HOW TO GET ENLIGHTENMENT THROUGH SAMĀDHI OR THROUGH PHENOMENAL HAPPINESS?

The three states may well be termed sensuous, mental and conscious states.

Even in the waking state when you suppose you enjoy something, you are not standing separate from Happiness, but as that Happiness itself. When you come out of that state, you interpret that non-dual experience in subject-object terms.

So also in nirvikalpa samādhi, there is no duality and there is perfect bliss. But on coming out of it, you express it in dual terms, in terms of subject-object relationship. This is wrong. It is not the experience by itself that really enlightens you, but it is the correct understanding of its significance. It is not possible to obtain the correct meaning of it except from the Guru; and until you obtain it directly from him, nirvikalpa samādhi will only be a source of transient happiness to you.

It is true you were in an egoless state, both during the experience of worldly happiness and in the nirvikalpa samādhi. But your subsequent interpretation posits the ego there retrospectively. That is because you rely more upon the mind's function and its satisfaction.

Therefore, coming out of samādhi, you must humbly and reverently wait upon the Guru, and place before him at his sweet convenience all your experiences. Then the Guru will explain the meaning of it, and you will understand that you were visualizing your own real nature and that you have never been bound. This is how one who is addicted to samādhi has to become liberated.

But he who follows the direct method of jnyāna can come to the same state of liberation by correctly examining any casual worldly experience of happiness, as instructed by the Guru, and by finding that it is one's own real nature of Peace that manifests itself as limited happiness in all the three states.

1210. HOW DOES ADVAITA EXPRESS ITSELF EVEN IN OUR WORLDLY ACTIVITIES?

You see a picture and enjoy its beauty. What does this mean? It means that, for the time being, you change your stand from the gross externals to the subtle idea, and that you forget your personal self or ego. It is only in such a state that you experience peace as beauty or Happiness.

At such moments you are standing in advaita. The original painter had first within himself an experience of advaitic beauty or Peace. This gradually condensed into an idea, which still further condensed into the gross picture. The onlookers are also taken, in the reverse order, to the same experience of advaitic beauty or peace experienced by the painter.

It is true you experience sublime beauty or happiness on witnessing objects like a mountain, the sea or a waterfall. This is because you forget your lower self for the time being and stand as one with the object, in the advaitic sense.

15th September 1956

1211. ASPIRANTS THOUGH MANY, THE LIBERATED ARE FEW.

All aspirants do not go in quest of the ultimate Truth. The large majority of them seek powers, mental satisfaction or mental happiness. Such persons get entangled in a subtle world of their own creation, or in the happiness experienced in the samādhi state. They are so completely satisfied with such fleeting happiness, at the mental level, that they do not even aspire for anything more real, in the beyond.

But the exceptional few, who fortunately sense something beyond, approach a Kāraṇa-guru, under whose instructions they easily attain liberation and get established in their real nature of Peace.

1212. HOW TO VIEW THE WORLD?

The awareness which is the witness of the three states is also the witness of every activity or inactivity, in each state. At every step, the witness asserts and proves that you are not the doer or enjoyer, but that you are always the knower. Thus the world, including life, can well be divided into two distinct entities: the one being the permanent awareness, and the other being everything else that appears and disappears.

Every statement of yours, if examined in the correct perspective, leads you to the ultimate Truth. Take for example the statement: 'I am walking.' What does it mean?

1. 'Walking' gets a meaning only from its source, 'non-walking'. So walking expresses only its source, 'non-walking'. So both walking and non-walking disappear as such, and you stand as that awareness beyond all opposites.
2. When one who has visualized the real 'I'-principle says, 'I am walking', 'walking' can only appear as an object of the 'I'. If one says 'I am the walker', the 'walker' is then the object. In any case, it is the changeless 'I'-principle that is emphasized and brought to notice.

Whenever you proceed to examine an object, take it to be an object first, and yourself the subject. An object can be an object of Consciousness alone. Therefore, when you take it as an object, Consciousness automatically comes in, the object loses its objectivity, and it shows you your real nature, Consciousness. This explains the whole world of objects, and it is not necessary to examine another object.

An object is a gross object when you are a physical being. But that is not the whole truth. You are at times a mental being. Then the object is only an idea. Even that is not the whole truth. You are at other times a conscious being. Then the object also becomes Consciousness.

So a strict and complete examination, of any object, leads you to the ultimate Truth.

1213. RELIGION AND ITS SCOPE

Religion rests upon blind faith in so called revelations, scriptures, and a personal God. Human tastes and tendencies differ, all over the world. Religions respond to the diverse tastes and tendencies, and so inevitably multiply differences.

Religions propose only to help man to lead a good, just and moral life on earth. For that purpose, each religion has invented its own temptations and threats, in the form of heaven and hell. They also recommend a strict code of ethics to guide their followers. Each religion insists upon the adoption of its ethics, just so far as it can serve its own limited, phenomenal purpose.

If pressed beyond these arbitrary limits, the same ethics destroy even the foundations of the religion and its personal God. This is what Vēdānta does. The practice of ethics involves a certain amount of self-sacrifice. When practised to the very end, every ethical law takes one to selflessness. This means the certain death of the ego, which no religion contemplates, but which Vēdānta wishes to achieve.

Therefore a Kāraṇa-guru can even make use of the ethics of religion, to lead its devotees to the ultimate Truth. Religion does not seem to recognize the scope and the potentialities of its own ethics. Though unknowingly, even religion, through ethics, advocates Vēdānta. Vēdānta is therefore the fulfilment of all religions.

1214. CAN THERE BE A UNIVERSAL RELIGION? YES, ONLY VĒDĀNTA.

The concept of a universal religion implies a personal God – being at the same time universal and also being acceptable to multifarious humanity. In fact a personal god is created by man in his own image, and heaven in accordance with his varying tastes. Most religions bank upon heaven and its glamours, peculiar to the country of its birth. The God and the heaven of one religion have no fascination for the follower of another religion. Therefore, no one religious conception can ever captivate the imagination of all alike. So a universal religion is impossible.

Vēdānta is the only such religion – if religion it may be called – appealing to the head and the heart alike, accepting the Guru (ultimate Truth) in place of God, the innermost being as the Self, and transcending all concepts and even the universe in its application. It welcomes all religions into its embrace and lends a helping hand to take them higher still, till all differences are reconciled and permanent Peace established.

Vēdānta alone is capable of explaining, strictly and rationally, the real significance of the tenets and ethics of a religion. Take for example, Jesus Christ's statement: '*Love thy neighbour as thyself.*' Love is the expression of the state of oneness. So to love another really, you must become one with the other. How is it possible to achieve that oneness, either in the physical or in the mental realm? Impossible! And religion does not go beyond these two realms.

Strict oneness is possible only in the realm beyond the mind. Vēdānta is the only gateway to it. Reaching its portals, you realize that you had ever been one with your neighbour in essence, and that love is your real nature. That love is already there and you have to do nothing to create it. You have only to know the truth about yourself and the so called neighbour. No religion can show you this truth. It is the subject of Vēdānta alone. So come to Vēdānta and cure all your ills.

16th September 1956

1215. CAUSALITY AND ITS ULTIMATE GOAL

The urge to search for a cause shows that you are dissatisfied with the effect and that you consider the cause to be more real. Therefore everything that comes under the category of effect is considered to be relatively unreal, and the ultimate cause or source is alone considered real. So you negate the effect and seek the real source, in the name of causality. Therefore, the enquiry of cause is also an indirect search for the ultimate Truth.

This may be pursued in different ways. Some of the important approaches (angles of vision) among them are mentioned in the following verse:

> yasmin sarvaṁ yasya sarvaṁ yatas sarvaṁ yasmāyidaṁ
> yēna sarvaṁ yaddhi sarvaṁ tat satyaṁ samupāsmahē

Upaniṣhad(?)

Any one of the above six modes of approach, if pursued steadfastly and sincerely, without deviating or stopping short on the way, will take one to the ultimate Truth, provided one is instructed by a Kāraṇa-guru. They may be defined as follows:

1. 'yasmin sarvam' – In what does all this appear or disappear.
2. 'yasya sarvam' – To what does all this belong.
3. 'yatas sarvam' – From what does all this arise.
4. 'yasmāyidam' – For what purpose is all this.
5. 'yēna sarvam' – Of what is all this made.
6. 'yaddhi sarvam' – What is all this?

'tat satyaṁ samupāsmahē' – That Truth I adore.

1216. EXPERIENCE AND SPIRITUAL SĀDHANA

It has been the bane of spiritual life, all over the world, to consider and extol as spiritual experience every kind of unusual expression of happiness, ecstasy or perception, external or internal. They are actually the result of mental exercises ignorantly called 'spiritual'. Every devotee, mystic or yōgin will naturally have any number of such experiences to narrate. None of these so called experiences have anything really spiritual about them. They are purely mental and may serve to purify the mind to a great extent. Even nirvikalpa samādhi of the yōgin is no exception to this rule.

Really spiritual experience is only one. Its tests are changelessness and self-luminosity. The only experience that stands these two tests is the real 'I'-principle or pure awareness. All the rest disappear in time, and so are unreal.

A spiritual aspirant guided by a Kāraṇa-guru is told, in unambiguous terms, always to test his experiences in the light of the question: 'Have you got the whole of what you really want?' If your experience – be it nirvikalpa samādhi – fails to answer this question in the bold affirmative, reject it and try again.

At last you come to that experience which never parts from you and which leaves no part of your want unfulfilled. That is the real 'I'-principle – pure Awareness.

17th September 1956

1217. RIGHT UNDERSTANDING

Ordinary understanding is supposed to be a function of the personality or the ego. But even science has of late come to admit that depersonalization is necessary for right understanding. In other words, science admits that understanding is the faculty or nature of the transcendental Awareness.

1218. WHAT IS THE TOTALITY OF ONE'S EXPERIENCES?

It consists of the experiences of the three states together with that Awareness which, while standing distinct and separate from the states, also lights up the states themselves. Therefore, the witness of the states is also the witness of each mentation or perception.

1219. WHAT IS THE RELATIONSHIP BETWEEN HAPPINESS AND THE EGO?

Even that which is supposed to be the enjoyment of happiness in the waking state occurs only when the ego or the lower self is forgotten or disappears. Whenever the ego disappears, it is the background – Peace – that shines in its own glory.

This is later on usurped by the ego and interpreted as enjoyment of happiness experienced by him. But in fact, the ego was nowhere on the scene at the time referred to.

1220. MIND IN DREAM IS DIFFERENT FROM MIND IN THE WAKING STATE. HOW?

The point was clarified by reference to two relevant dream experiences.

1. Mr. U.K. had a dream that his mother's sister died suddenly, and relatives and neighbours were gathered in the house for the performance of the last rites. Just then Mr. U.K.'s grand uncle, who was the head of the family, solemnly proposed that the cremation may well wait till her sister (U.K.'s mother who was then apparently in perfect health) also died, so that both could be cremated together. Mr. U.K. and the assembled relatives listened calmly to the uncle's declaration, perceiving nothing unusual or unreasonable in the proposal. It was accepted by all as being just the right thing. Even Mr. U.K.'s mother did not raise a protest, but calmly awaited her own death. The waking mind would never have accepted such a monstrous proposal.
2. Smy. P.A.'s father had another strange dream. He watched, most disinterestedly, the death of his own body in the dream. He saw his body being decorated and carried to the cremation ground, accompanied by several mourners. This is another instance of the dream mind, the nature and experience of which could never be reconciled with those of the waking mind. No more evidence is needed to prove that the dream mind is different from the mind in the waking state.

19th September 1956

1221. I AM MYSELF ALONE AS PURE CONSCIOUSNESS, IN DEEP SLEEP.

I, by my mere presence, illuminate all objects. When the objects are removed, what can I be but light itself?

When I am myself the sun, how can darkness approach me? I am myself alone, as Consciousness and Peace, in deep sleep. As such, how can I address deep sleep except as 'I'? Since there is no time in deep sleep, both questions, when did one go to sleep and when did one come out of it, are irrelevant.

1222. IMPORTANCE OF FULL AND CORRECT DATA

The data which is fractional cannot lead to anything but fractional truth.

Truth is one and indivisible. Therefore, what appears as fractional truth is nothing short of untruth.

Science, yōga, philosophy, devotion, mysticism and such other paths, all take into consideration only the waking state experiences and so work upon fractional data. Therefore their findings are not the truth. No intelligent man can seriously consider a bare one third of one's life's experiences alone, ignoring the remaining two thirds.

1223. OBJECT IS NOTHING BUT IDEA.

Even according to science, an object is only an idea.

Science says that the proof of the existence of an object can only be its perception by the senses. The perception, when it is examined, is found to be this. Certain rays of light passing through the eyeball fall on the retina, producing an inverted image there. The optical nerves take this impression to the brain centre, from where it is transmitted to the mind as a mere idea.

What you experience is only this idea. The idea does not prove the existence of the object at all, but only the idea. Therefore an object is nothing but an idea.

1224. WHEN DOES MY REAL NATURE SHINE AS IT IS?

Whenever the ego-mind subsides or disappears, the background Awareness shines as Happiness. Whenever objects of Awareness disappear, pure Awareness shines by itself, as pure Consciousness.

1225. WHAT IS THE END OF AN APPEARANCE?

Appearance can never merge in anything else. The non-existent snake can never be said to merge in the rope.

Shrī Gauḍapāda

24th September 1956

1226. WOULD IT NOT SERVE THE SAME PURPOSE IF I CONTEMPLATE THAT EVERYTHING IS MYSELF?

No. It will never be possible to transcend duality that way; because contemplation is thought and you cannot transcend the samskāra of everythingness (duality) in that realm. Thought, which is your only instrument if considered distinct and separate from you, will defy all attempt at absorption by another thought. Therefore the suggestion, though it may appear reasonable on the surface, is neither practicable nor enriching. On the contrary, it will lead you to a state of nothingness where you will find yourself helplessly stranded and deprived of all power of initiative to go beyond.

1227. SIGNIFICANCE OF THE TERM 'ADVAITA'

'Advaita' is the most significant term to denote the ultimate Truth. The ignorant man knows only the world, and everything beyond it is unknown to him. In this sense, Truth is unknown.

Still, he strives to attain that Truth. The world as known is the impediment to the attainment of Truth. Therefore the prakriyā adopted for this purpose is the scrupulous rejection (*neti*) of everything known.

At last, the principle which rejected everything else remains over as incapable of being rejected, and without a second. Looking from the known world, that principle can only be characterized as the 'not-known', in the negative. It is unknown, and not unknowable. If it is considered positive, it becomes known and then the knower comes in and duality is set up. Therefore, the most significant term to denote the characteristic of Truth is advaita (non-duality). The ultimate knower can never be known.

26th September 1956

1228. PRAKRIYĀS (PROCESSES OR METHODS) AND THEIR USE

Innumerable prakriyās have been prescribed in the shāstras, to help aspirants to the Truth. The indiscriminate use or comparison or mixing up of prakriyās are strictly prohibited. Ācāryas declare unequivocally that any *one* prakriyā, which suits the temperament and capacity of the person concerned, is enough to lift him up to the ultimate Truth.

1229. INSISTENCE UPON QUALIFICATIONS AND MENTAL STANDARDS FOR ASPIRANTS

Qualifications and mental standards, like dispassion and renunciation, are intended only for those aspirants who are temperamentally incapable of using their reason or discrimination in the right manner, and who do not pitch their goal as high as the ultimate Truth.

But in the case of one who has the earnestness and sincerity to attain the Truth, no other qualification need be insisted upon. In spite of all his apparent shortcomings, he visualizes the Truth, the moment he listens to the Truth from the lips of the Guru. Thereafter, everything necessary comes in spontaneously, when needed, as a result of the light that has gone in already. This leads him on till he is established in the Truth.

1230. THE TRUMPET CALL OF VĒDĀNTA

'*Awake, arise, and stop not, till the goal is reached*' is the trumpet call of Vēdānta.

All religions serve human tastes and ignorantly multiply differences. But Vēdānta alone serves the changeless Truth and reconciles all differences without exception. The wise saying goes:

> Where no two religions, mystics, yōgins, scientists or philosophers agree, no two sages have ever disagreed about the ultimate Truth.

1231. BODY REACTS DIFFERENTLY UNDER SAMĀDHI AND UNDER DEEP SLEEP. WHY?

Awareness cognizes ideas and co-ordinates the three states.

Question: The body of a person in samādhi sits up erect and seems controlled by the individual, while the body of one in deep sleep lies completely relaxed without any symptom of extraneous control. Why this difference?

Answer: Samādhi is artificial, being the product of preconception and intense effort. A part of the world, in the form of the samskāras of these two, go with you into samādhi.

But in deep sleep you leave everything as well as their samskāras and carry with you nothing of the world except *sat-cit-ānanda*. So deep sleep, which is *vastu-tantra,* is superior to samādhi, which is *kartṛi-tantra*.

All questions relating to the conduct of the body in samādhi are a spurious mixture: of the experience of happiness known to oneself alone, and of the body then known only to the non-self. They have no common ground, and so the question is not relevant.

1232. After visualization of Truth, how can I make the experience permanent?

Answer: Get acquainted with yourself, more and more.

Disciple: This is so simple, so intimate, so natural and so wonderful. But what shall I do to accomplish it in practice?

Answer: Say to yourself what you are, as often as convenient, adducing arguments and throwing yourself into that same state of visualization as you had on the first occasion. This will establish you there, in course of time.

1233. 'I know I am.' How to prove that this is no action?

I say I am the doer and I am the enjoyer. The doer is not the enjoyer. But I am both. So I am the non-doer background of both. I know doing and enjoying. This knowing is my nature – not an action – for it never parts from me.

Therefore, 'I know I am' means: 'I shine in my own light.'

28th September 1956

1234. WHAT IS MEANT BY SAYING THAT A THING 'EXISTS'?

An inert thing has to depend upon something else, in order even to exist.

That something is self-luminous Awareness. Therefore an object is Awareness itself. If a thing cannot exist in its own right, the existence part must come from elsewhere, i.e. from Awareness.

2nd October 1956

1235. NO BRIDGE BETWEEN TRUTH AND UNTRUTH

The relative world and the Absolute are in two entirely different levels, and there is no bridge or relationship between them. 'Jīvan-mukta' is a contradiction in terms. To correlate mind and its objects with pure Awareness – the Sage – is wrong. Even the 'he' is wrong, so far as the Sage is concerned. The 'he' is not. Therefore, his so called objects are also not. The jīvan-mukta himself is not. The principle called 'jīvan-mukta' has neither mind nor senses. It is jnyāna-svarūpa itself. Shāstras describe the jīvan-mukta only from a conceivable level.

(In spite of all this, the disciple of a Kāraṇa-guru can never deny his own experience that the apparent person of the Guru serves as the safest and the surest bridge to the Truth.)

1236. WHY DO SHĀSTRAS DILUTE THE TRUTH?

Most of the existing, recognized shāstras were not addressed to uttamādhikāris or to persons at a comparatively higher level of spiritual progress. They were addressed to persons who did not aspire to the ultimate Truth, who did not follow the direct path of jnyāna, and who did not see their Guru as the embodiment of that Truth. But one who has listened to the Truth from the lips of a Kāraṇa-guru, and has visualized the Truth himself, is well on the way to get established in the Truth.

Therefore, no written book will be of any help to him, in the work of getting firmly established in the Truth already visualized. The purpose of a spiritual book, be it an *Upaniṣhad*, is only to give the aspirant who has not obtained a Kāraṇa-guru an indirect knowledge (parōkṣha-jnyāna) of the nature of the Self, and to emphasize the supreme necessity of approaching a Kāraṇa-guru to help him to realize it. To one who has gone beyond both these needs, books are of no service whatsoever.

But this is not true of books written by your own Guru. They discuss the Truth in the same manner as it has been expounded to you; and that impersonal personality of your Guru as that ultimate Truth is there, so far as you are concerned, in every syllable of it, because the Guru is there in you already. Therefore, those books will help you every time, as much as a personal contact with your Guru would.

1237. WHAT IS PRATYAKṢHA?

Pratyakṣha (irrefutable perception) is of three kinds: *Sensual* pratyakṣha, *mental* pratyakṣha and *conscious* or *bōdha* pratyakṣha. You will lose your hold on the Truth if you cling on to any of the former two pratyakṣhas, but if you cling on to the bōdha pratyakṣha alone, you will never do so.

'*Sva-sthiti*' is a more significant term than the '*sahaja state*' to denote the natural state. The knowledge one happens to have about one's own Self can never be indirect. The knowledge that obtains as a result of adopting any of the prakriyās, like examination of the three states, is decidedly direct Self-experience itself. This is made possible only by listening to the Truth from the lips of the Kāraṇa-guru, with a deep sense of earnestness and sincerity on the part of the aspirant.

'*Shravaṇa*', or listening to the Guru, is alone said to be the '*sākṣhāt-kāraṇa*': the 'genuine cause' of liberation (if any cause could be attributed to liberation).

4th October 1956

1238. REALITY, HOW TO DEFINE IT?

Reality is beyond existence and non-existence. This is true even in the case of a so called object. How? Let us take an example. We say: 'A chair exists', and 'A chair does not exist.' The 'chair' is present in both these opposites. Therefore the chair is necessarily beyond the opposites. Beyond the opposites, there can be only one thing which is real. That is the real Self. Therefore, an object is that Reality itself.

If you say you have life and death, it means you have neither. Because you are in both. As such, you can only be something distinct and separate from life and death, and so necessarily beyond both. That is the conscious principle – the real 'I'.

5th October 1956

1239. *SAT*, *CIT* AND *ĀNANDA* PROVED TO BE ONE AND THE SAME

Ānanda is experienced by man in the name of 'happiness'. It is the knowledge of the existence aspect of the Reality in the form of an object that first attracts the ignorant man. He then begins to desire it, and strives to possess it. The moment he knows that he has obtained the thing he desired, the mind comes to a standstill and his real nature of Peace shines as in deep sleep.

But immediately, when the mind appears again, the memory of the desire and the effort that preceded its achievement colour the mind by contrast, and the pure Peace is therefore called 'happiness' for the time being. If that happy state is allowed to continue indefinitely, the sense of happiness will soon give place to deep Peace, as in deep sleep. Therefore, even the happiness supposed to be derived from objects is nothing other than one's own real nature of Peace.

The *jīvan-mukta* knows this Truth beautifully well and is established in that Peace. Therefore, he does not fall a victim either to desires or to objects. Whatever you experience as a result of effort, prompted by desire, is not Peace in its true nature. It is tainted to that extent. Whatever the heart enjoys is a limited and tainted Peace.

Real Peace is the experience of one's own real nature (ānanda-bhāva-svarūpa). *Ānanda* or *peace* is the experience one gets spontaneously on knowing, beyond the mental realm, that one's real nature is pure Consciousness.

Next, let us examine '*cit*' in the same manner. We say that objects of consciousness are diverse. But we are certain that the objects alone are diverse and that the Consciousness which cognizes these objects is changeless. This Consciousness is also uncaused; and it exists, all alone, even in the absence of all objects, e.g. in deep sleep. Therefore, it is Self-luminous and is *vastu-tantra*.

Lastly, let us examine '*sat*'. We say several objects exist. Every object depends upon pure existence for its own individual existence; but pure existence does not depend upon anything else for its existence. Look at deep sleep. The real 'I' exists all alone, without any other object, in deep sleep. And I know I exist. This pure existence is called *sat*. The *sat* is vastu-tantra and Self-luminous.

Life's activities are impossible without the help of *sat*, *cit* and *ānanda*. But *sat-cit-ānanda* is in no way attached to the objects concerned, which are but appearances upon *sat-cit-ānanda*. It shines all alone in deep sleep, as my real nature. Objects appear manifested in existence and in the light borrowed from my own Self. So they are not other than myself.

Sat, *cit* and *ānanda* are the one and the same. In order to say that *sat* is, *sat* must be known. To do this, Consciousness must come in. Therefore Consciousness and *sat* are one. When that Knowledge of *sat* dawns, a sublime peace filters down from that Consciousness, as the Sage poet sings:

> aṟivē, aṟivān adaivamē aṟivilūṟum ānanda vāriyē
>
> *Tāyumānavar*

Neither is this peace different from *cit*. Therefore *sat*, *cit* and *ānanda* are the one and the same Reality, viewed from the three different perspectives of life, thought and feeling.

1240. MENTAL SATISFACTION REGARDING A SPIRITUAL EXPERIENCE

Question: I have perfect certitude that I have understood and visualized the Truth. Still, I feel that there is something wanting. I do not know what. What is the cause and the remedy for this trouble?

Answer: You mean you do not get full mental satisfaction. Is that not so? Satisfaction is the outcome of the fulfilment of desire. It may result both from that which is right and from that which is wrong. It can, however, never be the identical experience in the two cases. Diversity is its rule, as with everything else which is phenomenal.

Satisfaction is a measure only of phenomenal enjoyment. It can never be a measure of the Absolute. Satisfaction always presupposes an object, with all its limitations. There is nothing phenomenal which can satisfy everyone, for all time. The many can never do this.

But there is only one thing – the Ātmā, the impersonal Self, by nature changeless, self-luminous, and being Peace itself – that can bring permanent Peace or satisfaction. Being changeless and uncaused, it cannot strictly be called satisfaction. It may be called 'objectless Happiness'. The knowledge that 'I am that changeless experience itself' is the svarūpa of satisfaction. This satisfaction is therefore self-luminous. No other satisfaction can be self-luminous.

The experience of being impersonal cannot be the object of any desire. It takes one beyond the mental level of satisfaction. But the memory of the age-long samskāras of satisfaction prompts us still to crave for satisfaction, even when we stand beyond it. Therefore, that false craving has to be ignored as illusion or destroyed in the light of the higher reason.

6th October 1956

1241. HOW TO UNDERSTAND EXPERIENCE?

Experience is of two kinds: vastu-tantra and kartṛi-tantra.

1. *Vastu-tantra* is begotten of Ātmā.
2. *Kartṛi-tantra* is begotten of doership.

All Experiences of duality, including even the yōgin's nirvikalpa samādhi, are kartṛi-tantra. The experience which takes me straight to my real nature, of Peace and Consciousness, is alone vastu-tantra.

vastutan vaśamāṁ jñānaṁ; karttradhīnam upāsanaṁ

[It's only on reality
that knowledge rightfully depends.
But meditation must depend
upon a doer of some kind.]

Bhāṣha Pancadashi, Dhyāna-dīpam, 73
(Malayalam translation)

Vēdānta alone adopts vastu-tantra; and that too, to destroy kartṛi-tantra and its creations that obscure the Reality. All other systems or practices or beliefs – karma, yōga, devotion, mysticism, religions... – all adopt kartṛi-tantra. Satisfaction is the goal of all these.

Vastu-tantra, being ātmic, is beyond feeling. Kartṛi-tantra, being mental, is capable of being felt, but is fleeting. Mental satisfaction can be derived both from Truth as well as from untruth. Vastu-tantra is not the result of any activity or inactivity. But kartṛi-tantra is always the result of activity, which takes the form of desire and effort for its fulfilment.

When the disciple – who is a waking subject – is told by the Guru that even his phenomenal satisfaction is not derived from objects, but that it is his own real nature shining in its own glory, his doership (which is the centre of kartṛi-tantra) crumbles for ever. Desires torment him no more, and satisfaction is transformed into permanent Peace.

When this sublime Peace, vastu-tantra, is sought to be brought down to respond to kartṛi-tantra, guided by varying tastes and tendencies, a host of new concepts in the form of religions, heavens, objects of pleasure and so on begin to appear. Therefore, give up your tastes, tendencies and desires – not violently, but by knowing, and by knowing more and more deeply, that all satisfaction is the expression of your own real nature of Peace – and you shall be for ever free.

The state of Peace in deep sleep is the most familiar experience of vastu-tantra in daily life. The annihilation of all kartṛi-tantra is the ultimate goal of Vēdānta. This establishes vastu-tantra without any positive effort whatever. Look at deep sleep. You have only to give up your attachment to body, senses and mind, in the waking and dream states. Immediately, Peace – vastu-tantra – dawns, permanent and self-luminous.

Deep sleep comes involuntarily, and without the help of discrimination. Therefore it disappears, after a while. Establish the same state voluntarily and with discrimination. When once you visualize it this way, it will never disappear.

9th October 1956

1242. WHAT IS THE WORLD (PRAPANCA)?

Answer: Dṛishyatva – perceivability. Dṛishyatva can never be in *dṛishya* [the seen] or the object. It can only be in *adṛishya* [the unseen]. This adṛishya (Ātmā) is alone the basis or background of dṛishyatva.

Dṛishyatva implies knowledge. Therefore it is Knowledge itself. The word 'percept' is the nearest English equivalent to *dṛishyatva.* A percept implies perception, and perception implies Knowledge.

1243. EVERY WORD DENOTES THE REALITY ALONE.

If I say 'I am *man*', I mean I am *sat, cit, ānanda.* How?

The essential precaution one has to take in order to understand a word correctly is to be prepared to understand just what is meant to be conveyed by the word, and nothing more or less. This is not what we generally do. We understand much more than what is conveyed by a word.

Let us take the same illustration: 'I am *man.*' It is the meaning of the word 'man' that we have to examine. 'Man' is unqualified, without number or gender. There is no diversity in 'man'. The word 'man' represents the whole man-kingdom. That which is 'man', in all men, is changeless. In this sense, 'man' is not limited by time or space. The only Reality, beyond time and space, is *sat-cit-ānanda.* Therefore, 'man' in its real sense is *sat-cit-ānanda* itself. So are all other words – 'animal', 'bird', 'table', 'pencil', etc. Every word in its strict sense means *sat-cit-ānanda*, the real Self.

It is never possible to make the apparent many into one. You need only understand that the manyness is an illusion, and that its background alone is real. The simple word 'man' is understood by everyone, no doubt; but nobody grasps its right meaning. It is not understood by the senses or mind, but by Knowledge alone. Knowledge cannot know anything other than Knowledge. Therefore what is understood by the word 'man' is Knowledge itself.

Ignorant man considers himself a particular being. He has been long trained in the habit of understanding even general statements in a particular sense, in accordance with his own tastes and tendencies.

But in order to understand a general statement correctly – for example 'man', 'water' etc. – one has to stand as a general being, beyond senses and mind. From that stand, one can never perceive anything other than one's Self – 'Consciousness'.

1244. QUOTING THE SCRIPTURES

The habit of quoting the scriptures and accepting their authority blindly is definitely a slavish mentality. The scriptures are only views of some of the ancients, recorded in books. They had their own particular ways of reasoning and modes of thinking. There is nothing wrong in your accepting their views, provided you understand them in the light of your own reason and make them your own.

You must yourself be able to establish those views, adducing arguments and illustrations – whether old or new it is immaterial. But you must not rely upon the names of the scriptures, or of their authors, to create conviction.

10th October 1956

1245. ILLUSTRATIONS EMPLOYED BY VĒDĀNTA

The illustration of 'earth and the pot' is usually adopted in Vēdānta to bring home the Truth that the world is nothing but Ātmā. But in applying the illustration to the problem of the world, mistakes often creep in. In this illustration, 'earth' should be taken to represent Ātmā; and 'pot' to represent everything other than Ātmā, gross or subtle, including name, form, utility etc., in other words 'object' in the most comprehensive sense.

The proposition is that there is no pot independent of earth. To disprove this, it is not relevant to bring in other objects, ignoring the fact that they are already represented by the pot in the illustration. Thus, all side issues like the potter's labour, utility of the pot, and contents of the pot are quite irrelevant, since they attribute independent existence to the pot. Therefore there is no pot as such at any point of time, but only earth. Similarly, there is no object or world as such, but only Ātmā.

It is best to see the pot to be nothing but earth, even when the pot remains as pot. It can also be seen to be only earth by destroying the pot as such. But the second method is rather crude and childish.

1246. WHAT IS THE NATURE OF REALIZATION?

The plainest and simplest way of putting it is this: 'I had mistaken myself to be a thinker, doer, perceiver and enjoyer. That misconception has disappeared.'

Here the question 'how' does not arise. But it has to be understood clearly that realization is no action.

11th October 1956

1247. THE STAND OF AN ADVAITIN

An earnest advaitin must studiously give up all contact with theology, scholasticism and mysticism, and take to pure *vicāra* alone, if he wants to get established in the ultimate Truth in the shortest time possible.

14th October 1956

1248. IṢHṬA-DĒVA

'*Iṣhṭa-dēva*' ['chosen deity'] is the form given by you to your own *iṣhṭa* (desire). Therefore, one who worships an iṣhṭa-dēva is virtually worshipping his own desire (liking).

So much so, a boy getting a vision of his iṣhṭa-dēva will invariably see him as playing with him in the sand or water. Because play is the then element and desire of the boy himself, at that age. No actual portrait of any iṣhṭa-dēva exists anywhere. Your own desire or fancy is your only guide in creating the form of your iṣhṭa-dēva.

Sculptors and painters have of course given us some models. But they are only forms of their own imagination. For example, M. Tampi has produced many portraits of Shrī Kṛiṣhṇa, Dēvī, Shāstā and other deities. He had never seen them in the waking state, and naturally he was at a loss to conceive their face and form. Therefore he thought of his own Guru and prayed to him to bless him so that he could paint a picture of the desired iṣhṭa-dēva. Straightaway he imagined a form and painted it. But it is strange that the prominent features in all his pictures – whether of Kṛiṣhṇa, Dēvī or Shāstā – have generally the stamp of the features of his own Guru.

This proves clearly that the iṣhṭa-dēva is nothing but one's desire personified. The worship of such a being can never take one beyond the mental realm of one's own likes and dislikes.

But if the worship is directed to the iṣhṭa-dēva as an 'Ātma-mūrti' ['embodiment of Self'], as explained and directed by a Kāraṇa-guru, one can rise to the Ultimate gradually by that and that alone.

23rd October 1956

1249. DREAMS AND WAKING BODY

A pandit took up a question discussed in the higher shāstras on Advaita.

Question: If dreams are quite unreal, why is it that they sometimes leave visible reactions on the waking body?

Answer: The shāstras try to explain this by positing a second dream in the interval between the dream and waking states. But this gives no satisfactory solution to the spirit of the question, because the answer is sought in terms of the waking state.

The question arises in the waking state, assuming causality to be real and the dream alone to be unreal. A correct solution is possible only by viewing the question from a higher level, beyond the dream and waking states, from the stand of the disinterested witness.

1. Viewing from there, both the dream and waking states seem equally unreal and therefore the question does not arise.

2. The dream was first examined and proved to be unreal, not in order to show that the waking state was real, but to show that it was equally unreal. Because it is impossible to find any difference between the two states at the moment of experiencing them.

3. Even in the waking state, it is never possible to connect two incidents; because the past remains only as an idea or dream, and the present alone appears as the gross in the waking state. As each appears in different states and at different points of time, the

two can never be connected. So also in the dream state, the so called cause and effect can never be connected.

4. The dream state is also a waking state, when experienced. Therefore, the waking and dream states may well be considered as successive waking states. Taking each waking state as one experience, no relationship can be established between two successive waking states, one being past and the other present.

3rd November 1956

1250. EXPERIENCE AND DISTORTION

The real experience of the Self is knowledge in identity. When the experience is expressed in words, as 'I enjoyed…', 'I perceived…' etc., in the form of subject-object relationship, it is a clear distortion of the experience itself. This distortion distances the ego far from the centre.

1251. A JĪVAN-MUKTA AND THE STATES

A jīvan-mukta does not destroy the states. He only illumines the states and understands them to be nothing other than the real Self.

But the onlooker might not perceive this internal change in the jīvan-mukta's perspective. He may still take him to be the old jīva, a subject of the changing states.

20th December 1956

1252. HOW IS A THING CONSTITUTED?

A thing may be said to be real only if it continues to be real in all the three states, that is at the sensual, mental and transcendental levels. In the subjective realm, the body is a percept, the mind is an idea and the 'I'-principle is Consciousness – the Reality. The senses, mind and the 'I'-principle each contribute their respective quotas to the make of any object.

The sense organ concerned contributes the one fundamental percept, the mind brings forth its store of former concepts and heaps them upon the first percept in the form of supplementary percepts, making the object a perceptual whole. The 'I'-principle contributes its quota – the sense of reality – to the object, and makes it appear real.

This last part is represented by the pronoun 'It', in the case of every object. The 'It' continues changeless, through all apparent changes.

26th December 1956

1253. THE STAND OF CĀRVAKA EXAMINED

Cārvaka asserts that there is nothing beyond the world perceived. Evidently, he takes into consideration only the waking, objective world.

But when his attention is drawn to the dream and deep sleep worlds, which are equally strong percepts when experienced, he is forced to admit that there is something beyond this apparent world. Then again, who is it that says that there is nothing beyond the world? Is that principle comprehended by the world, or not? *No.* It cannot be. It must certainly stand beyond the world. So Cārvaka's statement itself proves that there is a principle beyond.

If you say it is the brain that decides, the brain has to rely upon the body for its very existence. The dream body has also a brain. It has to be decided which brain is one to rely upon. The waking and dream brains disprove each other. Hence, that principle which stands beyond is the 'I' or Consciousness. It is the only thing that does not need any proof to establish its existence. This 'I' is not a percept, and so stands clearly beyond the world.

Vēdānta begins with that principle standing beyond body, senses, mind, and even beyond the witness. Nobody can deny his existence in the deep sleep state, when he is without a body, senses or mind. That is the 'I'-principle in one, beyond the body, senses and mind.

28th December 1956

1254. WHAT IS THE RIGHT APPROACH TO A PROBLEM?

Every problem has two standpoints. One is that of the ego; and the other is that of the 'I'-principle.

Suppose you desire an object. A desire shows your imperfection, at least to that extent. And the urge to become perfect comes from your own being deep below, which is by nature perfect, or one without a second. Therefore, desire points to your real nature, and you can realize it by viewing it in the right perspective. This is from the ego's standpoint.

Looking from the standpoint of the real 'I'-principle, you find that desire shows the pain of separation from the object desired, and a longing to end that separation by obtaining it. It shows an eagerness to establish that oneness or perfection, your real nature, whenever you seem to stray away from it by identification with body, senses or mind.

29th December 1956

1255. THE WORLD AND BRAHMAN SHOULD BOTH MERGE IN THE 'I'-PRINCIPLE.

The world, posited in space, is an appearance on the Reality. The term 'world' rightly comprehends also the generic space and time in which diversity is supposed to appear. The process of visualizing the Reality in the world is by completely separating the appearance part of it from the Reality.

But usually, in that endeavour, the world alone is eliminated, leaving behind unnoticed both space and time tagged on to the Reality. The consequent superimposition of the sense of time and space, on the Reality behind, gives it the idea of bigness. This is responsible for the fallacious concept and name, 'brahman'. When this sense of bigness is also eliminated, brahman itself stands revealed as the ultimate Reality, the 'I'-principle.

This is possible only by listening to the Truth from the lips of the Kāraṇa-guru.

1256. WHAT ARE INSIDE AND OUTSIDE?

The concept of inside and outside is born only with the inception of the body idea or the idea of space. When you transcend the body, even in idea, the space idea also vanishes, and with it the idea of bigness and smallness as well. In other words, you transcend all opposites.

1257. HAS TRUTH NO OPPOSITE?

No. The only possible opposite to Truth is untruth. But when you strictly examine untruth, you find it to be nothing but an appearance on Truth. Therefore Truth has no opposite.

1258. WHAT IS APPEARANCE AND WHAT IS IT THAT APPEARS?

Appearance certainly is not Truth. Because Truth can never appear or be subject to time and space. What else then can it be that appears? Can it be appearance itself? *No*. Because appearance is appearance only on appearance. Hence appearance can never appear. Therefore appearance is *not*. It is only an illusion. Truth alone is.

Memory proves that I am the witness. Suppose I make a statement, now, about a thought I had yesterday. In relation to the past thought, I am the witness. But in relation to the present statement, I am the sayer. None but the witness has the authority to say. Thus I am the witness, and as witness I stand identified with Consciousness.

5th January 1957

1259. THE UNANSWERABLE QUESTION

The question is often asked: 'Who is a Guru?' or 'What is a Guru?' But the answer is not so easily understood.

To the intellectual, the Guru is always an enigma. The Guru represents the ultimate Truth, and stands in non-duality. The question is raised in duality, in the mental level, about the Guru who is standing in non-duality. There cannot be any answer in either level. The question cannot be understood in the mental level since it pertains to the Guru in non-duality. And in non-duality, the question does not ever arise.

The Guru is beyond all questions and all duality. A question is the expression or synonym of duality.

1260. THE PSYCHOLOGY OF SUICIDE AND ITS REMEDY

Suicide means the killing of the self. Suicide is usually contemplated to avoid a dragging pain or dishonour. But instead, you are courting another pain of an intenser type, though for a shorter period, and with a most uncertain future. Therefore, if any other means can be suggested to get away from the pain, it would certainly be acceptable to one who contemplates suicide. Prove to him his identity with the changeless principle behind body and mind; and prove to him that the pain belongs to the mind alone, as a result of its identification with body.

Thinking of committing suicide means trying to kill the self. Who tries to do so? The self itself. Is it possible to split the self that way? *No*. Therefore direct your attention to the thought of committing suicide and kill it; in other words, 'kill the killer'.

Seeing a golden time-piece placed just below a photograph of Gurunāthan in his room, a lady disciple enjoyed the sight and said: 'It looks beautiful there.' Immediately Gurunāthan turned to her and said: 'But there is a deeper significance than you think. You see, the time-piece represents time; and I stand above it, transcending time. You must also stand likewise. Everything you see here will have a similar significance, if only you look deep enough.'

15th January 1957

1261. WHY DO SO FEW PEOPLE TAKE TO THE ULTIMATE TRUTH?

Answer: In this question you want to tie down the causeless to causality. It is impossible.

Question: Why does one go to a Guru?

Answer: To get beyond the why, and then the question disappears.

24th February 1957

1262. MIXING OF LEVELS

Indiscriminate mixing of levels is always to be discouraged. It leads to confusion of ideas.

But in every sādhana, there is mixing of the two levels [of Truth and untruth], to a certain extent. That mixing is helpful in establishing you in the Truth, since you emphasize the goal of Truth through all right sādhana and strive to eliminate all that is other than the Truth.

Thus even the mixing of levels, when done with discrimination, leads you to the background.

26th February 1957

1263. THE SPECTATOR AND THE ACTOR IN LIFE

Man is both the spectator and the actor in the drama of life. The spectator is real, but the actor is unreal.

27th February 1957

1264. WHAT IS LIMITATION?

The presence of objects and absence of objects are respectively termed limitedness and unlimitedness, or conditionedness and unconditionedness, of consciousness. The so called unconditionedness is also a limitation put upon Consciousness, and is generally called 'samādhi'. Truth is still beyond.

2nd March 1957

1265. KNOWING AND LOVING

Knowing and loving come in as a result of your not wanting to be separated from the thing. But there is a world of difference between the knowing in the relative level and knowing in the absolute level.

In the absolute level, to know is to be. In the relative level, there is the apparent distinction brought in between the existence and knowing parts.

If you continue to know as in the absolute level, the 'It' cannot stand as different from knowledge and non-duality is established.

1266. SHOULD NOT ONE WHO HAS KNOWN THE TRUTH BE KIND TO OTHERS?

The question rises out of a confusion of levels. The question tries to connect truth and untruth. Truth is in the absolute level, and the rest of the question is in the relative level.

You must see that it is not enough to be kind alone, but you should stand as one with others as Truth. Then the question will not arise. With change of state, the field of reference changes completely.

11th March 1957

1267. APPEARANCE AND DISAPPEARANCE

It is appearance that goes into the make of disappearance. So there is only appearance and no disappearance. Disappearance appears. That is all.

Appearance is 'seeing' itself, and 'seeing' is Consciousness itself. So all is Consciousness, the real Self.

14th March 1957

1268. WHAT IS THE NATURE OF THE EGO?

The ego is a spurious entity which does not exist and can never exist. It does not stand the slightest scrutiny. What is the difference between the ego and the other things which you have accepted to be illusions? Such things have at least a momentary appearance, in the mental level. But the ego has not even that. It is never experienced by anybody at any time.

You stray away from knowledge, down to the object known; and that is the ego.

18th March 1957

1269. WHAT HAPPENS WHEN YOU SEE AN OBJECT?

1. First, you see form. This belongs to the field of percepts, which is the outcome of the senses.
2. Next, you join it on to innumerable concepts, which belong to the realm of the mind.

3. Lastly, you attribute a permanence to it which belongs to your own Self and is denoted by the 'It' in relation to all objects.

All these together go to make the so called object. But when you emphasize the 'It' which was always there – all through – the other two naturally disappear; and the 'It', which was so long unknown, now becomes known in the real sense.

1270. HOW TO EXAMINE AN OBJECT?

The examination of an object must be conducted from all three states, with equal completeness. You are doing this, though unknowingly, all the time. You have only to note it and understand it correctly, as follows:

1. When the percept appears, the waking state sense organs function.
2. When the concepts (as ideas) are added on, the dream state is brought in.
3. At last, when knowledge dawns, the deep sleep state beyond the mind comes in.

Therefore, you confirm every object only after systematically examining it from all the three states.

23rd March 1957

1271. VALUE AND ITS APPLICATION

Values are of two kinds:

1. Truth value, and
2. Satisfaction value or happiness value.

They are essentially different.

Happiness depends upon one's tastes, which are different in different persons. Therefore the happiness value, as gauged by different persons, must also be different. Happiness is the criterion which guides the life of the great majority of persons – dominated as they are by the tastes and desires of the mind.

Truth, which is identical with the being in man, is of the nature of differencelessness. This is only one and self-luminous. It is only the one that has visualized the Truth that can adopt it. Therefore it is only vēdāntins, who are few in number, that can understand and apply the Truth value.

1272. HOW DOES *SAT-CIT-ĀNANDA* EXPRESS ITSELF IN EVERYDAY LIFE?

The first expression of the Reality in life is that 'something *is*'. This is the *sat* aspect. Beyond a vague 'is'-ness, it yields nothing more.

You want to know it and begin to search for more information about it. Then you know it, without the help of any light other than your own Self. This is the expression of *cit*.

As soon as that knowledge is complete, a spontaneous satisfaction oozes out of that knowledge. This is the expression of *ānanda*.

Existence, Consciousness and Peace express themselves in all experiences or activities of life. This happiness which flows from the mere knowledge of an existent thing is self-luminous happiness, which is 'vastu-tantra' ['coming from Truth'].

But the happiness which is the outcome of varied tastes and efforts is only worldly and a reflection of the *ānanda* aspect of the Reality. This is 'kartṛi-tantra' ['coming from doership'].

1273. OBSTACLE MADE A MEANS

Body, senses and mind are supposed to be the clothing of the real Self within. The ignorant man emphasizes the clothing alone and loses sight of the Self. But with the attainment of a spiritual outlook the position is reversed, and the very same clothes are made a help to visualize the Self within.

The way to achieve this is to make the clothing of the Self as thin as possible so as to see through them. Or, in other words, make the body, senses and mind function in such a manner that you can see through them. Then your attention is caught by the Self within; the mind and senses lose their significance as obstacles and become mere pointers to the Self.

1274. WHAT IS REAL DESTRUCTION?

The destruction of an object really means the disappearance of the object, without its leaving any trace, even as an idea. This is never possible in the physical or mental realms. But in the worldly sense, destruction only means disintegration in any manner.

Yōga and devotion accept the latter interpretation of the term; and they strive to destroy the mind by purifying or expanding it, keeping on the separateness once and for all. You can never destroy a thing by anything like cleaning, correcting or mending it in the same level. This is why yōga and devotion fail to destroy the mind, and lead one only to a state of peace limited by time and called 'samādhi'.

Real destruction is achieved only by jnyāna or Vēdānta – not objectively but subjectively – by eliminating the sense of duality once and for all, and thus seeing the object as nothing but your own Self.

1275. HOW DOES JNYĀNA HELP ME?

The jnyāna path does not claim to take you to the Truth or to illumine the Truth. You are always the Truth, and the Truth is self-luminous. So the jnyāna path claims only to remove the obstacles in the way – viz. the sense of separateness and its objects – by applying the correct tests of Reality, such as changelessness and self-luminosity. When all obstacles are thus removed, the self-luminous 'I' remains ever shining in all its glory. This is called visualization or realization.

Jnyāna alone is *vastu-tantra* [governed by Truth]. But devotion, yōga, karma and all other paths are *kartṛi-tantra* [governed by doership].

25th March 1957

1276. WHAT IS TRUE LOVE?

Love is deeper knowledge, and is usually considered to be feminine. The knowledge of the intellect, which is relatively superficial, is usually considered to be masculine. If you know the Truth with your own being, that knowledge itself is love, and is both feminine and masculine or beyond both.

If the ego takes leave of you in the course of an activity, it takes you straight to pure love. Love can be made permanent only if it is made unconditional and spontaneous, and if it expects nothing in return.

1277. WHAT IS BEING?

'Being' is being and is independent of its opposite, non-being. Non-being can exist only on being. But being can exist all alone.

30th March 1957

1278. WHAT IS THE TRUTH OF PERCEPTION?

I am Ātmā, the self-luminous Consciousness. It may be said that I first manifest myself as objectless Consciousness, by my own nature or self-luminosity. It is this objectless Consciousness that expresses itself as an idea or sensual object; and you say you perceive it.

But when the so called perception takes place, the apparent object loses its limitations; and its content, Consciousness, stands as the objectless Self. Therefore, it is nothing but the Self that you perceive.

1st April 1957

1279. BHĀVA AND ABHĀVA

Bhāva [being] and abhāva [non-being] as generic terms are Consciousness itself, indeterminate in nature and identical with the Self. They can never be conceived by the mind. When you know them or speak of them, they become determinate and distinct, and separate from you and from Truth.

1280. HOW DOES THE WORLD APPEAR AND WHAT IS ITS SOLUTION?

Pure Consciousness, which is the ultimate Reality, expresses itself first as self-consciousness, without admitting any medium whatsoever. This is the most immediate of all knowledge and is identical with 'being', completely beyond subject-object relationship.

This Consciousness seems to degenerate, by appearing to express itself through the mind and senses, as thoughts and perceptions. By accepting the medium of the mind and senses, the appearances – namely thoughts and perceptions – seem to be separate from the Self. This is how the world appears, though in essence it is nothing but the Self.

Therefore, the solution of the world does not lie in any objective search outside, by way of the sciences or philosophy, but in withdrawing into the real Self within one. This may successfully be achieved by following the ordinary mental knowledge itself to its very source, through the most immediate expression of knowledge, namely self-consciousness or objectless knowledge.

3rd April 1957

1281. WHAT IS 'VICĀRA' – 'DISCRIMINATION'?

It is a peculiar kind of activity, but not 'thought' as it might seem to be. Its purpose is removal of untruth (body, senses and mind) by arguments. What is left over is the real Self (absolute Truth) as the real background.

1282. WHAT IS REAL KNOWING?

'To know', in the real sense, is 'to be'.

You were Peace or Happiness in deep sleep. It is a fact and a certainty. How do you know it now? Whatever you think or say about it is wrong. Thought and statement both take place in the sphere of duality and refer only to objects distinct and separate from you. But at the point of knowing in deep sleep, you were in identity with Peace or Happiness. It is not possible for the mind to know it or remember it. It was pure being alone. Real knowing is always being, and answers only to the Truth.

But worldly knowing is always separate from you, and answers only to satisfaction in the mental level. Your goal should always be the 'Peace' of deep sleep, which is 'being' itself and not anything expressed or expressible.

You say you are a man, because you know you are a man. But when you know that you are a man, you can never stand as a man, but only as a principle distinct and separate from man. Therefore you are not man, but that principle which knows man, otherwise called the witness or knowledge.

Don't you say you 'feel pain'? But is not pain itself a feeling? Therefore the statement is redundant. It is also wrong to say you 'know the pain'. Because here knowing and feeling are both mentations. They are not possible simultaneously. But it is our experience that we know the mentations simultaneously. This is not known by the mind itself, but is known from a higher plane, by the witness.

The witness's knowing of a thing is 'being it'. It is the consciousness in the thought or perception of the thing itself that is the witness. The ego knows a thing only as subject and object. The ego is the false identification of the body, senses and mind with the real Self. The objects of the ego also suffer from the same false identification with the Reality. The purpose of the witness is to reveal this false identification of the object with the reality.

The witness has been defined as the consciousness in the object itself. Consciousness transcends both time and space. As such it can never see the object as separate from it – either in time or space. So it sees the object as itself. Thus it is the 'being' in the object itself that is called the witness, in order to eliminate the objectivity of the object. Then the object ceases to be object, as such, and stands as Consciousness.

1283. THE COURSE OF LIBERATION IN SHORT

The course of liberation, or the solution of the world, consists of only three simple steps.

1. Malady: *The wrong identification* with body, senses and mind, by which man appears to be bound and becomes miserable.
2. Remedy: *Separation*. Body, senses and mind are shown to be distinct and separate from the real Self, which stands as the perpetual knower or witness.

3. Recovery: *Right identification.* Standing as that witness, you stand identified with the being, and the witnessed disappears. Then the witness ceases to be witness, but stands as the ultimate Reality – Consciousness.

4th April 1957

1284. WHO KNOWS MY IDEAS?

Certainly not another idea. Because two ideas cannot exist simultaneously.

It is the transcendental Consciousness alone that can know an idea and know it not through the subject-object relationship, but by being identical with it. It is the non-empirical Consciousness that knows the idea; just as you know happiness in deep sleep, by being identical with it.

The moment an idea is known, the material part of the idea drops away and its essence – pure Consciousness – alone remains over. What you call an idea now is not really idea, as you presume, but only pure Consciousness. Because an idea is known by pure Consciousness, and Consciousness cannot know anything other than Consciousness.

Therefore, the ego's knowledge is also non-empirical. When you emphasize the Consciousness aspect, which is the essence of the ego, the ego gets immediately transformed into non-empirical Consciousness.

The moment you know Happiness, it is non-empirical and one with you.

Thus, whenever you know anything, you stand as one with the thing, as Consciousness pure.

1285. HOW IS AN OBJECT KNOWN?

An object can remain as an object only if it remains distinct and separate from you, and yet connected with you in subject-object relationship. The object has necessarily to give up its objectivity in order to be one with you, or to be identical with you, when known.

This happens both in the relative level of the ego and also in the absolute level, with identity established in either case. In the level of the ego, the ego loses itself in the object and becomes identical with it, for the time being. But in the absolute level, you make the object lose itself in you, as Consciousness for ever.

1286. THE DEEP SLEEP STATE IS ALWAYS IN THE PAST.

When you experience deep sleep, you stand identified with pure Consciousness or Peace beyond time. It can never be called the present in deep sleep. But when you refer to it from the waking state, you call the preceding state the 'deep sleep state' and then it is only an idea.

Similarly, every thought or perception is nothing but the ultimate Reality or knowledge, at the moment when you know it. But when you refer to it subsequently, you make an idea of it, which is not the thing referred to at all. This is the truth of the whole world, which – though a heap of thoughts, feelings and perceptions – is nothing but pure Consciousness.

1287. INDETERMINATE IGNORANCE IS ALSO THE REALITY.

Because ignorance of everything is the same as knowledge of everything, which is pure knowledge. 'Everything' is an empty word, incapable of limiting knowledge in any manner. The generic of bhāva [being] or abhāva [non-being] is one and the same.

4th April 1957

1288. REALITY CANNOT BE OBJECTIFIED.

It is thought and speech alone that obscure the reality. So cease these activities and the Reality will shine in its own glory.

Do not try to objectify Reality. The yōgin tries to objectify what refuses to be objectified.

1289. THE STATES ARE NOTHING BUT CONSCIOUSNESS.

The knowing act is the last act or link in the chain of any activity. There is nothing else, anywhere, to know it. The last knowing act, without itself being known, is non-empirical and is the ultimate Reality.

Every knowing in the relative level can be referred to a knowing beyond. The last one is transcendental Consciousness. The transcendental Consciousness alone can witness the states. Transcendental Consciousness cannot witness anything other than itself. So the states are nothing but Consciousness.

1290. HOW ARE STATES EXAMINED?

In deep sleep, the concept of general ignorance is destroyed, in order to show your real nature.

Ignorant knowledge gives reality to objects, forgetting its essence – knowledge. Here, in the waking state, your ignorant knowledge is destroyed, in order to show that you are the transcendental.

1291. WHAT IS *SARVA-JNYATVA* – ALL-KNOWINGNESS?

The 'all' here is only one object which has to be disposed of, like any other object, and shown to be nothing but Consciousness, the real Self. This is all-knowingness (*sarva-jnyatva*).

1st May 1957

1292. M.M.H. asked: I KNOW GURUNĀTHAN IS IN ME. STILL WHY DO I DESIRE TO GO TO TRIVANDRUM TO SEE MY GURU?

Answer: Your Guru is in you as yourself – the ultimate Truth. That is everywhere. But your Guru as he is in Trivandrum is something more than that. There he also has a living body which has been instrumental in liberating you, and towards which your love and adoration flow spontaneously. Therefore you have to go to Trivandrum to fulfil that desire, not any more to understand Truth. But, of course, your establishment in Truth gets firmer with every such visit.

Actually, whenever you think of your Gurunāthan you are at Trivandrum.

1293. HOW FAR CAN THE BOOK OF A SAGE HELP AN ASPIRANT?

There is as much difference between a Sage and his book as between yourself and your image in a mirror. The image is devoid of the life principle which is the very substance of the original. The image is a reflection of the exterior alone and has no interior.

Similarly, the book or language can convey only the mere exterior of Truth. But Truth has no distinctions such as exterior and interior. Therefore nobody can get at the essence of Truth through books or through language alone. A book, as such, is dead and inert, and cannot answer a new question arising from the one dealt with in the book. Whenever you read a book, you read something of your own sense in it. This, however, you cannot do when you read the books of your Guru.

Language is limited, but the Guru is unlimited. If anybody considers the Guru to be limited, by a particular body or mind, he is wrong and that conception is not the real Guru. But if body and mind cease to have their character as such, they are also the Guru.

2nd May 1957

1294. RELATION OF THE OBJECTIVE TO THE SUBJECTIVE

The objective world does not include the subject. But the subject includes the objective world. Therefore, you cannot find a correct explanation of the objective world from the objective world itself, but only from and through the subject.

1295. THE GURU THOUGHT

It is taken indiscriminately in more than one way.

One such way is the thought: 'I am the Guru.' *This is forbidden*; because, by that thought, the ultimate is crushed and the apparent 'I' gains in strength.

But in the next thought, 'The Guru is in me', the ultimate will gradually devour the 'me' and leave one as the ultimate Truth.

1296. THE VISION EXPERIENCED BY THE YŌGIN

When the world is examined objectively, emptiness is the background of all appearance, because it is there before and after appearance. Examining it subjectively, your Self – Consciousness – is the background.

This emptiness is thus Consciousness itself. This is why the yōgins see emptiness when the world disappears; because they look at all things objectively.

If you ask why the world appears, you must ask the world and not me. The world must explain itself to you.

6th May 1957

1297. WHAT IS LIFE?

A headache is a feeling. But we say: 'I feel a headache.' It is impossible to feel a feeling. But in fact you stand as that feeling. You are that. But then, the 'that' also disappears and you stand as yourself alone.

So feeling or thinking is being the feeling or thinking itself. This is the Truth. But you separate yourself from thought or feeling, and that is life. Whenever the mind functions, you are spatializing the absolute.

1298. WHAT HAPPENS WHEN YOU REMEMBER?

When you think of something you had perceived elsewhere, you are really in thought, taking yourself over there and trying to have the same direct experience of the thing as you had on the first occasion. It is never possible to take the thing over to where you are, as one ordinarily imagines one can.

20th May 1957

1299. I DO MY SĀDHANA IN THE WAKING STATE. HOW CAN THE DREAMER BE BENEFITED BY THAT?

A question in the waking state should have reference only to a waking subject or a waking object. A dream can never be either. So the question, as it is, cannot arise.

But the so called dream comes out as an idea in the waking state. An idea is nothing but Consciousness. A thought in the waking state about a dream comprehends only the dream state. But an answer to that on the spiritual level comprehends all the three states, because it takes you beyond all states.

A dream really means all that which has passed away. Therefore, the answer to a question about the so called waking state rightly includes the dream state as well. Whatever is past is an idea. A dream never exists in the present. So it is only an idea. A waking state experience may be said to have had a present, and it subsequently becomes the past. But the so called dream state has never had a present. If you say that during the dream you were in the present, I say it was at that point of time not a dream but a waking state. So, on that score also, there never was a dream. Therefore, there is only a waking state or only a dream state.

So there is no room for comparison. Reference can be made only to the past. By the time you perceive anything, the thing said to be perceived is in the past.

25th May 1957

1300. I AM CHANGELESS.

The very mention of one's age proves that one is changeless, at that period of time. Therefore one is changeless through all time. Space is derived from time. Therefore one is changeless as regards space as well.

If I say I am 57 years old now, it means that I have been changeless all through the apparent changes I have undergone – like childhood, boyhood, etc.

That which appears on Me is life. That which gets separated from Me is death. Looked at from a deeper level, even death forms part of life.

26th May 1957

1301. HOW IS THOUGHT EGOLESS?

During the occurrence of a thought, you do not have the thought that you are thinking. You stand identified with the thought itself, and so there is no duality or ego. It is after the event that the ego comes in and claims that he thought. This is a lie. Therefore, every mentation is egoless, at the moment it occurs.

You know every mentation just as you know Happiness in deep sleep. By being it.

1302. SPIRITUAL SPHERE AND SHĀSTRAS

The spiritual realm is covered by three progressive stages, namely:

1. *Ajāta-vāda* ['There is no creation' – the final, subjective stage],
2. *Dṛiṣhṭi-sṛiṣhṭi-vāda* ['Perception begets creation' – the intermediate, mental stage], and
3. *Vyavahāra-pakṣha* or *sṛiṣhṭi-dṛiṣhṭi-vāda* ['Creation is perceived' – the worldly, objective stage].

Most shāstras abound in the third (the lowest) stage of vyavahāra-pakṣha. Their variety and volume confound the ordinary reader with their innumerable arguments and counter-arguments – all purely academic. In all those arguments, the trace and colour of the waking state is felt and emphasized.

The correct approach is to stand as the awareness that witnesses the states. That alone is the Truth, and that alone has the right to speak of any state. When you know the waking state, you stand separate from the waking state, and then the waking state disappears as such.

'If you but open your mouth, advaita is gone.'

28th May 1957

1303. WHAT IS MEMORY?

Memory is past, and memory is about the past. Memory is something which upholds non-experience as experience, as though it has taken place in the past. The sense of experience is taken as the only proof.

But really there was no experience and memory can be no proof of it. Memory and experience depend upon each other for their very existence. So both are non-existent. Thus memory is a misnomer.

1304. HOW NOT TO FORGET THE TRUTH?

Suppose you light a cigarette and continue to talk. If you forget the cigarette, it will be extinguished. So you have to allow it frequently to remind you of itself. Similarly, you need only to allow Truth to come in uncalled, whenever you happen to forget Truth in the midst of activities.

1305. KNOWLEDGE OF OBJECTS, IF INTELLIGENTLY PURSUED, TAKES ONE TO TRUE KNOWLEDGE.

You know that there is a knowledge which stands knowing this limited knowledge. Immediately, you turn your attention to it. When you stand as that background knowledge, all the rest disappears and you are left alone in that pure knowledge.

Just as light has to be present before an object is seen, knowledge is there as knowledge or awareness, before it appears as the knowledge of an object. The knowledge of an object is changing; but the knowledge before and after the knowledge of an object is changeless, and therefore real.

Let the knowledge of objects turn your attention to that Reality behind, and you shall soon be established in it.

1306. THE BANE OF OBJECTIVITY AND ITS REMEDY

The knowledge that every mentation is nothing but pure, impersonal experience takes one to the height of Vēdānta. Objectivity, in any form, is the only obstacle to Truth. If you transcend it, the subjectivity also naturally disappears, and you stand as the Reality yourself.

Objectivity does not pertain to the object. Consciousness objectified is the object. The object is an object on account of you. The world of objects never affects one, except through one's own thoughts. Therefore the only thing needed, to be free, is to transcend thoughts. This is possible only by examining thoughts and disposing of them, without leaving even a trace behind. The trace is the objectivity attached to the thought. This objectivity can be eliminated only by examining thought subjectively; and finding that it is nothing but awareness, the Self, and that all appearance was illusion.

If the least trace is left behind, it sprouts up in the form of memory, which is but a fresh thought. Memory is the one thing that creates the whole world, and memory is the last link that connects one with the phenomenal world. If memory is understood to be nothing but a thought, which in turn is nothing but pure Consciousness – the Self – then memory, and the whole world with it, is merged into the Self.

29th May 1957

1307. TWO PERSONAL QUESTIONS AND THEIR ANSWERS

In the absence of our master, a stranger asked us: 'What difference can you mention between your master Shrī Kṛiṣhṇa Mēnōn and other great men of India?' Of course our answer had to be polite but frank. We said: 'Literally, our master disowns everything, while the others are found invariably to own some things, if not many things.'

Another day the same stranger asked our master himself: 'Well Sir! How is your philosophy different from the philosophy of Jesus Christ or Gāndhījī?'

To this Shrī K.M. promptly replied, with great personal respect towards the great men, but with greater regard for Truth itself: 'The answer depends upon the definition you give to the word philosophy. If by philosophy, you mean something meant to take you to the ultimate Truth, I have not known that either Jesus Christ or Gāndhījī had any philosophy.'

30th May 1957

1308. IGNORANCE A MISNOMER.

Ignorance is only in retrospect or in the past. You cannot say there is ignorance now. It is only the positive knowledge of something that can posit the precedent ignorance of that something. Therefore, to say that there was ignorance before any finite knowledge is absurd. Thus determinate ignorance is not. Indeterminate ignorance is knowledge itself. Therefore ignorance in any form is a misnomer.

1st June 1957

1309. MEDITATION

It is an activity of the mind and is purely yōgic in character. Its process consists of spatializing the object of its meditation, chiefly outside and in front of the one who meditates. Even if one tries to meditate on the formless, this idea of space and of the outside comes in.

If one who has heard the Truth from the Guru can transcend this tendency of spatialization, meditation can well be used to establish oneself in Truth. For this, the first thing one has to do is to give up the outside, and to draw the meditation within, into one's own inside or the Self. The inside is supposed to be the seat of the subject, and there the subject-object differentiation is not possible. Then spatialization ceases, and one stands as the real Self.

1310. DEVOTION

So also bhakti or devotion is a mental attitude directed to an object, generally an *iṣhṭa-dēva* [a chosen form of God]. This by itself does not give the ultimate result, mōkṣha.

Mōkṣha [liberation] is impersonal. To attain mōkṣha, the goal of bhakti has to be gradually changed to the impersonal, by understanding the nature of God. But the truth about God is that it is the highest concept of the human mind. Therefore, a subjective examination of the mind has to be gone through and its background, the Self, visualized. This can never be done by the mind alone, unaided.

Hence the truth of one's own real nature has to be heard from the lips of a Sage (Guru). By that, one's own svarūpa [true nature] is immediately visualized. It is then that incessant devotion has to be directed to that goal. That is real bhakti, and it enables one to get established in Ātmā. That is mukti (liberation).

14th June 1957

1311. FUTILITY OF USING THE MIND TO KNOW THE TRUTH

The mind functions in a long series of activities in the nature of subject-object relationship. But the last action of the series is an exception to this order, and it is not known or remembered by any other principle. This knowledge is not exclusive. It is an action of perfect identification, by being it – as knowing Happiness in deep sleep, by being it. This last knowledge is non-empirical and so is transcendental.

This knowledge is not opposed to anything else, but is the ground of all empirical knowledge. It is only from this stand – as this transcendental knowledge – that the mind can rightly be analysed. This stand cannot be acquired by any amount of mental exercises or watching. You get that stand only on listening to the Truth, from the lips of the Guru. All mental exercises and yōga only strengthen the mind and tighten the hold of the ego, while what you need is to transcend the ego-mind.

Even empirical knowledge is nothing other than this transcendental knowledge. But, with the inception of thought or memory, you make the transcendental appear limited and separate it from yourself. This is how the mind makes a mess of the Truth. To use such a mind to understand the Truth is foolish.

Even when the mind dies a natural death in deep sleep, one stands free as this transcendental knowledge. Therefore, create the same condition knowingly, by ignoring the mind and its vagaries altogether and going beyond it, in the light of the transcendental Truth as heard from the Guru. There is no other path to true liberation.

All the so called paths only pave the way, and some even obscure and distance the Truth. Therefore beware. Beware of promises, pleasures and powers achieved or anticipated. All these seduce you from the Truth.

17th June 1957

1312. WHAT HAPPENS WHEN I SAY, 'I KNOW HIM'?

It is not the body, senses or mind that is known. It is the mutual recognition of the impersonal 'I' in both, in sublime identity. It is non-empirical knowledge itself. No subject can become an object. Both are one and the same Absolute, beyond both individuality and universality.

The indeterminate (nirvishēṣha) knowledge or ignorance is Truth itself. Examine deep sleep. You are there, happiness is there and knowledge is there, but in identity with you. God is only a concept, while you are no concept but the Truth itself.

18th June 1957

1313. TRANSFORMATION

It is only the snake [illusion] that gets transformed into the rope [reality]. But, on the other hand, the rope never gets transformed into a snake.

1314. WHAT IS PRATYAKṢHA (DIRECT EXPERIENCE)?

Is it body, senses, mind, intellect or something still higher, which sometimes corrects even the intellect? Certainly the last is the nearest, and so relatively more direct (pratyakṣha) than all the rest.

1315. HOW TO ROOT OUT PAIN?

Question: Though I have been told that I am not the body, senses or mind, I am not able to escape from or forget suffering when it comes?

Answer: Evidently, you want to replace pain by pleasure. The truth is that both these are illusions, and that you stand as that Truth even when pleasure and pain come and go. It is not removal or forgetting the pain that is sought, but only the right knowledge that pain and pleasure are nothing other than your real nature – Consciousness. Therefore, you are not affected by whatever may come.

19th June 1957

1316. PEACE AND ACTIVITIES OF BODY AND MIND

One can be said to be perfectly healthy in body and mind only if no part of the body or mind makes itself felt. A part makes itself felt only when there is something wrong with it. You know that you have a head only when it aches.

You know things in the waking and dream states by separating them from yourself. That is when duality comes in. So in the case of the healthy man, the body and mind continue to function smoothly, without making any one of them specially felt; and in this way, he remains in a state of external peace, short-lived though it may be.

But in deep sleep, you stand in your own glory, when neither the body nor the mind comes in to disturb your real nature of Peace. Even with phenomenal knowledge, at the moment of knowing, you stand in identity with the object, in perfect non-duality. It is only subsequently that you import thought and separate the thing known. When there is identity, thought or recognition is impossible.

All this is concerning the involuntary experience of peace one has occasionally, though this peace depends upon the incidental subsidence of activity. This is made permanent and independent of the presence or absence of activities in the case of the jīvan-mukta, by his conscious experience of the nature of Peace, his own real Self. The apparent activities of his body, senses and mind do not disturb the tranquillity of his nature.

When you really know a thing, you stand identified with that thing. But, when you *say* you know, you do not know.

1317. HOW TO MAKE USE OF ANALOGY IN A SPIRITUAL CONTEXT?

Every analogy in a spiritual context should immediately be applied to the subject, and the truth revealed thereby.

Take for example the snake in the rope. The snake is symbolic – representing the whole world, including all appearances. The rope is the changeless background 'I' or Consciousness. Nothing other than the rope has ever been there. Therefore the snake is *not*, and so also the world is *not*. You are alone the ultimate Truth.

22nd June 1957

1318. INCOMPETENCE OF DUAL YŌGA AND BHAKTI TO LEAD TO THE ULTIMATE TRUTH

Both yōgins and bhaktas utilize their mind as their only instrument of sādhana. Their attempt is to concentrate upon a set ideal or the form of an iṣhṭa-dēva. Both these are nothing but concepts of the mind, even though it may be as expansive as brahman.

Relatively speaking, a concept is only a fraction of the mind. The goal of yōgins and bhaktas is to merge the *dhyātṛi*, the one who meditates (including his whole being of *sat* and *cit*), in the *dhyēya*, the object of the meditation. This is impossible.

But what happens is only a long forgetfulness of oneself, as in deep sleep. This state does not profit you any more than the usual deep sleep. Coming out of it, you are exactly the same old individual. Therefore yōga as such never takes you anywhere beyond the mental realm. This inefficacy of meditation is exposed by Shrī Aṣhṭāvakra in the verse.

acintyaṁ cintamānō 'pi cintā-rūpaṁ bhajaty asau
tyaktvā tad bhāvanaṁ tasmād ēvam ēvā 'ham āsthitaḥ

[In thinking of what can't be thought
some form of thought must be involved.
So too that last-remaining mode
of thinking must be given up,
to stand in truth where I abide.]

Aṣhṭāvakra-samhitā, 12.7

1319. THE APPROACH OF THE JNYĀNIN COMPARED TO THAT OF THE YŌGIN

The condition of the jnyānin is expressed in the luminous line of Shrī Aṣhṭāvakra.

sama-duhkha-sukhaḥ pūrṇa āśā-nairāśyayōḥ samaḥ .

[You are that being which is perfect:
just the same in pain and joy,
the same in hope and in despair...]

Aṣhṭāvakra-samhitā, 5.4

The yōgin tries, by dint of exercise, to be callous to pain as well as pleasure, or to forget both. This does not help him for long. Because he comes back to his body and mind after some time, and then they affect him adversely with redoubled force. But the jnyānin sees by discrimination that he is the witness to both pain and pleasure even when they appear; and so he remains ever unaffected by the opposites. This was illustrated by the following incident which actually took place recently.

A Sage who was also a great yōgin had a cancer and was operated upon by the doctor without anaesthetic. He stood the operation with such composure as though nothing was happening. This strange conduct surprised an eyewitness who was also a disciple, who was himself on the way to the Truth. This disciple later narrated this incident with visible emotion to his Guru himself, when he had recovered. The Guru wanted to correct the disciple without wounding his feelings. So he asked the disciple in all apparent seriousness: 'What part of the great man was performing the miracle of taking the mind away from the centre of operation and escaping from the pain? Was it the yōgin in him? Or was it the jnyānin in him?'

Disciple: 'Certainly the yōgin in him.'

Guru: 'How was it possible?'

Disciple: 'As a result of his long yōgic sādhana and the resulting powers.'

The Guru continued: 'But the jnyānin in him was absolutely unconcerned about either pain or pleasure, since they do not affect him as their background.'

Composure and consternation are both mental. The yōgin sticks to the former and remains in the mental realm. The Jnyānin stands beyond, clearly transcending the opposites. The exhibition of miracles by the yōgin has no truth value at all, and the appearance of the common place in the activities of the Jnyānin does not take away even a grain from his absolute Truth value.

Shrī Vidyāraṇya immortalizes this truth about a Jnyānin in the words:

irunniṭṭō, kiṭanniṭṭō, paṇippeṭṭō, peṭāteyō,
smariccō, vismariccōtān cākāṁ bhramam udicciṭā

[Seen sitting up or lying down,
remembering or forgetting things,
in trouble or untroubled, no
confusion can arise at body's
death, for one who has realized.]

Bhāṣha Pancadashi, Mahābhūta-vivēka, 119
(Malayalam translation)

'The "I"-principle or awareness is the real revelation – the revelation of the three states.'

'The subject is constitutive of the object.'

'The moment you perceive and know the object, the object abolishes itself (disappears by self-sacrifice) and reveals the Awareness.'

'The very word "appears" signifies Awareness, and that Awareness is my real nature.'

'Objects point to you – abolishing themselves.'

'To become aware of the fact that I am birthless and deathless is real liberation.'

'To get established in that certitude is *jīvan-mukti*.'

1320. KNOWING THE 'I'

When I say 'I', I know what I mean. So also when you say 'I', I also know what you mean, because the 'I' is already familiar to me. This knowledge is obtained by identity alone. Therefore even if the sayer means only his body and mind, still one who knows the Self, knows him also to be that Self.

Knowledge of Self is knowledge *as* Self.

22nd September 1957

1321. SIGNIFICANCE OF 'AUM'

'Aum' has three distinct parts: 'a', 'u' and 'm', representing the waking, dream and deep sleep state experiences. Examining each part separately, you find that each part is a twisted manifestation of pure sound which represents Ātmā – the ultimate Reality. It is the sound itself that appears twisted as 'a', 'u' and 'm'. This sound is thus in the manifestation, between the three parts and beyond them. Knowing that this pure sound represents Ātmā, the real 'I'-principle, if you repeat or listen to the repetition of 'aum', you will get more and more firmly established in the Reality.

> 'I shine in my real nature between mentations, as mentations, and beyond mentations.'

15th October 1957

1322. SOME ASSERTIONS

Religion, scholasticism, yōga, devotion etc. can never by themselves take you to the ultimate Truth. But of course they help you in their own way, to prepare the ground to receive the Truth at last from the Guru.

The totality of one's experiences consists of the three states, together with the most important factor – awareness – standing out of the states as the knower or witness thereof. But this factor is usually ignored.

The name 'deep sleep' is only a synonym for the real 'I'-principle.

The Awareness is the witness or knower of the appearance and disappearance of the states, and also of the content of each state.

22nd October 1957

1323. THEORY AND PRACTICE

> *Theory* is speculative thought or mere supposition existing only in the realm of the mind, in order to explain something in the phenomenal.

Practice is that which brings thoughts to the body level.

Truth is beyond practice and theory. To bring down the 'I'-principle to the mental level as theory, and still further to the body level is absurd. You learn swimming from theory in books. It is only he to whom body is all important that wants practice and depends upon theories. It is the ignorant man that does so.

If you begin to theorize or practice Truth, it ceases to be the Truth as such. Is 'I am' a theory? What is more immediate and intimate to you than 'I am'? So it is beyond theory and practice. 'I am jīva' is theory. 'I am body' is practical to the layman.

To apply theory and practice to 'Truth', upon which they themselves depend for their very existence, is absurd. Don't follow the line of error, by reversing the process of the line of Truth. Body is comprehended by mind and mind is comprehended by Self, in the Jnyānin. In the ignorant man, body holds mind and mind holds Self.

Even thinking or meditation distances the 'I' from you. So you are asked only to repeat what you are, and not to think or meditate. The knowledge of the 'I'-principle is experiential knowledge, and even 'Consciousness' may be called theory.

29th October 1957

1324. WHAT IS THE KNOWN?

When the variety is seen and reality is attributed to it, see that you are an ego-ridden being.

Without the 'I' (aham) being there, there can never be the 'this' (idam). So the this is nothing other than the Truth (the *svarūpa* of the 'I').

The 'I' is known only in identity. The generic of anything is neither space limited nor time limited. The known, when it is known, ceases to be known, abolishing itself as such.

23rd December 1957

1325. ARE YOU HAPPY?

When you say you are happy, you are not happy. For then, you stand away from your happiness and are objectifying it. When you are happy, you are not happy in the literal sense, but you are happiness in identity, and then you do not know it.

Similarly you do not know the states. Take for example the waking state. You know the objects in the waking state. But do you know the knowing of the object? *No*. Remaining as part of the waking state, you can never know the waking state as a whole. So the waking subject can never know the waking state. But the transcendental principle beyond all states can alone know it. That principle cannot know anything other than itself, and that only in identity. So nobody knows the states. Therefore the states are *not*.

A Sage elevates his disciples not through tattvōpadēsha alone, but by all varieties of activities and inactivity. Truth is *differenceless*. The interpretation that deep sleep is the experience one had in the past is purely a construction of the ego in the waking state.

1326. THE SUBJECT IS CONSTITUTIVE OF THE OBJECT.

The object is made an object only by the presence of the subject as such. Therefore, to say that an object exists, when there is no corresponding subject to objectify it, is absurd.

Ignorance is an object only in retrospect, and there is never a subject to support it. This position is anomalous. Therefore ignorance is *not*.

24th December 1957

1327. WHAT IS THE SUBJECT?

The last of a series of acts, without itself being known, is the subject.

1328. THERE IS CONNECTION EVEN IN SEPARATENESS.

Even concerning the so called phenomenal knowledge, it is knowledge in identity. We say A and B are there, without any apparent relationship between them, except the recognition of the existence of each other. So there is this connection established between consciousness and existence. Thus, knowledge bridges the gulf of separateness.

1329. HOW TO SEE THINGS IN THE RIGHT PERSPECTIVE?

Suppose you see this stool. The following activities take place there.

1. The sense organs supply the form.
2. The mind supplies concepts or ideas.
3. The Self supplies the sense of Reality.

Of these three, the first and second items are disconnected and get connection only through the third, the Self. So, to see through the changeless Self is the right perspective. If you see through either of the first two items, which are changing, you cannot come to any definite conclusion.

The first is in space, the second is in time, and the third is beyond. So through the first two items, you come progressively closer; and in the third, you become one with your own Self – the Truth.

26th December 1957

1330. WHO SEES THE STATES?

The subject who sees objects is called the 'object-self', which is in turn perceived by the real Self. The subject who sees objects is never seen by the subject himself.

If you say you are in the waking state, you are then *not* in the waking state, for certain. Because when you say so, you know the waking state as your object. The real Self alone can know it. But there is nothing else for it to know. So what appears as the waking state is the real Self. So are all states. The waking subject has no authority to assert this.

When you say you know the waking state, the ego who asserts this either stands out and ceases to be the ego, or what he sees is only part of the waking state.

29th December 1957

1331. WHY IS IT MORE DIFFICULT TO RECONCILE WITH TRUTH THAN WITH UNTRUTH?

Question: You reconcile yourself in a moment without any effort with the world which is a lie. But you find it very hard and take long to reconcile yourself with the Truth, even after visualizing it. Why is this?

Answer: Because you are yourself a lie and look upon Truth as something alien to you. Hence the delay in reconciling yourself with Truth.

30th December 1957

1332. EXPERIENCES OF TRUTH

Truth is experienced in three ways:

1. Truth is before you, as objects of perception.
2. Truth is in you, as knowledge of objects.
3. Truth is yourself, as objectless knowledge, as Self.

3rd January 1958

1333. THINKING AND KNOWLEDGE

Knowledge unites, in being or in identity. Thinking separates, in subject-object relationship.

Knowing has no place in the ordinary thought process. Thinking about something which has to be known is wrong, since it moves in a vicious circle. You cannot think of anything you have not known. Such thinking can never take you to the Truth.

But when you direct your thought to something (say yourself) which you have otherwise visualized, the thought loses its own characteristics and limits, and stands revealed as that Self (Consciousness) itself. Thought is thus reduced into its essence.

5th January 1958

1334. THOUGHT AND ITS APPLICATION

Thought is applied usually in two ways, with opposite results.

1. It is applied *objectively*, in order to know something that is not already known.

   The mind's natural tendency is to project the object of its thought into space, in terms of its own stock of former concepts. Therefore, when thought is applied with effort in this manner, to know any phenomenal object, gross or subtle, the object you consequently arrive at is pre-eminently an object of your own mind's creation. It is changing and so an untruth.

2. Thought is applied for the purpose of *recognizing the Self*, which you have already visualized on listening to the words of the Guru.

   But when you direct your thought to the Self you have already visualized, it is a sudden switch-over to the real subject, which can never be objectified. The mind, in that attempt, loses its own sense of objectivity. Thus deprived of its own dross, the mind stands revealed in identity with the real 'I'-principle. Here, thought ceases to be thought, and helps you to get established in the Truth you have already visualized.

   Suppose you decide to visit the seat of your Guru you know already. The moment you take that thought, you are there – at the feet of your Guru. Even the picture of the house of the Guru and all the long way to it vanish into insignificance. Your body treads the road mechanically, but the heart is at the goal. The thought directed to the Truth already visualized has the same effect.

7th January 1958

1335. WHAT DO I WANT AND HOW TO SECURE IT?

You want to know only something which is existing. If you want satisfaction in the mental level from something which leans towards virtue, you become religious-minded and get momentary satisfaction. But if you want to know that which really exists, by the knowing alone you get something called 'Peace', which is the source of all happiness. It is of the nature of knowledge and existence. If you seek it, you limit it and miss it. If you want to know without any purpose, you spontaneously get Peace.

If you lose yourself in any knowledge, be it apparently limited, you get to Peace. Therefore, 'Lose yourself, lose yourself' in any kind of knowledge. That is all that you have to accomplish, and you get to Peace instantaneously.

Satisfaction is personal or private, and creates the many.

Truth is impersonal or public, and destroys diversity.

10th January 1958

1336. WHAT ARE THE STATES AND HOW TO KNOW THEM?

The waking subject is the chief constituent element of the waking state. So he cannot know it. The 'I'-principle beyond cannot also know it, since there are no states in its realm. Similarly, the dreaming subject cannot know the dream state. The deep sleep state is also not known by the sleeper, if there is one. So the three states, as such, do not exist.

In fact all the three states are only one and the same background principle – Consciousness – and not states as they appear.

In the deep sleep state, you stand as that. But in the waking and dream states, you stand on memory and miss the Truth. Therefore, dispense with memory, and you are at once beyond all states and in Truth.

14th January 1958

1337. THE TURĪYA STATE AND HOW TO KNOW IT?

In the turīya state or nirvikalpa samādhi, which results from the yōgin's meditation, the subjectivity merges in the objective ideal – a mere concept – set before him. Thus the subjectivity vanishes for the time being, leaving objectivity all in all. But still you are no nearer the Truth than before. You may even be said to be at a greater disadvantage in that state, because you have lost all power of initiative to help you to transcend the state.

Truth is beyond subjectivity and objectivity. It can be visualized only by the deep discrimination and reason one obtains on listening to the Truth from the lips of the Guru, in the waking state.

The yōgin's artificial states are all great obstacles to the smooth visualization of Truth.

17th January 1958

1338. WHY THE PATH OF NEGATION?

A positive knowledge of Ātmā is impossible. Therefore the path of negation is adopted. Your position after negation of body, senses and mind is 'being it', though it is generally called 'knowing it'. There 'to know' is 'to be'.

1339. THERE WAS NO DREAM! HOW?

The so called dreamer was never dreaming, from his own standpoint. The dream is only a thought of the waking subject when he was not dreaming. So there was no dreaming, at any point of time. Therefore, there was no dream.

1340. WHY DO DOUBTS SOMETIMES TEASE EVEN A JĪVAN-MUKTA?

Question: Though I have clearly visualized the Truth, why is it that doubts still seem to arise often?

Answer: It is only in certain weak moments of the mind or ego, when it lays greater emphasis on its material aspect, that questions regarding certain parts of the world arise.

1341. WHY CAN'T ONE OBTAIN TRUTH FROM THE BOOKS OF A SAGE?

This can be answered in many ways:

1. Who asks the question? Of course the ego-mind. The mind can understand only in terms of the mind. The Truth transcends the mind and so cannot be understood in terms of the mind. You read books and understand them only at the mental level. Therefore Truth cannot be understood from books.
2. Truth cannot be understood from anything other than the Truth. Because everything other than the Truth is untruth. Thus book, as such, is also an untruth; and anything understood from it, by the mind, is also untruth.
3. The question itself is the product of ignorance. The question presupposes that Truth can be obtained from somewhere else, as an object of the mind. But the fact about Truth is that it is the Self. You are that always, and the question of obtaining it is wrong and does not legitimately arise. It is the activities of the

body, senses and mind that obstruct your visualizing the Truth, your real nature.

Then you might ask how does the Guru help you. Truth being your real nature, it has not to be obtained from elsewhere, but the obstacles on the path have to be removed; and then the Truth, being self-luminous, shines in its own glory. This is actually what the Guru does.

If a child asks where its body is, no book can teach it where it is. The nurse has only to remove the child's clothes and nothing else has to be done to show the child its own body. Similarly, the Guru creates the conditions wherein your real nature of Truth shines in all its glory, and the mind with all its questions disappears for ever.

15th February 1958

1342. LIFE

(A casual statement.) The ordinary man's life is a swing between a tear and a smile.

17th February 1958

1343. HAVE THE STATES ANY LESSON FOR THE SPIRITUAL ASPIRANT?

Answer: Of course. The three states give us lessons capable of establishing us in the ultimate Truth. But it needs a Kāraṇa-guru to direct our attention to those lessons and to interpret them correctly.

The lesson of deep sleep is that I get to my real nature of Peace and Consciousness, when I transcend body, senses and mind.

The lesson of dream and waking states is that it is the one Consciousness – my real nature – that divides itself into the subject series and object series, and that I am witness to all mentations.

1344. BONDAGE AND LIBERATION

Bondage is identification with body, senses and mind.

Liberation is the giving up of that identification, by visualizing what you are, in the regular order.

1345. The known from different perspectives

The lowest: Whatever is known is the knower himself.
Higher still: Whatever is known is knowingness itself.
And ultimately: It is pure Consciousness, the Self.

1346. Is the silencing of the mind our goal?

No. It is only a means. It is achieved in two ways:

1. By utilizing meditation or yōga as the means to silence the mind. The mind gets into a state of nothingness or blankness where, it wrongly presumes, it identifies itself with the Ultimate. But no, the Truth is far beyond.
2. By utilizing right discrimination and reason to analyse the mind. The mind as such disappears, and you stand in your real nature. The activity of the mind is the only obstacle; and when it disappears, for whatever reason, you imagine you have silenced it. But really, the mind is dead.

1347. What is the Truth about the states?

A state as a whole can never happen to its own subject, which is comprehended in that state itself. It cannot happen to Awareness either, since they are in two different planes. And there is no third party concerned in the affair. Therefore the states are not.

A disciple: Is there any benefit in using good words and extending blessings and help to others?

Answer: Yes. If they come from you spontaneously.

1st March 1958

1348. What are problems, their source and remedy?

It is you (the ego) who create your own problems, and you yourself in turn get entangled in them. The teacher (the Guru) has only to draw your attention to that principle which created the problems, and immediately the creator and the created both vanish. Then you stand by yourself alone – free from all problems, and for ever.

2nd March 1958

1349. WHAT IS MEANT BY EXAMINING A PERCEPT?

A percept, at the outset, is distinct and separate from you. The process of examination is to bring it nearer and nearer the Self, and at last to merge it in the Self.

You examine the percept, identifying yourself with the perception; and then the percept vanishes, getting merged in the perception. Then the perception is examined in its turn, yourself standing as pure Consciousness. Then the perception also vanishes, as such, getting merged in Consciousness, ultimately leaving Consciousness alone.

> parāg-artha pramēyēṣu yā phalatvēna sammatā
> saṁvit sai 'vē 'ha mēyō 'rthō vēdāntō 'kti pramāṇataḥ
>
> [Where any object is admitted
> among others to be known,
> what there results is consciousness
> and that alone. Just that needs to
> be known. That's what Vēdānta
> demonstrates, in everything it says.]

Pancadashī, Kūṭastha-dīpa, 11

1350. THOUGHT IS IMPOSSIBLE. HOW?

Answer: Thought is possible only in terms of language. Language is possible only in terms of continued sound. But sound can exist only at a single point of time. Thus language as such is impossible, and so is thought.

1351. WHAT IS THE RELATIONSHIP BETWEEN 'FORM', 'SEEING' AND 'CONSCIOUSNESS'?

'Seeing' is the verb-form of 'form', because seeing goes into the make of form.

'Consciousness' or Awareness is the noun-form of 'seeing'; because, without Consciousness, seeing cannot be seeing.

6th March 1958

1352. ĀTMĀ IS ANYHOW UNAFFECTED. THEN WHY CAN'T I LIVE AS I CHOOSE?

What does it matter to you if Ātmā is unaffected? You are miserable only when you are affected, and it is only then that you seek a remedy. Or in other words, it is only then that you earnestly want to be unaffected. For this, there is absolutely no other means except to be the Ātmā itself. Know that you are that, and be free.

1353. '"I" AS ĀTMĀ AM UNAFFECTED.' (*PANCADASHĪ*) THEN WHY SHOULD THERE BE ANY BREAKING OF THE 'KNOT OF THE HEART' ('HṚIDAYA-GRANTHI')?

Answer: Don't forget the former part of the statement. That itself is the cutting asunder 'the knot of the heart'.

The former part of the statement is: '"I" as Ātmā ...'. It means 'I' identifying myself with Ātmā, which is by nature unaffected. Here the knot already remains cut. Therefore, if that preamble is accepted, there is no need for any further effort in that direction.

1354. WHAT IS THE SECRET OF ALL PROBLEMS, AND HOW TO DO AWAY WITH THEM FOR EVER?

Answer: The world is nothing but a bundle of problems raised in an unbroken chain by the ego, while he himself always eludes recognition.

All sciences and yōga run after analysis and the examination of individual objects, ignoring the arch-usurper – the ego – altogether. Their methods can never exhaust the world problem, nor end in any reasonable conclusion.

Therefore, the only right approach to solve problems is to direct attention to the subject of all this trouble, the ego. The moment you begin to do that, you unknowingly take your stand in the Awareness beyond the ego or the mind. Then the ego sheds all its accretions and stands revealed as that Awareness itself. Looking from that position, the baffling world problem disappears like mist before the sun, never to appear again.

1355. WHAT IS SPACE?

The ignorant man thinks of objects as existing in space. But space as 'this' or 'that' cannot remain over, independent of the objects themselves. Space and objects both being mutually dependent for their very existence, they can both be disposed of as unreal. Then Consciousness alone is left over, as real.

Therefore space is a misnomer, and what appears as space is nothing but Consciousness.

1356. WHAT IS 'MAHĀ-BUDDHI'?

When the mind ceases to objectify, it is *mahā-buddhi* itself. The other terms – higher reason, vidyā-vṛitti and functioning Consciousness – are only synonyms of mahā-buddhi. This is the only instrument to help one to visualize the Truth; and this, though the birthright of all human beings, can be awakened to active function only with the help of a living Kāraṇa-guru.

1357. WHAT IS MONISM?

It is only a mental position, being the opposite of dualism. It is often mistaken to be non-dualism. Non-dualism is pure Advaita, which is a clear negation of both dualism and monism and stands beyond both. Advaita is what remains over, after rejecting all that stands as 'this' or 'that'.

1358. WHAT IS THE SAFE ASYLUM FOR THE TROUBLED MAN?

There can be only two asylums for anyone. They are the 'I' and the 'this'.

The 'I', being impersonal and standing beyond the mind, cannot hold anything else. But the 'this' holds all the diversity of this world. Therefore, standing as the impersonal 'I', you have to examine the 'this' dispassionately. Then the 'this' gets reduced into the 'I' itself, which is nothing but the ultimate Truth.

1359. HOW IS THE COSMOLOGICAL OR TRADITIONAL PATH OF JNYĀNA DIFFERENT FROM THE DIRECT PATH?

In the *direct path* (also called *vicāra-mārga*), if the aspirant is found to be tolerably sincere and earnest to get to the Truth, he is accepted as a disciple by the Kāraṇa-guru. Then the whole Truth is expounded to him; and the aspirant, who listens to the talks of the Guru with rapt attention, is made to visualize the Truth then and there.

Having secured the strongest certitude and affirmation from his own 'Being', regarding the correctness and intensity of his experience of Truth, he is asked to cling on to it in his own way. This clinging on, in due course, makes his own real nature of Truth more and more familiar to himself; and thus he gets gradually established in the Reality. There is nothing that can be an obstacle to him, at any stage.

But the case of the aspirant following the *traditional or cosmological path* to the Truth is quite different. After a long and arduous course of preliminary exercises, the Guru one day explains the meaning of the aphorism '*Tat tvam asi*', and proves that the substance of the individual and of the cosmos is one and the same. But this knowledge remains with the aspirant only as indirect (parōkṣha) or objective knowledge. In order to make this knowledge direct and to experience the Truth, he has to continue his efforts for very many years, by way of contemplating on the three different aphorisms one after the other, each for a different purpose.

The main difficulties in the indirect experience of Truth (as '*Tat tvam asi*', meaning *kūṭastha* and *brahman* are one) are:

1. The distance and strangeness of brahman;
2. The smallness of kūṭastha or 'I' as usually understood; and
3. The bigness of brahman, which is also a limitation.

Remedies: By deeply contemplating on the aphorism '*Ahaṁ brahmāsmi*', brahman is brought into immediate and intimate contact with the 'I'.

Next, by contemplating on the aphorism '*Brahmaivāham asmi*', the sense of smallness usually attributed to the 'I' is sought to be removed.

Lastly, by contemplating on the aphorism '*Prajñānaṁ brahma*' the sense of bigness (the natural corollary of the concept of brahman) is also eliminated, leaving the Self as Ātmā, the ultimate 'I'-principle.

But according to the *direct method*, it is expounded at the very outset that 'I am Consciousness' (corresponding to the meaning of the last aphorism in the cosmological path). This does not leave any room for any subsidiary problem, and the aspirant visualizes the real nature of the self instantaneously. He has only to cling on to that experience, in order to get established in it.

8th March 1958

1360. HOW ARE HAPPINESS AND CONSCIOUSNESS ONE?

From the experience in deep sleep, we see that Happiness is self-luminous, or that Happiness lights itself up. This 'lighting-ness' of Happiness is what is called 'Consciousness'. Both are intrinsic in the Self. This is how one knows Peace in deep sleep. This is knowledge in identity. Therefore, '*Happiness can never be unintelligent.*'

1361. IS 'VICĀRA' THINKING ABOUT THE TRUTH?

No. It is entirely different. '*Vicāra*' is a relentless enquiry into the truth of the Self and the world, utilizing only higher reason and right discrimination. It is not thinking at all.

You come to 'know' the meaning and the goal of vicāra only on listening to the words of the Guru. But subsequently, you take to that very same knowing, over and over again. That is no thinking at all. This additional effort is necessary in order to destroy samskāras. When the possessive identification with samskāras no longer occurs, you may be said to have transcended them.

You cannot think about anything you do not know. Therefore thinking about the Truth is not possible till you visualize it for the first time. Then you understand that Truth can never be made the object of thought, since it is in a different plane. Thus, thinking about the Truth is never possible. The expression only means knowing, over and over again, the Truth already known.

1362. A disciple asked: WHEN CAN I BE SURE THAT I AM SECURE?

Gurunāthan: Do you ever think that you are that tree?

Disciple: No.

Gurunāthan: Similarly, knowing what you are, equally strongly, you are quite secure in the real 'I'.

10th March 1958

1363. HOW DOES KNOWLEDGE FUNCTION?

Knowledge is of two kinds:

1. Of the nature of subject-object relationship.
2. Of the nature of identity.

The former comprehends all phenomenal knowledge, and the latter pertains to spiritual experience alone. In the latter, 'consciousness of self' is to be understood as 'Consciousness as Self'.

Peace in deep sleep can exist only if Consciousness is also there. That is, it must be understood as consciousness of Peace. But this is also 'knowledge in identity'. Therefore the expression 'consciousness of Peace' has to be understood to mean 'Consciousness *as* Peace'. Thus, Consciousness and Peace are one and the same, intrinsic in the Self.

1364. HOW IS SAMĀDHI BROUGHT ABOUT AND WHAT IS ITS REACTION UPON THE INDIVIDUAL?

acintyaṁ cintamānō 'pi cintā-rūpaṁ bhajaty asau
tyaktvā tad bhāvanaṁ tasmād ēvam ēvā 'ham āsthitaḥ

[In thinking of what can't be thought
some form of thought must be involved.
So too that last-remaining mode
of thinking must be given up,
to stand in truth where I abide.]

Aṣhṭāvakra-samhitā, 12.7

When you begin to think of the unthinkable, the mind is thrown into a state of nothingness, accompanied by a sensation of peace as pleasurableness. This state is called samādhi, which is nothing but a thought form.

Aṣhṭavakra and all other Jnyānins advise you with one voice to ignore it altogether. According to the Jnyānin, one can never get out of one's own real nature, whether in samādhi or in the waking activities. Therefore, the Jnyānin is indifferent about both. But the yōgin can never claim to be that Reality, since he has not known it in the right perspective. Therefore, the yōgin is bound as much by samādhi as the ordinary man is by the world.

1365. WHAT IS THE PURPOSE AND SIGNIFICANCE OF THE 'OBJECT-SELF'?

When you ask a question, you are the 'object-self' in the mental realm. Even an answer to the question from that level does not take you beyond, but keeps you in the same vicious circle. The object-self is always entangled in the whirls of diversity.

In order to extricate you from the object-self, you are told that you are the subject-self; and it is proved that you are, as such, a permanent and conscious principle. Being enabled to stand as that principle, all questions disappear and you find yourself free.

13th March 1958

1366. HOW TO VIEW OUR STATES?

Our so called waking and dream states are in fact only a succession of waking states, all equally real. In the same waking state, we subsequently correct some of our experiences. E.g. the snake in the rope. Similarly, one waking state may be corrected from another waking state; but we are never to take one state as waking and the other state as a dream.

1367. HOW IS THE SUBJECT CONSTITUTIVE OF THE OBJECT?

It means that the subject goes into the constitution of the object. When you examine the object in the right manner, the subject is also unknowingly being examined. Then both disappear, leaving Awareness alone. The same argument applies to the whole world. Thus the whole world stands explained, as Awareness pure.

If the Awareness is directed to anything apparently different, that other thing becomes Awareness at once.

1368. WHAT DOES MY NAME DENOTE?

Every name represents the Ultimate. The name given to me by my parents at my birth is the only one changeless thing that still continues with me, in the midst of the ever-changing body, senses and mind. Therefore, the name pertains to the real Self in me, and not to the body, senses or mind.

16th March 1958

1369. WHAT IS THE SCOPE OF REASON?

Reason is generally of two distinct kinds. One is vēdāntic, and the other intellectual.

> *Vēdāntic reason* is tri-basic in character, having sway over the experiences of all the three states.
>
> *Intellectual reason* is only mono-basic in character, being applicable only to the experiences of the waking state.

21st March 1958

(A casual statement)
1370. 'WHAT YOU ARE, YOU SEE OUTSIDE.'

Think over this.

1371. HOW DO THE OPPOSITES MEET AND WHERE?

Love and hate are supposed to be opposites, in the phenomenal sense of the terms. Both need the presence of an object outside, in order to be worth the name.

Love, if expanded encompassing the whole universe, ceases to be love, having no external object for its application; and then it stands as the ultimate Truth.

Hate, likewise, if expanded encompassing the whole universe including one's own body, senses and mind, ceases to be 'hate'; and stands again as the same ultimate Truth.

Thus the opposites meet in the background. You must transcend both passivity and activity, in order to understand the Truth. Having first understood the Truth from the Guru, you can again visualize it whenever you want, either by extreme passivity or by extreme activity. But without first having that understanding, no kind of activity or inactivity can be of any avail to you.

23rd March 1958

1372. A REFLECTION OF OUR OWN STANDARD

Any desire or effort to know the Truth will certainly taint your visualization of Truth, to that extent. An effort amounts to desire. Both of them posit their own standards. The result will only be judged by such limited standards of satisfaction as are directed by the preceding effort or desire.

1373. WHAT IS THE RELATIONSHIP BETWEEN THE 'I'-NESS AND THE 'THIS'-NESS?

Life is a complex mixture of the 'I'-ness and the 'this'-ness. The 'I'-ness being the real subject is first explained by the Guru to the true aspirant, as the impersonal 'I' or real 'I'-principle or pure Consciousness or the ultimate Truth. Immediately he visualizes it.

The 'this' is something appearing distinct and separate from the 'I'. While the 'I' can exist independently in its own right, the 'this' cannot have a separate existence even for a moment. Therefore, in order to know the content of 'this', you have only to separate the 'this'-ness from the 'this'. It can be done with effort and sometimes without effort. Then the pure 'I' remains over, proving thereby that the 'this' is in essence nothing other than the 'I'. Therefore the world is nothing but the real 'I'.

1374. WHAT IS REAL RENUNCIATION?

Renunciation, as it is usually understood and practised, is only renouncing or discarding distant objects in which you have a genuine interest, in favour of some other objects nearer and dearer to you, namely your own body, senses and mind. This is but a farce, not real renunciation; and it does not help you to approach the Truth.

The goal of renunciation is certainly to get at the Truth. In order to do that, you have to renounce the untruth in full. The apparent world is a mixture of subject and object. Of these, the real subject alone is the Truth; and all else is untruth appearing as objects, gross or subtle, including one's own body, senses and mind.

All worldly experiences can be reduced in terms of 'consciousness of objects' – 'Consciousness' being the real subject and the rest apparent objects. Therefore, in order to get at the Truth (Consciousness), you have only to renounce the 'object' from 'consciousness of an object'. Then Consciousness, the ultimate Truth, remains over in all its glory.

This is one of the accepted prakriyās (modes of approach) in the path of knowledge. If it is adopted under instructions from a Kāraṇa-guru (which rule has no exception), you will visualize the Truth *then and there*.

You are warned in this context that Consciousness should never be associated with the sense of outside or inside, as in the case of the objects.

1375. WHAT IS THE RELATIONSHIP BETWEEN TRUTH AND SACRIFICE?

It is the way of the world to applaud anything that involves the least sacrifice of the comforts of the body, senses or mind. Accordingly, 'courage' in the phenomenal world is applauded because the interests of the body, senses or mind are partially sacrificed for the attainment of a particular goal.

But in the spiritual quest, one's stand is even beyond human courage. The spiritual aspirant knows that he is deathless; and by the mere thought of that fact, he transcends his own body, senses and mind, and stands in Truth. It is well beyond the realm of mind and sacrifice.

From the standpoint of Truth, all sacrifice is unreal. But in the relative level, it helps much to attenuate the ego; and to that extent, of course, sacrifice is welcome.

2nd April 1958

1376. IT IS OFTEN ASSERTED THAT NOBODY KNOWS ANYTHING. BUT HOW TO ESTABLISH THIS?

Gurunāthan: Take any example you like.

Disciple: I know I am a man.

G: All right! But before answering the question, don't you think it essential that a clear definition of 'man' has to be agreed upon?

D: Of course.

G: Then please define 'man'.

D: (After a pause) … I find it very difficult.

G: Then I shall help you. You admit you are a man, he is a man, I am a man, don't you?

D: Yes, I do.

G: But individually, each one of us have different attributes. Still, there must be something in common to all men. That something is clearly attributeless. That is the real 'man'. That is the ultimate Reality. That is the real 'I'-principle. That can never be known and can never be defined, don't you admit?

D: Yes.

G: Then, don't you see that your position is quite untenable?

D: Yes indeed.

G: Therefore nobody knows anything, and all names are only names given to the absolute.

5th April 1958

1377. VISIONS OF THE GURU AND OF THE IṢHṬA-DĒVA

A disciple asked: The vision of the iṣhṭa-dēva gives one ecstatic joy. I know that the Guru is far beyond the iṣhṭa-dēva and that he is the only Reality. But why does it not give me the same ecstatic pleasure, each time I see my Guru?

Answer: We are brought up from childhood on a fund of samskāras which extol the personal God, and we have all along nourished an intense desire to visualize him. It is on this background that we get a vision of the iṣhṭa-dēva, all in the mental realm. The depth of the desire and the glory of the iṣhṭa-dēva, as conceived by the former samskāras, together create the excitement and joy in the mental plane.

But the darshana of the Guru is beyond the realm of the mind and of samskāras. It is spontaneous, and not the result of any long cherished desire or meditation. The darshana of the Guru at once takes you beyond the mental realm; and you experience by identity that ultimate Peace, one's own real nature. Therefore no spectacular joy is expressed there, as in the case of the vision of the iṣhṭa-dēva.

3rd May 1958

1378. INSIDE AND OUTSIDE

Question: What is the meaning of inside and outside (in the spiritual context)?

Answer: Refer to *Ātma-nirvṛiti*, chapter 15, verse 1: 'Experience and knowledge are inside. How can their objects be outside?'

What does '*inside*' signify?

'Inside' strictly means not separate from the Self. Therefore, '*Experience is the Self.*'

1379. WHAT HAPPENS WHEN I PERCEIVE AN OBJECT?

Answer: The 'perception of an object' brings the object nearer and nearer to the Self, through the instrumentality of perception. But perception itself, when examined from the standpoint of the Self or

Consciousness, is brought still nearer the Self, without the services of any instrument whatsoever. Just as 'perception' lights up the object, the 'I' in turn lights up 'perception' itself.

Both 'perception of objects' and 'perception itself' do not stop till each has touched me and merged into me, as Consciousness. Just as an object is reduced to perception, so also perception is reduced to Consciousness.

The illustration of the dream state proves this abundantly. If you begin to examine the dream objects disinterestedly – in the strict sense of the term – you unknowingly transcend the dream state and stand beyond.

Similarly, when you start to examine any object in the waking state, you spontaneously and unknowingly stand beyond the waking state.

1380. DISCARDING IDENTIFICATION WITH BODY

Question: What is the difference, in discarding identification with the body, between an ignorant man and a jīvan-mukta?

Answer: In order to discard one's own body, one must first become convinced of the unreality of the body. One cannot be deeply convinced about the unreality of the body without being already conscious of the reality of the Self.

If an ignorant man discards his identification with his present body, he is sure to continue as another space-limited being, identifying himself with a body, gross or subtle, or with the absence of all bodies as in samādhi. The absence of a body, like the possession of a body, leaves a samskāra behind and is still illusion.

But when a jīvan-mukta discards the body idea, he stands in all his glory in his own real nature, without assuming any other body. He is deeply convinced that it is his own Self – the ultimate Reality – that appears as the body; and so he rests in Truth.

1381. EXPERIENCES OF DEEP SLEEP AND OF SAMĀDHI BY THE IGNORANT MAN

Question: What is the difference between the experiences of deep sleep and of samādhi, by one who does not know the nature of the content of either?

Answer: The experience in 'deep sleep', being spontaneous and uncaused, is purely vastu-tantra (creation of Truth itself), and leaves no trace of samskāra behind it.

But 'samādhi' is the product of severe effort, and leaves a strong samskāra behind which binds one to the object, viz. samādhi. This is called kartṛi-tantra (caused by effort).

Therefore, of the two experiences, the experience of deep sleep is infinitely superior to that of samādhi.

1382. THE REACTION OF TECHNICAL TERMS AND TERMINOLOGIES UPON THE IGNORANT

Question: What is the reaction of technical terms and terminologies upon persons who have not studied the shāstras directly under a Kāraṇa-guru?

Answer: To such persons, they are invariably deceptive. For example, take the phrase 'aṇōraṇīyān mahato mahīyān' ['smaller than the smallest, greater than the greatest' – from the *Kaṭha Upaniṣhad*, 2.20]. Literally, the description is mentally incomprehensible. The real significance can be understood only from the experience of Truth. It really means that the Ultimate is neither small (aṇu) nor big (mahat), but is clearly beyond both concepts. This is Consciousness, the real 'I'-principle. This, being beyond all concepts, can never be explained by the shāstras, nor understood by the mind.

30th May 1958

1383. SOCIAL SERVICE AND THE SAGE

(Extract of a talk with Shrī A.P. at Bombay in 1950)

Question (A.P.): Why does not the sage do anything to alleviate the misery of the millions in society?

Gurunāthan: You have to establish your data, before calling for an answer to the question. Still, I shall take it up. So you take for granted that there is a society of millions, there is much suffering in society, and that each one should act to alleviate that suffering.

A: Yes.

G: Which society please? Don't you sometimes experience an equally real society in your dream, with even greater sufferings? Do you now do anything to alleviate the suffering there?

A: No.

G: Why not, please?

A: Because it is not real.

G: And this?

A: This we see as real, here and now.

G: And didn't you see that as equally real, then and there in the so called dream?

A: Yes.

G: Is there any difference between the two at the moment when each is experienced?

A: No.

G: Who is legitimately qualified to make any remark on the experiences of each state?

A: Only one who has been consciously present in each state.

G: Can there be any difference between the opinions of the two perceivers, regarding the reality of the realms each perceived?

A: No.

G: Then what is your evidence for saying that one state alone was real?

A: None.

G: Now do you admit that both states are equally unreal?

A: Yes.

G: The Sage, knowing this, does not run after his own shadow, and so appears to be indifferent.

Let us examine the problem from still another standpoint, confining ourselves to the waking state alone. Now what is it that really prompts you to do social service? Examine your heart dispassionately and tell me. You should give me the nearest source of the prompting.

A: I want to see them all happy.

G: Why? What would happen to you if they are not happy?

A: If they are unhappy, I am also unhappy.

G: So that alone makes you happy. Is it not?

A: Yes.

G: Now tell me, is it the prospect of your being happy or of their being happy that really prompts you? Or is it their happiness alone irrespective of its reaction upon you?

A:. Both!

G: No, no, that cannot be. Suppose the government promulgates an ordinance prohibiting all kinds of social service activities. What would you feel?

A: Certainly, it would make me quite unhappy.

G: Now then tell me, is it your own happiness or the society's happiness that really prompts you?

A: Certainly my own happiness.

G: Now, have you known any instance of one who has attained perfect and permanent happiness through such objective means?

A: No. It is only temporary.

G: Now then, if one (the sage) has attained perfect and permanent happiness through other means, have you any other charge against him from your own standpoint?

A: No. Excuse me for my impertinent question.

G: But I have not finished, and I do not propose to leave you there. Let us look at it from still another standpoint. So you take society as a means or a medium to make you happy. Is it not a fact?

A: Yes.

G: Certainly this medium will often fail you, for different reasons beyond your control.

A: What else can we do to be happy?

G: Supposing you can rest in perfect happiness, without seeking the help of any medium whatsoever. What do you say about the prospect of it?

A: Wonderful! But how is it possible?

G: That exactly is what a Jnyānin does. He is dead not to society alone, as you suppose, but is dead to his own body, senses and mind as well. He is alive to his real nature alone, which is conscious Peace, the abode of Happiness. What more does he need, and what more can he aspire for?

A: Nothing. But a Jnyānin alone can be so.

G: No. Not so. You can also have it now and here, if only you really want it. If your desire to know the Truth is deep and sincere, you have only to take instructions from a Kāraṇa-guru (Sage) and listen to his talks which expound the Truth of one's own real nature. Immediately, you visualize the Truth and become free. Thereafter, for some time more, you have only to ward off the obstacles whenever they appear, clinging on to the Truth you have already visualized. Is it so difficult, if you really want it?

A: No, certainly not.

G: Now let us examine the problem from a still lower and human level. Social service usually functions on two planes.

The first is in the body level, catering to the basic bodily needs of society alone. This is the lowest and the most transitory form of service.

The second and slightly higher type of service is by extending education to the poor, so as to make them self-dependent and capable of acquiring better standards of life and comfort.

But this is also impermanent and uncertain, in the strict sense. Quite a small minority of society will still be dissatisfied even with this. To them remains always open the last and the best resort, the never failing royal road to Peace. This is on a still higher plane, beyond even the mind. There you stand beyond want, beyond pain and pleasure, as absolute Peace or objectless Happiness.

You can also attain this, but only by listening in person to the words from the lips of a Kāraṇa-guru. This is the realm where the sage always rests. He is never satisfied with giving dreamy doles, as social service workers do. He never encourages any propaganda inviting aspirants. He shows nothing spectacular about himself, though he can easily excel any yōgin in the field of powers. Naturally therefore, very few, who really want his help, alone come to him. He leads them to the state of perfect Peace, even in this life, here and now. He cannot give anything less; and when he gives, he gives only to those who really want it.

Now what do you think about your question?

A: Excuse me. I withdraw the question in all humility.

G: A word of clarification may still be desirable. Standing in my real nature, I stand as one with the whole world, and their suffering becomes mine. Is this not infinitely superior to your keeping others separate and trying to sympathize with them, much less to love them? You preach to others to 'love thy neighbour as thyself' and never tell them how to do it. Love is a sense of oneness with the object of your love. Is it ever possible to be one with another at the body level or at the mental level, where the sense of separateness persists? *No*. You can, at the most, sympathize with them in their suffering. And what is the result! You succeed in inviting some suffering to yourself also, without alleviating the suffering of others.

All these remedies at the physical and mental levels are adopted without enquiring about the Truth of the suffering, and therefore serve only to hide or cover the so called suffering for the time being.

The ultimate remedy is to examine whether the suffering is real or not. This is what the sage does. He examines it impartially, from the standpoint of Truth, and finds it all a dream, being confined to one state alone. Thus, for the sage, the suffering loses all its pangs. He invites the so called sufferer to wake up from his dream, and to see that the suffering is an illusion. This is the only permanent remedy for all ills.

But I do not deny that your social service activities have one redeeming feature about them. It helps the helper to attenuate his own ego, by giving him an opportunity to sacrifice his own comforts. But, it has to be said, the method is long and arduous, and the pitfalls are innumerable. Of course it helps to prepare the ground, as any other path does; and the aspirant has to take instructions from a Kāraṇa-guru to reach the Ultimate, the earlier the better.

1384. THE BLURTING OF AN INFLATED EGO

A young man X, under the pangs of some phenomenal desperation, once said to his friend Y: 'It is indeed terrible to live under the shade of a great man.'

To this the friend retorted: 'Of course, excepting the Guru, in whose luminous presence it is simply marvellous to be living-dead.'

X: How do you say that?

Y: Please listen to me for a moment. If you meekly welcome slavery of any one kind, you cannot help being harassed by innumerable other slaveries from all around. According to your own statement, you admit yourself to be a small and helpless ego, reluctantly subservient to a greater ego. Indeed such a life cannot but be slavery of the first order. But slavery to what? Not to the apparently aggressive great man. But slavery to your own inflated ego (constituted of a bundle of thoughts and feelings arising out of your wrong identification with your own body and mind). Withdraw first from that servitude and thenceforward slavery shall be a misnomer to you. Slavery is the offspring of duality.

In the presence of the Guru, be it in thought, it is perfect non-duality that obtains. Your ego in that presence is dead, for the time being, and the shadow of your ego continues to serve the Ultimate (the Guru) under all apparent conditions. Thus you are living and dead simultaneously, and your condition is all Happiness and glory of the Ultimate. So please look deep and revise your opinion, and cease to be a slave to anything.

1385. Be a child in knowledge.

What was Lord Kṛishṇa? He was a child in knowledge.

It is the absolute Ātmā and Ātmā alone that is the background; and it is Ātmā that seems to express itself and function without functioning. This may seem incomprehensible to the mind. But nobody can help it. Still, it can well be experienced directly. The mind must die in order to know it by identity alone.

Such a child was Lord Kṛishṇa, all through his life. An ideal sketch of his apparently phenomenal life, without losing its spiritual significance, is given in the following verse:

> iṭatumiṟiparattunniprapañcaṁ samastaṁ
> palatumiṟi vamikkuṁ vahniyil bhasmamākkuṁ
> karumanapalatēvaṁ kāṭṭiyātmasvarūpē
> śiśutaviśadamākkuṁ vastuvē satyamāvū

Shrī Ātmānanda, Ātmārāmam, 1.42

> 'This entire universe, projected out of the left eye, is burnt to ashes by the fire emitting from the right. That alone shall be the ultimate Truth which stands established by such and many other pranks of a like nature, shown in pure childish innocence, never budging an inch from the real nature of Ātmā.'

Thus, he was the embodiment of Truth. But others saw him in diverse ways – according to their own tastes, tendencies and standards. The following verse by Shrī Veda Vyāsa pictures some of those:

> mallānām aśanir nṛṇāṁ nara-varaḥ strīṇāṁ smarō mūrtimān
> gōpānāṁ sva-janō 'satāṁ kṣiti-bhujāṁ śāstā sva-pitrōḥ śiśuḥ
> mṛtyur bhōja-patēr virāḍ aviduṣāṁ tattvaṁ paraṁ yōgināṁ
> vṛṣṇīnāṁ para-dēvatēti viditō raṅgaṁ gataḥ sāgrajaḥ

Bhāgavata Purāṇa, 10.43.17

> mallanmārkkiṭivāḷ, janattinaracan, mīnāṅkanēṇākṣimārkk-
> illattil sakhivallavarkkarikhalarkkannandanōnandanan,
> kālan kaṁsanˇ, dēhikaḷkkihavirāṭˇ, jñānikkutatvaṁparaṁ,
> mūlaṁvṛṣṇikulattinennukarutī mālōkarakkaṇṇane

Malayāḷam translation of above, by Shrī Ātmānanda

'He was the sword of lightning to the ruffian wrestlers, King to the subjects, cupid to the loving feminine folk, comrade to the Gōpas and Gōpīs in their own homes, enemy to the wicked, son to Nanda, God of death to Kamsa, universal *virāṭ* to yōgins, ultimate Truth to the Jnyānin, and the source of the Vṛiṣhṇi community. Such were the manifold ways in which the world looked, simultaneously, upon the boy Kṛiṣhṇa.' And they were all true – each at its own level. But to Kṛiṣhṇa himself, he was a child in knowledge, pure and simple.

The same idea is expressed in the statement: 'Ātma-bhāvē śiśu-svarūpō 'ham.' ['In the play of Ātmā, I am the true nature of the child.'] It was a statement made by Shrī Ātmānanda from the majestic heights of a spiritual mood called the 'child's mood'. The word 'mood' here should not be confused with anything like the complex modifications of the human mind, be it even the highly applauded state of mind 'nirvikalpa samādhi' itself. The word 'mood' is simply used for want of a better word in English and to draw your attention to something, and not to make you understand anything about its condition.

Question: And what is the nature of that child's play?

Answer: The child in knowledge himself said one day. 'The child's play is heaven's pride.' It explained that immediately in its own language, as follows:

Nearest and immediate expressions of the absolute

1. Light and joy,
2. Love and power,
3. Splendour and majesty,
4. Beauty and goodness,
5. Harmony and peace,
6. Rich and full,
7. Grand and noble,
8. Pure and innocent,
9. Calm and serene,
10. Sweet and soft,
11. Cheerful and happy.

Don't mistake any of these for the Self. But you can certainly see me, the Absolute, through any of these expressions of Myself.

2nd July 1958

1386. IṢHṬA-MŪRTI – ITS SCOPE, LIMITATION AND PERFECTION?

God is logically defined as the highest manifestation of the human mind. Similarly, the *iṣhṭa-mūrti* [the form of God chosen for worship] is also the creation of one's own mind. You give to it the form and qualities you like most, and therefore it is called 'iṣhṭa-mūrti' [literally 'embodiment of liking']. It has exactly the same characteristics as an ordinary object, but with this difference – that it is highly magnified.

Let us examine an object. It is not an intrinsic, indivisible whole. It is constituted of three distinct and separate elements, namely:

1. Form (percept) which is the immediate creation of the sense organ concerned;
2. A fund of ideas (concepts) thrown out by the mind to supplement the former percept; and
3. A sense of existence (Reality or permanency) which forms the background upon which the former two can appear.

This last one – permanence or existence – can never be the contribution of either the changing senses or of the changing mind. It is the contribution of Consciousness, beyond even the mind. In order to get at the truth of any object, it has to be analysed till its generic form is reached, eliminating the changing parts in the process. Then the object gets reduced to its essence or substance.

Neither the individual nor the 'iṣhṭa-mūrti' is an exception to this rule. But the 'iṣhṭa-mūrti' has one particular advantage over all other objects, in that it has no sensual or perceptual form to begin with. It has only a form of ideas or concepts, with universal qualities like all-knowingness, all-pervasiveness, almightiness etc. attributed to it. In order to understand the iṣhṭa-mūrti correctly, one has to eliminate the form made up of ideas and qualities from the background 'existence'.

But this existence which is left over is, for the time-being, recognized by the aspirant only as nothingness or blankness. The meaning and the essence of this blank wall of ignorance still remains a mystery to the mind. The mind can never unravel it, by its own unaided efforts.

This same state is attained by following very many other paths and by exercises like meditation, devotion, chanting of mantras, and yōgas of different types. The aspirant is invariably stranded in this apparently pleasurable state, taking it for the highest or being unable to get beyond or being attracted by the sense of pleasurableness in the state.

In all these instances, the enquiry is made purely objectively, ignoring the subject altogether. It is true that the object is reduced to its most generic form. But the subject still remains as a subject. As long as the least trace of subjectivity remains, objectivity cannot disappear. And until objectivity disappears completely, the real nature of the object can never be visualized. This is the fundamental error committed by science as well as philosophy, both in India and outside, in trying to approach the Truth through the medium of the mind.

Remedy: It is only the 'Kāraṇa-guru', who is established in the ultimate Truth and who is prepared to lead another to it, that can help one out of this darkness. The aspirant has so far been examining things outside himself, from the self-assumed stronghold of the mind. But the 'Kāraṇa-guru', if one is fortunate enough to secure one, draws the attention of the aspirant away from the object, to the subject so far ignored. The truth about the real nature of this 'subject' is then expounded to the aspirant in the most unambiguous terms, in the light of the aspirant's own personal experiences.

He is thus enabled to visualize his own real nature, beyond the shadow of a doubt. He is then asked to review his former problems from his own real and permanent stand, just visualized. But to his utter bewilderment and joy, he finds every problem standing self-solved to perfection and himself free from all bondage. What appeared first as an insurmountable blank wall of ignorance, now appears as the most concrete and self-luminous Truth within.

1387. SOME OF THE PATHS USUALLY ADOPTED

1. *The path of meditation*, as enjoined by the Ācāryas of old, has three distinct and progressive stages:

a) 'Pratīka-dhyāna' (dhyāna or meditation in strict conformity with the gross model before the disciple): Here, by mere concentration, the aspirant tries to make a mental picture of the gross model in front of him.

b) 'Dhyēyānusṛita-dhyāna' (allowing full freedom to the creative and decorative faculties of imagination, without impairing the skeleton of bare fundamentals): Here the gross model is completely dispensed with. The attention is slowly diverted from the dead form to its live features. All kinds of dualistic visions are experienced at this stage. All aspirants guided by 'kārya-gurus' (those dealing only with any particular aspect, art or trade) get stranded here, not knowing the way beyond, and satisfied with the limited experiences of happiness accompanying the visions. But the fortunate few, who happen to get a Kāraṇa-guru at least at this stage, slowly enter into the third state.

c) 'Aham-gṛiha-dhyāna' (in consonance with one's own experience): There is neither gross form nor subtle quality in one's experience. Experience is knowledge or Peace alone. Therefore, one gives up here the mental part of one's meditation as well, and one is directed to cling on to the substance (knowledge) behind all appearance. This is possible only if one has already become familiar with the same knowledge or Self behind the mind. The aspirant, under positive instructions from the Guru, visualizes the Self and, by clinging on to it, is gradually established there.

2. *Devotion* is the most popular method adopted all over the world; but unfortunately, for the vast majority of aspirants, it is left incomplete.

It is usually inspired by phenomenal religion, ethics and blind faith; and therefore is inevitably blind in its application. It takes into consideration only the physical and mental aspects of the object of its devotion. These two aspects are transitory and therefore yield only transitory pleasures and transitory powers, though all this is in all humility attributed to the Lord. Most devotees usually get enamoured of this pleasurable state; and being afraid of losing the glamour of it, they stubbornly refuse to examine the content of their experience in the light of right discrimination. Thus they get stranded in that state of empty and fleeting pleasurableness.

Even Shrī Caitanya was no exception to this. His super-mystical experiences were the result of blind devotion, which kept the world spellbound for years, but at last they faded away. For a period of about twelve years, he was immersed in virtual stagnation. He is then reported to have approached a Sage (from a Shrī Shankara order), who initiated him into the ultimate Truth. The path being beautifully prepared and his heart being sublime as a result of his former experiences of selfless devotion, he could imbibe the spirit of vēdāntic instruction and instantly visualize the Ultimate.

This is the one path of liberation open to all devotees, if they earnestly desire to visualize the Truth, which alone can be called real salvation or liberation.

3. *The path of sound* is yet another common approach. Here, the chanting of a 'mantra' is the exercise adopted. It is done in four distinct stages.

a) 'Vaikharī': Here the mantra is pronounced repeatedly in clear audible tones, and attention concentrated on the audible sound.

b) 'Madhyamā': Here the gross, audible part of the exercise is given up, and the mantra is chanted silently or mentally. Late in this stage, one gets pleasurable experiences through the realm of sound, by way of ecstatic music, agreeable sounds etc. If the aspirant emphasizes the sound part of the mantra alone, he will be stranded in this harmony of sound. But if he is fortunate enough to secure a Kāraṇa-guru, the attention of the aspirant will immediately be directed to that which manifests itself as sound. The meaning of the mantra and the source of sound are explained to him, and thus he is lifted up to the next stage.

c) 'Pashyantī': Here the objectivity completely vanishes, and he visualizes the impersonal Truth which stands as the background of the harmony of sound.

d) 'Parā': Where the aspirant gets established in this Truth, by clinging on to it.

4. *Yōgas (e.g. Kuṇḍalinī yōga):* Still another class of aspirants take to the path of meditating on the various nerve centres or ādhāra-cakras – gross as well as subtle – assumed to be situated along the course of the spinal chord. This exercise is supposed to arouse the vital energy

called 'kuṇḍalinī' – which lies dormant at the lower extremity of the spinal chord – and to raise it in gradual stages to the crown of the head. The aspirant obtains a variety of phenomenal experiences, as the kuṇḍalinī passes from centre to centre.

The whole process depends upon the concept of the centres; and the centres in turn depend upon the body, even for their very concept. Therefore, this exercise can never be expected to yield anything but relative results in the dual plane. This exercise also falls short of the ultimate goal.

On reaching the crown of the head ('brahma-randhra'), the yōgin finds his progress blocked by a blank wall of ignorance or nothingness. Therefore, he seeks a Kāraṇa-guru, and under his instruction visualizes the ultimate Truth and gets established in it.

Comparing all these so called paths and exercises, we come to the conclusion that they only prepare the ground for the aspirant, by purifying his mind and heart. He can then imbibe the ultimate Truth. The real light can be imparted only by the Kāraṇa-guru, '*in person*'. There is no exception to this.

6th July 1958

1388. THE HELPLESS FALLACY IN EXPRESSING IN WORDS A SPIRITUAL EXPERIENCE

'Spiritual experience' is only one. It is visualizing or knowing the real Self. It is knowing the self in identity, without the least trace of subject-object relationship.

Subsequently, the ego attempts to express that experience in words, without itself ever having been present in the realm of experience at all. In this attempt, the ego miserably caricatures the spiritual experience, in terms of the only standard available to it – the subject-object relationship. Here, name and form must come in. The ego poses itself as the subject, and tries to make the impersonal Self its object, by calling it 'happiness'. Thus the ego says it 'enjoyed happiness'. This statement is nothing short of a veritable lie, since the experience was unique and indivisible.

The ego is a spurious mixture of Reality (the Self) and unreality (body and mind). The presence of Reality, in the ego itself, enables the ego to remember something of the real experience. But the memory gets blurred, by the identification of the real with the unreal, in the ego. It is further distorted in the attempt to express it through the narrow media of mind and language.

Thus the experience, when expressed in words, appears to be what it was not.

8th July 1958

1389. 'SARVA-JNYA' (THE 'ALL-KNOWING')

'Sarva-jnya' is a term often misunderstood and misapplied. Though spiritual in concept, it is more often used in the limited yōgic sense. It has two clear and distinct implications, 'yōgic' as well as 'jnyānic'.

In the yōgic sense, it is invariably used as a personal noun. It presupposes a person as the knower and an 'all' (usually excluding his own personal self) as the known. Here, the knowing is purely of the nature of subject-object relationship. The first thing to be considered is whether such a knowledge – regarding the supposed 'all' – is humanly possible. The 'all' must imply a multiplicity of distinct and separate units or entities. The mind, by the very nature of its constitution, can conceive only any one thing at a time. Then the 'all', composed of infinite separate units, can never be the simultaneous object of the mind.

But they say it is objectified. How is this made possible? There is only one solution to the problem. The multiplicity of the composition of the 'all' is ignored completely; and the 'all', only in name, is conceived as an integral unit. This unit, recognizing no other object by its side, cannot have any of the distinct qualities of a sensual or mental object. Thus the 'all' takes the form of generic space, or mere absence of objects. For all practical purposes, this affords sufficient objectivity for the mind to hold on to. Having transcended diversity, there is the agreeable though reflected sense of pleasurableness attached to it. The helpless yōgin considers this as the Ultimate and tenaciously clings on to it, giving the artificial state different names and being blissfully ignorant of his own relationship with that state or object.

The problem may also be examined from the standpoint of time. Time appears in its three forms: as the past, present and future. Mental knowledge functions only in the present. Experiences of all kinds also take place in the present. In the same manner, 'sarva-jnyatva' is also an experience in the present. It may allude to what you may call the past or future, but your experience is only *in* the present and *of* the present. Therefore, to say that you experienced the past or future, as comprehended by the term 'all', is absurd.

If the knower's identity and the separateness of objects are preserved, the said experience of an 'all' is impossible. It may be possible, by dint of exercise, to expand the limits of the mind; so as to comprehend, within the limits of its 'present', many things which might legitimately belong to the past or future, according to the standards of others. But this offers no real solution to the problem. It only makes it all the more complicated. You are not enriched by any such experience of the 'all', in a yōgic manner.

But a *Jnyānin's* view of 'sarva-jnyatva' is entirely different. The Jnyānin is one who has visualized his own real nature, as nothing but pure Consciousness and Peace. He knows that an object, when known, no longer remains separate, but gets merged in him as knowledge. He knows also that the ego or personality called his own is only one such object. Therefore, to him, the 'all' is only another such object; undergoing the very same process of transformation as any other object when known, and thus leaving only himself, not as knower, but as knowledge pure.

Thus to him, *sarva-jnya* means *sarva-jnyāna* or Consciousness pure.

31st July 1958

1390. THE PRESENCE OF A SAGE IS SURCHARGED WITH LOVE AND KNOWLEDGE.

It may be said to be highly 'love-active' or 'knowledge-active'.

Mr. Bose asked Gurunāthan: I feel attraction and joy when I come near you. But I feel the opposite when I go near some others. Why?

Answer: When you come near me, you are spontaneously taken beyond body, senses and mind; because that is the gist of my teaching to you, and that may be said to be the realm in which I rest. Thus, you unknowingly dive deep into yourself when you see me, and you thereby touch your own background – the 'Self'.

I am also standing as that background – the 'Self'. The Self is only one. It is indivisible and is of the nature of Peace. This contact with the background gives you peace, which you call joy from the waking state.

But when you meet others, they are only the objects of your senses and mind, and you yourself remain as the ego in the mental level. Therefore you are always subject to the tribulations of the mind.

4th August 1958

1391. SEEING AND UNDERSTANDING OF THE WORLD

Question: How do the ignorant man and the Sage see this world?

Answer: The ignorant man and the Sage both face the world, apparently in the same manner, but with one fundamental and subtle difference.

The ignorant man understands everything – including knowledge – in terms of the object, and experiences objects alone.

But the Sage understands everything in terms of knowledge, his own real nature.

5th August 1958

1392. DEVELOPMENT OF JNYĀNA

Question: What are the progressive stages and their significance, in the development to Jnyāna?

Answer: The path of jnyāna has three distinct and separate stages, in their order of progression. They are:

1. *Sṛishṭi-dṛishṭi-vāda:* Perception of objects already existing. This is called 'vyavahāra-pakṣha' – giving full credence to the world of objects, including God, Māyā etc. All experience in this realm is only indirect (parōkṣha). This is intended only for the ignorant man who is attached deeply to the body and senses. This path only prepares the ground to receive the Truth in the next stage (dṛishṭi-sṛishṭi-vāda).

2. *Ḍṛiṣhṭi-sṛiṣhṭi-vāda* holds that the object appears only when perceived, and that the essence of perception is Consciousness alone (the Real). This is visualized only on listening to the Truth from the lips of a Kāraṇa-guru. Having thus visualized the Truth, you are asked to look back upon the appearances below, from the ultimate stand of the Self. Then you find that the apparent world is all an illusion. This resolution is called 'ajāta-vāda'.
3. *Ajāta-vāda* holds that nothing other than the real Self (Consciousness) was ever born, ever is, or ever shall be. This is the highest stand of Advaita, in relation to the apparent world.

1393. WHAT IS THE COMPOSITION OF THE WORLD, AND ITS RELATION TO TRUTH?

Answer: The world appears as a connected chain of Consciousness, perceptions and objects.

When Consciousness functions through the sense organ 'eye', the object of perception is usually called 'form'. In the chain of form, seeing and Consciousness, the 'seeing' is unknown to 'form', because 'form' has to give up its grossness in order to become 'seeing'. Then it ceases to be 'form'. Again, Consciousness is unknown to 'seeing'; because 'seeing' has to give up its objectivity completely in order to stand as Consciousness, and then it is no 'seeing'. But 'seeing' is not unknown to Consciousness and 'form' is not unknown to 'seeing'.

The process of analysing form – and reducing it to seeing – is much facilitated by substituting the word 'sight' in place of 'form', because no explanation is needed to show that sight is not different from 'seeing'.

1394. WHAT IS THE RESULT OF EMPHASIZING CONSCIOUSNESS IN IDEAS OR OBJECTS?

Answer: Consciousness is absolute and is only one.

Consciousness + something = idea.

Emphasizing Consciousness means looking at the idea from the standpoint of Consciousness.

When Consciousness begins to look at the idea, Consciousness being only one and that being already in the idea as its essence, that Consciousness has to stand out of the idea. Then, the idea being divested of its essence 'Consciousness', the idea becomes extinct.

Consciousness is the essence of both the idea and the object. If Consciousness stands as the idea, the object disappears. If Consciousness stands as Consciousness itself, the idea also disappears. Consider the illustration of the figure in the rock.

It can well be said from one standpoint that *Consciousness by itself never illumines ideas or objects, but only kills them.* Let us apply this process in our daily life. You say in the waking state that you remember your past dream. But what exactly is it that you remember? You remember only the 'seeing' of objects in the dream. What else was there in the dream? Nothing. All that appeared as gross object in dream was nothing other than the 'seeing' itself. This fact needs no further proof, when you wake up. This is typical of every so called 'waking' experience also.

Therefore, it is only 'seeing' that appears as object; and similarly, it is Consciousness that appears as 'seeing' in both the states.

1395. WHAT IS SPHURAṆA?

Answer: Sphuraṇa [shining], in whatever level it manifests itself, is the Ultimate. Sphuraṇa in the mental level is understood and is interpreted in terms of subject and object. But in the spiritual context it is viewed only in identity. Therefore all phenomenal illustrations can only mislead one, regarding the significance of *sphuraṇa.*

It may be said to be the objectless manifestation of the light of Consciousness.

1396. WHAT IS THE GOOD OF KNOWING 'I AM HAPPINESS', IF I CANNOT ENJOY IT?

Answer: It has been proved already that one's real nature is objectless happiness, and that one can experience it. It is experienced not through subject-object relationship as in the waking and dream states, but in identity as in deep sleep. In deep sleep, the mind is dead.

The questioner evidently wants to know the happiness, herself standing separate as the knower and to feel the joy of it as the enjoyer. This is possible only in duality, as in the waking or dream states.

Even there, a deeper examination will show that the so called enjoyment of happiness is being one with it. Happiness is never enjoyed. To know that 'I am Happiness' is a spiritual experience. Spiritual experience is only one. It is non-duality. Its real nature is pure Happiness itself, and you know it there in identity.

On coming to the waking state, you seem to know it objectively. Immediately, happiness is separated from you as your object – a mere idea. You have actually lost the happiness, by trying to know it or feel it. Therefore, never objectify happiness by trying to separate it from you, in any manner.

31st August 1958

1397. MANTRAS AND THEIR EFFICACY

Mantras are designed by the great seers. They are composed of groups of sounds with an active life principle, capable of producing specific forms and effects when pronounced in the proper svara (tune).

Mantras have a double purpose. At the phenomenal level, emphasis is on the audible part of the mantra. The form created by each mantra (called its 'mantra dēvatā') is possessed of certain particular powers. The mantra dēvatā, in exercise of some of its powers, confers upon the devotee certain benefits prayed for. But in the course of this process, one has to guard against innumerable possible slips, of commission and omission.

Mantra, if properly utilized, helps one to approach the ultimate Truth. Just before and after every mantra, there is a visible gap into which the sound merges. In this gap, there is nothing other than one's own Self or Consciousness. Having once visualized before the Guru this nature of the Self, if you pronounce the mantra emphasizing not the audible part but the content of the apparent gaps, you are easily taken to the centre of your visualization – the real Self – and this helps you gradually to get established there.

Though the mantras, in the great majority of cases, are utilized as instruments of action (pravṛitti), they can also be utilized for the purpose of liberation (nivṛitti) if handled with sufficient discrimination and insight. In the former, the centre of emphasis is the object; and in the latter, it is the background.

1st September 1958

1398. REPENTANCE

Repentance in the phenomenal level, though recommended by most religions, is in practice a dangerous and colossal blunder.

In doing the wrong, you are prompted by the irresistible craving of the heart. But in the usual expression of repentance, it is an empty intellectual argumentation. The moment you start to repent, you recall the past incidents in all their detail. This provides a fresh opportunity for the heart to enjoy the cherished pleasure, at least in a subtle manner. This amounts practically to a repetition of the wrong, in the subtle form. At last, you express an empty verbal repentance and rest contented with it.

This sort of repentance only aggravates the evil and inflates the ego. Therefore it has to be avoided at all cost, and every attempt must be made to forget the incident altogether. This is the golden rule of progress.

2nd September 1958

1399. WHAT IS THE NATURE AND PURPOSE OF ART?

> *Art* is only that which tends to merge the other into yourself.
> *Mundane* is that which separates the other from you.

Therefore real art takes you to the unity of the subject, and so it is really a preparation of the ground for initiation into the ultimate Truth.

1400. WHAT IS THE ESSENTIAL DIFFERENCE BETWEEN JĪVA, ĪSHVARA AND JNYĀNIN?

The *jīva* remains a slave to avidyā (ignorance) and helplessly oscillates between pain and pleasure.

Īshvara – possessing a clear preponderance of sattva-guṇa – holds māyā always under his sway.

The *Jnyānin* – being pure sattva alone – remains master of the mind which is of the nature of vidyā (knowledge), and he sometimes allows that mind to function in its own way.

4th September 1958

1401. CAN THERE BE ANY RELATIONSHIP BETWEEN MISERY AND HAPPINESS?

Misery as such is purely man-made. It is born and maintained in *dvaita* (duality) alone.

Happiness is *advaita*, and is natural to man.

Duality is never experienced by anyone, because no two things can be experienced simultaneously. Misery is duality, and is therefore an illusion. But non-duality is brought in to enjoy misery.

Consciousness itself appears as 'perception'. You think of it as separate from Consciousness and give it the different name 'perception'. But no, it is Consciousness itself. Even this perception – considered independent of the perceiver and the percept – is no perception at all, but Consciousness itself.

This process can be shortened further. The intermediary steps can be dispensed with, and the knower and the object alone taken into consideration. The object can never exist independent of the knower, consciousness; and it is therefore Consciousness itself.

5th September 1958

1402. WHAT IS THE FUNCTION AND THE FATE OF AN OBJECT?

Answer:. An object is there always pointing to the Consciousness of the perceiver, as 'You, You, You...', meaning thereby: 'I am here merely on account of you.'

But the moment you stand as Consciousness and turn back to the object, the object vanishes; in other words, the object commits suicide.

1403. CAN I REMEMBER?

Answer: No. But speaking loosely, we say that we remember past incidents. To remember something exactly as it was perceived, the time which has passed and the past sense perceptions must occur once again in the present here. But they are past and gone. Of all that was then and there, Consciousness alone is here and now. Therefore memory, as ordinarily understood, is a misnomer.

23rd September 1958

1404. HOW IS MISERY RELATED TO LOVE?

Answer: Misery is love itself. But how? Let us examine misery. Take any experience of misery. You say the thought of your departed father creates misery. But does it always do so? If your father, when living, was cruel and inimical to you, the thought of his demise would hardly make you miserable. Therefore it is clear that it was not the thought of the father that was the cause of the misery, but it was the thought of your father's love that was the real cause.

But love is attributeless and indivisible. It is wrong even to call it father's love, and it has been proved that the thought of the father was not the cause of misery. Therefore it was love and love alone that was the cause of the misery, if it could ever have had a cause. But you experience only one thing at a time – love or misery – and therefore there can be no causal relationship between the two [as different things].

Hence it is love that expresses itself as misery, and not your father [that causes it, as something different from love]. The father is forgotten in love. To find the source of misery, you must go beyond body and mind. If you emphasize body and mind, you are fixed in the expression of Truth. The substance is beyond.

Misery and happiness are both expressions. Love pure is the background of both. When you cling on to love, objects vanish. But when you cling on to objects, love is not perceived as such.

Where there is no love, there is no misery. So love goes into the make of misery; misery is love itself. It is the illusory concept of time that makes love appear as misery. If you separate love from misery, misery is *not*.

25th September 1958

1405. DOES THE PATH OF PHENOMENAL LOVE TAKE ME ANYWHERE?

Answer: Yes. To the Ultimate, if followed diligently and intelligently.

Love is the feeling of oneness with the object of one's love. Following the path of phenomenal love means expanding the sphere of your love. This course, logically, takes you to a stage where your love becomes universal. In the concept of the universal, the last vestige of the ego, your individuality, is included.

This fact can be perceived and duality transcended only when a Kāraṇa-guru points out the Truth. Then the ego is merged into the universal and universality vanishes, leaving love alone supreme. Here, you may be said to stand in identity (as one) with that love. This love, being all comprehending, is objectless and pure. This is the Ultimate.

But it has to be said that the path is long and arduous, and the pitfalls are many.

1406. HOW TO JUSTIFY SHRĪ RĀMA IN ABANDONING SĪTĀ'?

Question: In the epic of *Rāmāyaṇa*, Shrī Rāma is depicted as an ideal of manhood. But he is found in the end to abandon his innocent wife Sītā alone in the deep forests, even while she was about to have a child. To all existing cannons of human justice, this was an ignoble act. But this can never be. How can we justify Rāma, without sacrificing Truth and justice?

Answer: Rāma the individual and Rāma the King were two distinct and separate entities; sometimes their interests clashed. Whenever their interests clashed in this manner, the lower interest (that of the individual) had to be sacrificed and the higher interest maintained. The King has no human wife. His spouse is the country and the people.

Therefore, in the abandonment of Sītā, the interest of the individual Rāma was sacrificed; and the interest of Rāma the King was maintained, by upholding the cause of the country, of the people and of justice. It was an incomparable act of self-sacrifice, on the part of Rāma. Divorce was ordered by Rāma the King, and Rāma the individual suffered the dire consequences – the pangs of separation. Can this be called selfish?

1407. HOW TO EXAMINE A THING? AND WHY?

A thing is not independent in itself. It is inextricably connected with the rest of the world. Therefore, in order to understand the entire truth about the thing, either the whole world has to be examined, or the thing has to be examined independent of the rest of the world.

The former is literally impossible. Therefore, the only possible course is to examine the thing as representing the whole world. This cannot be done in terms of time, space and causality, which are but the most generic standards accepted by the world. They are but parts of the world itself, and go into the make of the thing. Such an examination could never yield true results.

The examination therefore has to be conducted, not from the level of the world, but from a level beyond. Such a level can only be that of Consciousness. Taking your stand there and looking at a thing, the thing along with the world no longer appears as such, but stands transformed as Consciousness itself. Therefore, the thing and the world are nothing but Consciousness.

A thing has to be examined, not to find out its composition or potentialities, but to find out its truth value or the changeless in it. The absence of this perspective is the cause of the failure of science, yōga, arts, philosophy etc. to reach the ultimate Truth.

Another approach: The world is a world of perceptions alone. The unit of each perception is composed of perceiving, the perceiver and the percept, all three constituting the so called 'triputī'.

Triputī is supposed to appear simultaneously and also to disappear likewise. This viewpoint is rather vague, and not intended for the uttamādhikāris. Examining the triputī more closely, we find that it is perceiving that produces the perceiver and the perceived. So perceiving is more important than, and even the source of, the other two.

But when perceiving itself is examined more closely, from the standpoint of Consciousness, the perceiving disappears and stands transformed as pure Consciousness. Thus perception is nothing but Consciousness, and so is the world.

12th October 1958

1408. HOW CAN AN OBJECT BE EXAMINED, TO FIND OUT ITS TRUTH?

It can be done in two distinct and separate ways, from two different standpoints. They are:

1. The standpoint of the ego
2. The standpoint of the real 'I'-principle

1. The ego, in trying to examine an object, first splits the object into its two component parts, the permanent and the impermanent. Then it tries to separate the impermanent parts from the permanent. But in so doing, an unconscious transformation comes over the ego itself. Simultaneously with the shedding of the impermanent parts from the object, the accretions or the impermanent parts of the ego itself drop away.

   Finally, the changeless in the object alone remains over, and that is the *sat* aspect of the Reality. Then the ego also stands as that Reality, divorced of all its accretions. Therefore the object is nothing but the Reality – the Self. This argument applies equally to the body also, which can be reduced to the real 'I'-principle. Thus the world stands revealed as the ultimate Reality.

   But this examination can never be conducted successfully and in its entirety until you have listened to the Truth from the lips of a Kāraṇa-guru. Because, without visualizing the truth of the Self and without being able to cling on to it, the ego can never shed all its accretions. This is why, at the end of all their enquiries, the yōgins, scientists and philosophers all knock against a blank wall of ignorance.

2. The second examination, from the standpoint of the real 'I'-principle, is easy. Because, if you examine the object or the

world, neither will appear as such, but each stands as one with the Reality – the 'I'-principle. Thus also, the object world is *not.*

1409. WHAT EXISTS BETWEEN THE 'HERE' AND THE 'THERE'?

Answer: Only that which supports the two. That is *sat* [existence] alone. Similarly, pure Consciousness exists between two mentations and supports the mentations as well.

1410. WHAT IS BHAKTI?

Answer: You cannot have bhakti for something non-existent, nor can you have it towards anything you do not know. Every object of bhakti has two aspects:

1. The impermanent or non-existent form, and
2. The permanent or the real consciousness.

Bhakti should be directed to the latter aspect, and the former can be blissfully ignored when it has fulfilled its legitimate purpose. The purpose of the 'form' is only to arrest your attention and to enable you to direct it to Consciousness, which is its background. The Consciousness can never be objectified. That is always the ultimate subject (viṣhayin). It is in the devotee himself and indivisible.

Therefore, a real devotee can only and need only direct his attention to the Consciousness in him. This is real bhakti; and it immediately yields Peace or *ānanda*, which is Consciousness itself. This is vastu-tantra, the outcome of Truth. Shrī Shankara defines real bhakti of the highest order as follows:

mōkṣa-sādhana-sāmagryāṁ bhaktir ēva garīyasī
sva-svarūpā-'nusandhānaṁ bhaktir ity abhidhīyatē

[Among all ways of seeking to be free,
it's love that is the best, one must agree.
To question one's own truth, to ask what's there,
that is the love of those who ask with care.]

Shrī Shankara, Vivēka-cūḍāmaṇī, 31

'Incessantly clinging onto one's own real nature is verily termed bhakti.'

Bhakti for anything other than this is really unworthy of the name. It may, at the most, be called a fascination as unreal as the object itself.

1411. CAN DUALISM AND NON-DUALITY EVER REACH A COMPROMISE?

The centre of dualism is an assumption of the separate and independent existence of subject and object. The world of diversity is built upon this concept. Non-duality is the background and support of duality itself. It is the seeing of objects in the right perspective and is never an assumption. It is rightly called in Sanskrit '*darshana*' or visualization of Truth. Therefore, no compromise is possible between the two.

The attitude of non-duality is sāttvic and magnanimous, even towards this hostile duality. Non-duality liberally lends its own light to duality, in order that it may appear and thrive, even to oppose the source of duality itself.

However, there have been of late certain attempts in social circles to effect a compromise between dualists and non-dualists. Poor friends! They have not gone deep into the workings of either party. Society, which is dualist by nature, can only align itself with the dualists, because it knows something about them only. But it is ignorant of the stand of non-dualists.

The non-dualists, on the other hand, know the stand of the dualists quite well; since they were themselves dualists earlier in life. Therefore the non-dualists might even be prepared for a compromise, to the extent that duality is only an appearance.

This does not help the dualist in any way, and to go any further the non-dualists will have to sacrifice the essence of their own stand. The dualists cannot even conceive of non-dualism. Therefore a compromise between the two parties is impossible.

> ananyāś cintayantō māṁ yē janāḥ paryupāsatē .
> tēṣāṁ nityā 'bhiyuktānāṁ yōga-kṣēmaṁ vahāmy ahaṁ ..

Bhagavad-gītā, 9.22

The verse in the Gītā quoted above is a typical example of the non-dual approach. It means: 'Whoever thinks of Me as none other than "himself", his worldly and spiritual well-being will be safe-guarded and looked after by Me (Ātmā, the Absolute).'

1412. WHAT IS THE SOURCE AND REMEDY OF PASSIONS?

Love is pure, and by nature objectless. It is one with *ānanda* or Peace.

But when mental desires are brought to bear upon love, that love becomes degenerate and objectified as rāga [passion] or kāma [desire]. Out of rāga arise the manifold passions of enmity, anger, avarice etc.; and you groan under their weight. The only way of escape from this malady is to trace back the course to love, by relinquishing desires and their objects. Then rāga gets sublimated, passions disappear, pure love shines in all its glory, and you stand as one with it in identity.

12th November 1958

1413. VĒDĀNTIC TRUTH IS NEVER A MEANS TO ANYTHING ELSE.

Questions:

1. What is the meaning of achieving the unification and advancement of mankind?
2. How can vēdāntic truth and teaching be applied to the good of the community, the state and the word at large?

Answer:

1. Mankind always stands united and centred in 'man'. Disunion creeps in only where 'man' is misunderstood or misinterpreted. Therefore, the only means of achieving the goal is to know the real significance of 'man' and to let it be known.

   'Man', when dispassionately examined, is found to mean the most generic form of man and comprehends all mankind. Being generic, it is the ultimate Truth itself – the real Self.

   Vēdānta alone helps you in this endeavour. Therefore follow Vēdānta, realize your own Self, and save your 'mankind' – if it still remains. But you, for certain, will be saved as a result of such effort.

2. Vēdāntic Truth is only one. It is Consciousness, the nature of the real Self. It has no teachings, so to say. It must first be understood that vēdāntic Truth – being ultimate, beyond all relativity – can never be used as a means to any other end.

   The vēdāntic approach is strictly individual and never social or communal. By visualizing the ultimate Truth (the Self) through Vēdānta, the individual realizes his own perfection and automatically transcends society and the world. He finds the world a mere illusion. But he allows the illusory world to continue to exist, merely as a matter of concession. He can undo it by withdrawing his own consciousness from it any moment.

   Therefore, so far as the vēdāntin is concerned, the question of improving the world does not arise.

15th November 1958

1414. WHAT IS LIFE?

Answer: Life, thought and feeling are but the expressions of the ultimate Reality, through the respective perspectives of existence, knowledge and peace. Life can never be correctly examined from the standpoint of any of the states, which are but parts of the apparent life itself. It can be examined correctly only from the standpoint of that which is permanent or changeless in life (pure Awareness). This may be done in many ways.

1. Taking for granted that the three states are real, let us examine life. The totality of life consists in the experiences of the three states, together with an Awareness which records the appearance and disappearance of each state. The waking state as such is only a fraction of the totality of life. Therefore no enquiry limited to the waking state experiences alone can be fair; nor can it be expected to yield any reasonable result. Of the totality of life's experiences, the experiences of the three states are each independent of the other two and change or disappear completely.

   The only permanent or changeless part of life's experiences is the Awareness which stands as the background of the states and even beyond. This is the real 'I'-principle, the ultimate Truth. Therefore, the essence of life is the Reality itself.

2. Existence appearing limited is life. But the appearance is an illusion. So the essence of life is pure existence or 'being' itself, or the real 'I'-principle. The disappearance of the limitation of existence may be called 'death'. Life and death being both appearances, they cannot exist without a real background. That background is existence itself and that is the essence of both life and death.

3. Existence manifests itself in varying degrees of intensity, from the god-man kingdom down to the mineral kingdom. Every kingdom '*is*'. The 'is'-ness alone is the changeless part or essence of each kingdom, and all the rest are mere appearances and therefore unreal. This 'is'-ness is the background of life, and that is the Reality which has neither birth nor death. The term 'life' really comprehends both birth and death, and stands transcending both.

26th November 1958

1415. I KNOW I AM NOT AN IDEAL DISCIPLE. BUT SHOULD I NOT SEE THAT MY ACTIONS DO NOT BRING DISCREDIT TO MY GURU?

Answer: No. You may think that you are not yet an ideal disciple, and even pray to the Guru to help you to reach that goal. But what exactly that goal is, you do not know. It has no test, either mental or ethical. That goal shall always remain unknown, in the sense in which knowledge is used ordinarily. Therefore it is futile to try to verify your progress towards that goal. But what you can do and must do, is to continue to keep incessant contact with the Guru, in whatever manner convenient to you – in the gross, in the subtle or beyond.

28th November 1958

1416. CAN CAUSALITY FUNCTION UNDER ANY CONDITION?

Answer: No. Not even in the same order of time, much less when the order of time also changes. For example, the sun sets and darkness comes. Can the preceding sunshine be said to be the cause of darkness, or vice versa? No. Both are absurd. Therefore, causal relationship cannot be established between such changing states, which have no connection whatsoever between them.

1417. IF I AM THE ULTIMATE TRUTH, HOW DOES AN OBJECT APPEAR?

Gurunāthan: Does the object appear at all? Who says so?

Disciple: It is the ego that says so.

G: What is the ego from your own standpoint as the real 'I'-principle? Is it an object or is it the subject?.

D: Certainly the ego is only an object.

G: Therefore, including the ego also in the category of objects, does the question arise at all?

D: No. It was a stupid question.

30th November 1958

1418. WHAT CAN I DESIRE?

Answer: Nothing.

Desire shows want and that shows your own imperfection. But you are Consciousness which is by nature perfect; and you cannot desire to know anything else, there being nothing else beside Consciousness.

Again, you are Peace or Happiness which is also perfect; and you cannot desire to have any other happiness, there being nothing else beside Happiness – your own real nature.

1419. I KNOW I AM HAPPINESS AND CONSCIOUSNESS; STILL I AM SOMETIMES MISERABLE. WHY?

Gurunāthan: Which 'I' is Consciousness or Peace?

Disciple: The real 'I'-principle, Ātmā.

G: Is that 'I' ever miserable?

D: No. Not at all.

G: If somebody else (for example the usurper 'I') is miserable, why should you, the real 'I', be worried?

Now listen. I will explain your confusion. The ego is sometimes miserable, because it desires to enjoy transitory sensual pleasures and at the same time to avoid their opposite, misery, the inseparable counterpart of pleasure. That is impossible.

Pleasure and pain are the obverse and the reverse of the same coin. You cannot choose one side alone. Either you accept both together or reject both together.

1420. HOW CAN WE DISTINGUISH THE SPIRITUAL FROM THE PHENOMENAL?

Answer: The real 'I'-principle (also called Ātmā, Truth, real Self, Consciousness, Peace, etc.) is alone spiritual. Everything else, including even the much applauded nirvikalpa samādhi, is phenomenal.

In other words, the ultimate subject alone is spiritual, and everything with the least trace of objectivity is phenomenal.

1421. VICĀRA-MĀRGA

Vicāra-mārga is an enquiry by the 'being' itself into the experiences of the totality of life.

1st December 1958

1422. WHAT IS VĒDĀNTA?

Answer: Vēdānta is a deep and relentless enquiry into the ultimate Truth. The enquiry is made with the aid of pure discrimination and reason alone. The reason employed for the purpose is tri-basic reason, which is applicable to all the three states. But the reason employed in science, yōga, arts, philosophy etc. is only mono-basic reason – applicable only in the waking state.

1423. TRUTH IS THE ONLY ANTIDOTE FOR ERROR.

1424. MENTATION (COMPREHENDING INTELLECTION AS WELL) IS AN ACTIVITY OF THE MIND.

2nd December 1958

1425. WHAT IS THE PURPOSE OF THE PROCESS OF NEGATION?

Answer: Negation of the objective world gives you a disinterested and tranquil stand from which to start the enquiry. Otherwise, there is the danger of the mind coming in uncalled for, in some form or other, to pollute the enquiry.

15th December 1958

1426. THE QUALIFICATIONS ESSENTIAL FOR AN ASPIRANT TO GET TO THE TRUTH

They may be roughly classified into four.

1. The aspirant should know for certain that there is 'something' beyond the appearance of the world of objects.
2. The aspirant should steadfastly keep away from all personal predilections, notions and information about the object of his enquiry.
3. The aspirant should be free from all kinds of religious hankering.
4. The aspirant should have a firm determination to overcome all obstacles to the Truth.

1427. DEATH – WHAT IS ITS SIGNIFICANCE?

Answer: Death is a misnomer. Death may be examined from the standpoint of life. Life, as such, knows no death. Therefore, from life's own standpoint, death is a misnomer.

Nobody has ever experienced death, nor can anybody think of his own death. On this account also, death is a misnomer.

To know that there is no death, you have only to refer to the so called dream state, in which you see your own death or that of a relative. But on waking up, you know that the dream persons and their death were both illusions. It is in the same way that we should view death in the waking state.

Therefore, *death is a misnomer*.

1428. CAN DEATH BE COMPARED TO DEEP SLEEP?

Answer: No. It is fallacious to do so. The experiences of death and of deep sleep are both unknown to the waking mind, and so they are wrongly supposed to be identical by the ignorant man. But in fact, they are poles asunder.

Deep sleep is the unique and the independent experience of a whole state. It is the experience of non-duality in identity. But death is only an incident in the waking state. Therefore they occur in two entirely different planes, and can never be compared one with the other.

2nd January 1959

1429. WHAT IS A PERCEPT?

First answer: No percept really exists – either in the present, the past or the future. A percept is the result of perception and it cannot exist independent of perception. Therefore there cannot be a percept either before or after perception.

Perception goes into the make of the percept itself. Therefore, if you attempt to perceive the percept, the perception part of the percept has to be withdrawn and placed outside it, in order to perceive it. But when the perception part is thus withdrawn, the percept crumbles and disappears. Thus there is no percept during the perception also. It is the perception itself appearing as the percept, for the time being.

Therefore 'percept' is a misnomer. There is only perception. And perception being dependent upon Consciousness for its very existence, it is nothing but consciousness.

Similarly, Consciousness itself appears as an idea; and when Consciousness tries to perceive the idea, the idea disappears and Consciousness alone remains over.

Therefore, all is Consciousness.

A shorter approach: A percept is nothing but the object and is representative of the whole world. Perception goes into the make of the percept, and therefore the percept is perception itself.

Consciousness goes into the make of perception, and therefore perception is Consciousness itself.

Similarly, Consciousness goes into the make of the idea, and therefore idea is Consciousness itself.

Therefore the world, gross as well as subtle, is nothing but Consciousness.

4th January 1959

1430. HOW IS AWARENESS DISPASSIONATE?

Answer: Because it has nothing to gain by emphasizing any of the three states.

1431. WHY DOES NOT THE PEACE EXPERIENCED AT THE MOMENT OF LISTENING TO THE TALK OF THE GURU CONTINUE WITH ONE? AND HOW TO RESUME IT, IF LOST FOR THE TIME BEING?

Answer: At the moment of listening, the ego is crushed by the dazzling brilliance of the ultimate Truth which is proved to be your real nature. But as soon as you get out of that presence, the old samskāras of the ego – which were kept away for the time being – make their appearance again, to establish their supremacy over life.

You have only to look straight at them and say, 'You are only my objects and I am the changeless witness' or 'You do not exist without me – pure Awareness – and so you are nothing other than myself', adducing arguments if necessary for either position. This will at once take you to the same old experience of Consciousness and Peace.

Continue this as often as the ego springs up, to obstruct your perspective. You may stop all such exercises when you feel your position in the ultimate Truth is secure.

23rd January 1959

1432. HOW TO KNOW A THING?

Answer: In the phenomenal sense, we do not know the thing at all. But we know only something about the thing, or in other words we know the appearance alone.

To know the thing, we have to go deeper, even beyond the appearance, into the background; and there all appearances disappear, leaving the background alone. That is the real thing; and that is known by identity alone, there being nothing else beside it.

1433. HOW DOES CAUSALITY FUNCTION?

Answer: Causality is a misnomer, and it never functions. (This is said from the highest level.)

Viewing it from a lower plane: When one object is supposed to produce another, the former is said to be the cause and the latter the effect. But the relationship between cause and effect has to be examined more closely, though from the standpoint of the waking state. There can be only two possible positions, if we adopt this approach.

1. That the cause and effect are entirely different one from the other.
2. That they are not different.

If we accept the first position, causality cannot function, because a cause cannot produce an entirely different effect. And if they are not different, as in the second position, then causality has no meaning. Therefore, in either case, causality is a misnomer.

1434. WHAT IS THE BEARING OF THE WORLD UPON TRUTH?

Answer: The world is a compromise between opposites; life is impossible without reference to opposites. But Truth is beyond opposites and unlike the world in its characteristics.

The characteristics of the world, when strictly analysed and reduced to the generic standards, are found to be: changeability or impermanence, inertness, and misery (*anṛita-jaḍa-duhkha*). All these terms make unconscious reference to their opposites. But the characteristics of Truth are utterly different; and so they are represented as the opposite of these, viz. Permanence, Consciousness, and Peace or Happiness (*sat-cit-ānanda*).

These by themselves are only lakṣhaṇas (pointers) to the Truth, and so have to be transcended, in order to get established in the Absolute. The purpose of the term '*sat-cit-ānanda*' is only to divert your attention away from the phenomenal, to the substance beyond. When the world has disappeared, the characteristics of the Truth – *sat*, *cit* and *ānanda* – also vanish; and you stand in the ultimate Reality, originally pointed to by these terms.

25th January 1959

1435. 'THE EGO ALWAYS RUNS AFTER THINGS ADVENTITIOUS TO IT AND NEVER TURNS TO ITS NATIVE SOIL.'

3rd February 1959

1436. I KNOW THAT EVERY ACTIVITY IS MADE POSSIBLE ONLY BY CONSCIOUSNESS BEING THERE, BUT HOW DOES THAT KNOWLEDGE PROFIT ME?

Gurunāthan: Profit whom, please?

Disciple: Profit the ego, of course.

Gurunāthan: But that is not the goal of Vēdānta. This is the answer from the highest level. But it may be answered from a slightly lower level also.

Of the three – the object, the activity and your own Awareness of both – you see that the object and the activity are adventitious to you or distinct and separate from you, and that they only come and go, so far as you are concerned. But the Awareness alone never parts with you and is intrinsic in you.

Therefore, you are that Awareness – pure. How can anything else be more profitable to you than yourself? Therefore even from the utilitarian point of view, Awareness is the most profitable of all.

The ego desires to be permanent, and to lord it over everything. But, as the ego has only a fleeting existence, it can never do that.

Vēdānta enables even the spurious ego to fulfil its desire, not by satisfying it in its own terms, but by helping it in the light of unassailable reason to shed all its accretions. Thus it stands in its own essence, as Awareness, which is by nature permanent and above everything else.

13th February 1959

1437. WHAT IS AN OBJECT?

Answer: You are told that the object (body) is nothing other than seeing, because the object cannot exist independently of seeing.

Then you are asked to go deeper, meaning thereby 'deeper into seeing', because the body as object has been proved to be non-existent.

Going deep down into seeing, you see that there is only Consciousness there, and therefore Consciousness may well be said to be the object of seeing.

22nd February 1959

1438. WHAT IS REALLY PRACTICAL?

Answer: The 'practical', in the ordinary sense, is opposed to the 'theoretical'. Of the two, the latter is considered to be less real than the former and more liable to change.

These terms are applicable only at the relative level. Applying the tests of relative reality and permanency, the proximity to the Self may be said to be the test of practicality. Thus the senses being nearer you than objects, the senses may be said to be more practical than objects. In the same manner, mind (as thoughts and feelings) is more practical than senses and objects.

But all these are only relative and changing. The ultimate test of practicality is permanency, or unchangeability. In this sense, the real 'I' is the only practical thing, being the only changeless Reality.

Of course, this might be diametrically opposed to the concept of the ignorant man. But truth is no respecter of personalities or majorities. It is the smallest of all minorities, being the one without a second. What is 'experiential' is alone real or practical, and whatever is intellectual is only theoretical.

The world consists of four component parts, viz. the three states and an Awareness that gives light to the three states. Of these four parts, that light-giving principle alone can be real or practical, being alone capable of shining in its own light. The other three depend upon that light for their very existence, and are therefore theoretical.

24th February 1959

1439. WHAT IS APPEARANCE?

Answer: The ordinary statements 'I knew the object', 'I thought the idea', 'I felt the pleasure' etc. are all redundant and wrong, in the strict sense of the terms.

Because an object is nothing but perception, idea is nothing but thought-form, and pleasure is nothing but feeling. As such, one and the same thing cannot remain as subject and object simultaneously.

Therefore, all appearance is nothing but an illusion.

1440. WHY DOES THE ORDINARY MAN PREFER FEELING TO KNOWLEDGE?

Answer: The subject-object relationship is the characteristic of perception. This relationship is clearly evident in the case of all mental knowledge; and it is indistinguishable in the case of feeling, though not dead.

One prefers feeling to knowledge because one really wants the subsidence of the subject-object relationship without one's knowing it. It is the deep urge from one's own being. This is partially satisfied in the case of feeling, by the temporary subsidence of the subject-object relationship. But this by itself does not help one. It is no better than the ignorant man preferring deep sleep to the waking state.

But, on the other hand, when you go from knowledge of object to feeling, the subject-object relationship alone should be allowed to fade away, and the knowledge part should be kept alive, in the form of right discrimination or higher reason. The content or significance of feeling should be discovered with the aid of this reason; and the absence of the subject-object relationship in apparent phenomenal knowledge should also be visualized, in order to make one's experience complete.

For the ordinary man, knowledge is represented by the head (or reason) and feeling is represented by the heart. But it is only a harmonious blending of the head and the heart that may be called realization. Therefore, an academic and one-sided development of the head alone makes one a dry pandit, and a similar development of the heart, divorced of the head, makes one an ecstatic devotee or mystic; both being far away from the Truth.

But if one is already directed by a Kāraṇa-guru, the blending of the head and the heart comes spontaneously, without any effort. As regards reason and feeling, the former must always be there to guide the latter.

27th February 1959

1441. HAS PROOF ANY BEARING UPON TRUTH?

Answer: No. Proof can exist only in the relative realm.

Everything phenomenal is recognized as a result of proof offered by the senses or mentations. But there is a unique exception to this general rule. There is an experience of self-consciousness just preceding every perception or mentation, without which an activity would never be possible. This self-consciousness never calls for a proof to establish itself; and its existence in its own right can never be denied, even in thought. It is this that stands as the ground of all relationship, and it is this that is called the *silent witness*.

Therefore, the need for a proof of an object is itself the proof of the unreality of the object.

1442. WHAT IS THE CONCEPT OF YŌGIC MEDITATION?

Answer: The yōgin takes the waking world alone to be real and starts from the waking body, trying to expand and exploit the potentialities of the mind. The method adopted is meditation, and the goal is the merging of the meditator in the meditated. During the meditation, as it is usually practised, the mind never ceases to objectify and duality is never transcended.

1443. (A disciple asked) TRUTH IN ITS PURITY IS UNTHINKABLE. THEN WHAT CAN I DO TO GET ESTABLISHED IN IT?

Gurunāthan: After visualizing the Truth, it is true you are told that you need not think about it. Because you cannot. But it only means that you should not forget it at any time. Can't you undertake that much?

Disciple: Yes, of course.

G: That is the last sādhana you have to do. Do it and be at Peace.

3rd March 1959

1444. HOW IS LIFE A CONNECTED WHOLE?

Answer: Life consists of independent and disconnected appearances – of actions, perceptions and mentations upon Ātmā, the changeless background. Thus it is 'Ātmā' that keeps the continuity of phenomenal life.

8th March 1959

1445. WE GENERALLY SAY 'I AM HAPPY' AND 'I AM CONSCIOUS.' IS IT ULTIMATELY TRUE?

Answer: No. It is only at the moment when you are happy that you are aware of the fact that you are happy. That knowledge is in identity, where 'knowing it' is 'being it'.

But when you say that the happiness is past, the subject-object relationship sets in. It is this kind of knowledge that people want. Because the ordinary man stands as the empirical subject and is incapable of thinking of anything beyond. Thus, when you say you are happy, you are really *not* happy.

Similarly, when you know Ātmā, you stand as Ātmā or you *are* Ātmā. But when you say so, your stand changes and you cease to identify yourself with Ātmā. Still, Ātmā, as self-awareness, stands as the background of even the saying of this.

Thus, self-awareness is the ground of awareness of objects. Even when objects vanish, Awareness continues. In all the three states, Awareness is the only principle that does not change or die out; and

Awareness is indivisible. Therefore it is this self-awareness itself that appears as, or is the ground of, awareness of objects.

11th March 1959

1446. WHAT IS IT THAT MAKES THE DIVERSE WORLD APPEAR AS A HOMOGENEOUS AND MEANINGFUL WHOLE?

Answer: The nature of every little object is the nature of the whole world as well. Therefore, let us take any one object – let us say a book – as representative of the whole world, and examine it. The book consists of chapters, a chapter consists of paragraphs, and a paragraph consists of sentences. What is it that gives meaning to a sentence? The truth of the sentence is applicable to the book as a whole and to the world as well.

Now let us examine a sentence in detail. It consists of several words, each independent and disconnected as such, but connected by something beyond the mind. The word, likewise, consists of several sounds – each in itself being independent, disconnected and meaningless. But these different sounds are also connected by that same principle which connected the different words in the sentence. The sounds themselves appear as sounds as a result of the existence of the connecting and lighting-up principle, and therefore the connecting principle goes into the make of the sound.

Thus, the substance of the sound, and therefore of the world as well, is that connecting and lighting-up principle – the Ātmā, also called self-consciousness. Therefore, whenever you do anything or understand anything, you are standing in your real nature. And when you do not do anything or do not understand anything, then also you are in your real nature. When exactly, then, are you not in your real nature? *Never*. How then can worries torment you?

This truth is beautifully manifested in the chanting of the *praṇava* [the mantra 'aum']. During the chanting, the senses and mind are arrested by the sound, which slowly vanishes into the inaudible. Along with the sound, the mind also vanishes into its background, one's own real nature; and you are left there as Peace. Knowing well this prakriyā (process of enquiry) of sound, even if you pronounce any other sound, you will see that you are left in your real nature.

Thus, even in activity, you are in your real nature; and in inactivity also, you cannot be elsewhere.

Ātmā connects and lights up disconnected sounds. But it is the ego that attributes particular meanings and limitations to words and sentences. Therefore, a word is Consciousness to Ātmā, and a mere object to the ego. Thus when you know a thing, you know yourself. In other words, self-awareness is the ground of all knowledge or experience.

1447. WHAT IS THE RELATION BETWEEN KNOWLEDGE AND IGNORANCE?

Answer: Both knowledge and ignorance are supposed to exist as indeterminate, and to manifest themselves as determinate forms in the waking and dream states. The indeterminate being the source of the determinate, the former alone need be considered.

The indeterminate can never be understood through the subject-object relationship, but only in identity. Everything known in identity is the real 'I'-principle, and therefore indeterminate knowledge and indeterminate ignorance are one and the same as the real 'I'.

Moreover, between knowledge and ignorance, knowledge has to be relied upon, even to prove or disprove ignorance. But knowledge never needs the help of anything else to establish itself. It is self-luminous. Therefore knowledge alone is real, and ignorance is unreal. Taking ignorance to be unreal, it would be ununderstandable to say that indeterminate ignorance is real. Therefore it would be better to say that 'indeterminateness' is Reality and 'determinateness' unreality.

Ignorance of a thing appears only in retrospect and never in the present. It is posited in the past, only after perception of the object concerned in the present. Therefore ignorance is never experienced by anyone; and something which has never been experienced can never be considered real.

18th March 1959

1448. WHY CAN'T THERE BE A SUBJECT BEYOND THE 'I' OR THE 'ĀTMĀ'?

Answer: The 'I' or Ātmā – as the ultimate subject – does not know that it knows, or that it is the subject. This 'I' or' Ātmā' refuses to be objectified under all conditions, and therefore there cannot be another subject knowing this.

28th March 1959

1449. HOW DOES DISCRIMINATION FUNCTION?

Discrimination functions in two ways – through the head, where it is called '*buddhi-vivēka*'; and through the heart, where it is called '*hṛidaya-vivēka*'.

Buddhi-vivēka functions through the medium of the intellect, in the realm of the phenomenal mind. As this function takes place in duality, it is liable to all kinds of uncertainties and interpretations.

Hṛidaya-vivēka functions through the medium of the heart. The heart being nearer the inner being and duality in that realm being indistinguishable, it is capable of over-riding buddhi-vivēka. It points straight to the beyond and if one had already had the direct experience of non-duality before the Guru, he gets the same experience over again by this. Frequent repetition of the same helps him to establish himself in the real background.

1450. HOW TO VIEW DESIRES, SO AS TO MAKE THEM A HELP TO SPIRITUAL ADVANCEMENT?

Desire is always for an object, and its goal is happiness. Thus an object is only the means, and happiness is the goal. The ignorant man perceives and emphasizes only the means, namely objects, and awaits happiness as a necessary corollary. One does not get enriched by this sort of enjoyment of happiness.

But the spiritual aspirant takes an entirely different approach. First, he understands from the Guru that Happiness – the goal of all desires – is one's own real nature; and he directs his attention to the goal, even in the case of happiness which appears limited by objects.

He notes with satisfaction that the limited happiness expresses itself not when the desired object is gained, but only after it is lost (or forgotten). Therefore he is not disappointed like a layman, even when the desired object is sometimes not obtained. This practice – of emphasizing the disappearance of the object as the necessary prelude to the expression of happiness – gradually helps him to cling to the goal which is objectless Happiness, his own real nature.

Therefore desire, if viewed in the right perspective, is a great help to one's spiritual advancement. All the trouble creeps in only when the ultimate goal is forgotten and the means itself considered as the goal.

'Desire you may, but only don't forget the goal.'

29th March 1959

1451. HOW TO VIEW THE DESCRIPTIONS OF THE FORM, EMBELLISHMENTS AND FEATURES OF PERSONAL GODS TO THE BEST ADVANTAGE?

Each item of the above, taken by itself, is distinct and separate from all the rest; and the only connecting link between all these is the permanent living background which is the essence of the deity itself.

If any such verse or description is read, chanted or meditated upon, emphasizing the appearances alone, as is done ordinarily, you are not enriched by that. On the other hand, if you do the same exercise, emphasizing the living background connecting all these, you transcend the appearances and reach the background yourself.

But this is not possible until you have heard the Truth from the Guru and visualized your own background, the real nature. Thus, to the jīvan-mukta, all personal Gods, mythology and even history and sciences are but sparks of the glory of one's own real nature.

Even a hypothetical assumption of the existence of such a background, and the direction of the attention to that background, would take one a long way towards obtaining a Kāraṇa-guru.

Some spiritual statements of Shrī Ātmānanda

A statement of the Guru helps you not when you take it,
but when you leave it.
(from note 529)

Related to note number:

1. Deep sleep is the key to the ultimate Truth.

   Sleep knowingly.

2. Remembrance is forgetting.

3. I see Me where the 'where' is not
   I see Me when the 'when' is not
   I see Me when 'I see me not.'

8. The absence of any objective perception, thought or feeling – which is wrongly called 'nothingness' – is the svarūpa [true nature] of real, unconditioned Happiness.

   The ajnyāna [ignorance] of Truth is the jnyāna [knowledge] of objects.

9. Deep sleep is the touchstone of one's real nature.

10. Mind as mind knows no peace, and mind at peace is no mind at all.

13. To become a Jnyānin [Sage] means to become aware of what you are already.

14. One should be equally alive in samādhi as well as in worldly activity.

15. You realize the moment you hear the Truth from the Guru.

16. That which was called 'unknown' is in the known as well and is still unknown. It is the Reality itself.

18. All activities of the mind and body of the Sage are but expressions of the Absolute, and therefore purposeless in themselves; while the activity of the worldly man is purposeful as a means of enjoyment.

19. You cannot express the Truth by word of mouth, by thought or feeling. But the Truth expresses itself, in all these varied activities.

20. All the world is my object, and I am the changeless subject.

21. Diversity is only in objects. Consciousness, which perceives them all, is one and the same.

22. You come to real experience only by reducing either the subject or the object into the 'I'-principle.

25. Knowing or loving an object really means absorbing the object into your own Self, thereby destroying all illusion and separateness.

27. You cannot be liberated by knowing your *sat* [existence] aspect alone; but your *cit* [consciousness] and *ānanda* [happiness] aspects have also to be known.

    Reality can be expressed only by negative import, because it is nameless and attributeless. But it expresses itself in all names and forms.

28. To have deep peace and not to be disturbed from it, even for a moment, is the end and aim of life.

29. You are always in perfect dispassion, and that in the most natural and effortless manner.

30. Ātma-tattva [truth of self] is not something to be imported or acquired; but it already *is*, as the real 'I'-principle.

36. Realization is only here and now. Only know it and hold on to it, till it becomes your natural state.

40. That alone is the real experience which never changes in all the three states – waking, dream and deep sleep states, or the physical, mental and transcendental states.

42. In every experience, the expression is the objective part, which is changing; and the background is the subjective part, which is the changeless Reality.

The test of every experience is to see whether it is strictly subjective or objective.

43. The 'I'-principle alone really lives and knows no death.

The Jnyānin alone really lives and knows he lives. His advice to every man is: 'Die, in order to live.'

46. Water does not flow.

47. Knowledge can know only knowledge.

54. Every man is a jīvan-mukta [free within, while living as a person in the world]; but he has only to know it.

55. The world and Ātmā [Self] are only apparent contradictions. Whatever you assume yourself to be, so you will see outside you.

56. Wealth without right discrimination may be an obstacle to spiritual progress; but not otherwise.

66. Going beyond the existence and the non-existence of anātmā [objects], one reaches the Absolute.

67. Karma-sannyāsa [renunciation] is the perfection of the supposed passive principle in man; and karma-yōga (the usual path of the householder) is the perfection of the active princi-

ple in man. But realization is beyond both passivity and activity.

75. If you want misery, be a worldly man. If you want happiness, be a spiritual man, understanding that happiness is in misery as well.

76. Unity is the cause of diversity and not the other way about. The 'thing in itself', the Reality, is beyond both diversity and unity.

77. The 'present' is only a mere word representing an agreement – so to say – between the past and the future, to provide a common meeting ground for them.

78. After realization you may live apparently exactly as before; but you will never be able to resist the reaction of the subjective transformation you have undergone.

79. Knowledge that dawns on the subsidence of the ego can never cease to be.

84. Realization consists in becoming deeply aware of the fact that you have never been in bondage. Because realization can never happen: it can never occur in time. To the question: 'When shall I realize?', the answer can only be: 'When the "*when*" dies.'

85. Realization is not a case of understanding at all, but of being one with the Truth.

87. He who wants to get to the Truth does not crave for the fulfilment of individual desires.

88. God remaining as God, creation as ordinarily conceived is impossible.

89. Repentance is no road to progress.

92. The best way for the best living is to cling on to the living alone, forgetting the 'how' and the 'why' of it completely.

96. In every question, you forget your real Self.

Every question brings with it its own answer.

98. You love your Guru for your true death, allowing your body and mind to continue.

99. When Shiva is visualized as the ultimate Truth, the world is reduced to a mere appearance – making Shiva's title of destroyership literally significant.

102. All names denote the right Absolute.

103. Science wants to establish oneness outside in objects perceived. But Vēdānta wants to establish oneness inside, outside and everywhere.

106. When the thought that you are Ātmā, the Reality, becomes as strong as your present thought that you are the body, then alone are you free.

107. Worldly knowledge is nothing other than giving a name to the unknown and dismissing it immediately from your mind.

112. Self-luminosity is the particular prerogative of consciousness alone. Consciousness is the light of lights. Therefore Consciousness is self-luminous.

If memory leaves you, you become an idiot in ignorance. But become an idiot in the beyond and you are blessed.

Sleep away the whole world, clinging on to consciousness.

116. It is only when you consider things just as they appear, that any problem arises.

117. It is he who has the ego present in him that does or does not do. He who has destroyed the ego in him knows neither doing nor non-doing.

120. You should never try to know that you are the knower. Your knowership is objectless and can never be objectified.

Witnessing is silent awareness. Do not try to make it active in any way.

121. Space begets objects, and objects beget space.

125. The disinterested witness alone enjoys the picture exhibited for sale. Neither the vendor nor the vendee enjoys it.

134. Spirituality replaces the object by the subject.

142. No amount of effort, taken on your own part, can ever take you to the Absolute.

144. The basic error is the false identification of the 'I'-principle with the body, senses or mind – each at a different time. This is the pivot round which our worldly life revolves.

158. Diversity can be diversity only through Me, the 'One'.

168. Personality rests with body, senses and mind. If you think you are impersonal, if you feel you are impersonal and if you act knowing that you are impersonal, you *are* impersonal.

182. Advaitic philosophy does not talk in terms of opposites. It always means only what it says. When it says 'It is not active', that does not mean 'It is inactive.'

197. Negatives can never subsist independently, by themselves. They want a positive something, as their background.

202. Desirelessness is the goal of all desires.

203. Beware of happiness in samādhi. Enjoy it if it comes unsought. But never desire that happiness or court samādhi for that.

205. Ethics has always unselfishness as its goal. But witnesshood takes you even further, and makes you selfless or egoless.

208. Visualization is there when the effect that is produced in seeing is produced by depth of understanding.

219. The body does not exist, either when you stand separate from the body, or when you think about the body.

226. Science starts upon the basic error of giving independent existence to the world of objects, leaving the subject and the thing nearest to it – the mind – to themselves. Science examines only remoter things.

227. The sage has both worldly and spiritual activities. To him both are recreations each in relation to the other (on an equal footing).

233. When you know a thing, the thing is covered by knowledge.

When you say you perceived an object, the object is not there and you are not elsewhere.

243. The world is the manyness of the one. [Caṭṭampi-svāmi]

251. A disciple need never bother himself about what the Guru is doing for him. A disciple can never conceive or understand it, in its real significance. You need only know that the Guru takes you from the phenomenal to the Absolute.

255. Love becomes divine when personality is not emphasized.

259. In deep sleep, 'I am I'; and I can never come out of it.

266. Mind and senses are but names of functions. *Sat*, *cit* and *ānanda* – when manifested – become life, thought and feeling.

272. Action proceeds from inaction and inaction proceeds from action. So both are non-existent as such. 'All the world is relative. I am the only Absolute.'

275. The past is past only in the present.

277. In your childhood you were a child in ignorance; but on listening to the Truth from the lips of the Guru, you become a 'child in knowledge'. So only a Sage can really be said to have a second childhood.

282. Realization is the harmonious blending of the head and the heart, in Peace.

288. Only if your knowledge of your own Self is correct, can you hope to know anything else correctly.

Sat [existence] is that which is incapable of being even thought of as non-existent. 'I' alone am the one such.

307. On listening to the Guru you realize the Truth, now and here. You have only to cling on to it, in order to take it to then and there.

308. A dream is no dream to the dreamer.

315. A Sage who has left his mortal coil can never be a Guru to a new aspirant.

317. A thought about the Guru, just before any activity, brings the living presence of the Guru to preside over the activity or to illuminate the experience that follows.

319. If you can see the entire world – including your own body – as only dṛishya or the 'see-able', you are free; and you have accomplished what has to be accomplished.

For the ignorant man 'ignorance of consciousness' covers up the object. But, for the Sage, 'Knowledge' covers it up.

320. It is in and through Me that all activities take place. But the mistake is made in the attempt to objectify that non-doer self and its experiences.

323. Beauty is personalized when you perceive it. But, in itself, 'beauty' is an expression of the Absolute. It is harmony itself and is not perceivable.

Knowledge (in the relative sphere) is becoming one with another with one's intellect.

Love is becoming one with another with one's whole being. So love is relatively deeper. Deeper knowledge is love.

Direct perception is silent knowing.

327. Man alone, of all living beings, exists and knows he exists.

329. From inactivity (even of nirvikalpa samādhi) you cannot get to the beyond without something active coming to your help. But from the active sphere (the waking state), you can rise straight to the Ultimate, merely by understanding it aright.

335. You can be really good only on reaching the ultimate Truth, when even the 'good' loses its 'goodness' and becomes transformed into that ultimate Truth.

336. Children have to be educated at School on '*avidyā*' ['false learning'] relating to varied subjects, and at home on '*vidyā*' ['true learning'] regarding the 'I'-principle, the permanent background of all that is taught at school.

337. Memory is double edged. It is a thought like any other thought, and it is a cheat, outright.

339. Misunderstanding cannot know understanding. But, on the contrary, understanding alone can know misunderstanding. When understanding begins to know misunderstanding, misunderstanding becomes understanding itself.

342. Each sense organ perceives only itself. Knowledge knows only knowledge. And love loves only love. In short, the instrument utilized is itself perceived by the instrument. So also, you see only yourself in others.

348. As long as you attach an attribute to God, He remains only as a mental concept; and together with the attribute it becomes a percept.

357. Language is the art of concealing thought, and thought is the art of concealing Truth. Transcending or giving up language and thought together with their samskāras, you reach the Truth direct.

Bondage is the conviction that the object remains over, after every experience of knowledge or Peace. Liberation is the conviction that not even a trace of the object remains over, after every such experience.

362. 'I am' is the source and the end of all experiences, devoid of the experiencer and the experienced.

363. Every activity is recorded in knowledge, your real nature, before another activity commences.

364. Vital energy (prāṇa), seeing, hearing, touching, tasting, smelling, thinking etc. are all verbal nouns.

367. The vēdāntin alone is the real communist. He clings to his ideal steadfastly, and establishes it unquestionably in the ultimate Reality, the 'I'-principle.

374. A thing can prove the existence of nothing other than itself. Sensations can prove the existence of sensations alone. So you also can prove only yourself.

377. The general can well be said to be in the particular; but the particular can never be in the general.

378. The deluge [pralaya – cosmic dissolution into unmanifested causal potency] is the last refuge after the misguided search, through the cosmological path; for the cause of the objective world.

379. Mantra is a harmonious sound or group of sounds, with or without an intelligible surface meaning, but capable of creating and applying some definite and potential energy if properly uttered.

391. If, when you think of consciousness, the 'I'-thought comes in spontaneously and vice versa, then you are free. And if, when you think of the body, the 'I'-thought comes in spontaneously and vice versa, then you are bound.

396. Real art is that which sets its expression in perfect tune with the external harmony in diversity, without doing the slightest violence to the inner harmony which is the absolute Reality itself.

404. Vēdānta dispossesses one completely of his phenomenal address.

408. The 'I'-principle is the only concrete thing, and all else is but illusion.

410. Jīva [the personal ego] is he who thinks or feels; and Ātmā [the real self] is he who knows both these activities (and is no 'he' in fact).

413. To get to perfection, the ignorant man has to reverse completely his perspective of the world.

419. Realization is nothing but shifting the centre of gravity or emphasis from the object to the subject in every perception.

420. You have to give up all that you deem to possess, before you are let into the ultimate Truth.

426. You have to gain liberation only from the appendages: namely body, senses and mind. The officer is an appendage of the man, who is relatively the witness of the officer.

441. Renunciation, instead of proving the unreality of the world of objects, makes it more real and frightful; though you may gain temporary relief by being kept away from parts of it.

444. A 'smile' has the aroma of consciousness in it, and therefore it naturally turns the attention of the aspirant towards the impersonal.

450. If only you observe and recognize impartially and without prejudice all that you do as a layman, you shall stand established in your centre by that and that alone.

451. In the 'you', the 'I' is always present. But in the 'I', the 'you' is not present.

452. A householder Sage is inwardly a perfect sannyāsin [renouncer], and outwardly a man of the world.

The Sage has renounced his life completely, but has kindly permitted 'life' to cling to Truth for the time being, to be dismissed without notice whenever he chooses.

The Sage is always *in* the world, but not *of* it. You should also learn to live in the same manner.

458. The best way to do charity is to do it and forget all about it immediately.

459. Worship of God ensures the pleasures of heaven (dṛishṭa-phala-sādhya). But worship of the Guru ensures permanent happiness (including the former if desired, though in fact they are never desired – dṛishṭādṛishṭa-phala-sādhya).

464. The ultimate ideal is not '*not* to see' when objects appear, but to be deeply convinced that the Reality is far beyond both seeing and not-seeing by the senses.

470. Vēdānta is verily a spiritual 'atom bomb'; and it is no wonder that the intellectuals cautiously avoid it, for fear of blundering into the Right.

You are the only noumenon, everything else – from the intellect down to the body – being the phenomenon.

477. Reality alone has the right to come into your mind unbidden; because that is the subject and the Reality.

481. If you lose yourself in any action, that action will be the most successful.

486. 'One in the one is not one.' An individual who has reached the Ultimate no longer remains an individual.

488. God, as he is ordinarily conceived, is the highest manifestation of the human mind.

493. The best time for meditation (if necessary) is at waking from deep sleep, but before becoming fully awake to the world.

494. Nature works normally and regularly. Your sādhana should never be pitched against or contrary to the current of nature.

495. The ignorant man and the vēdāntin each consider the other a lunatic. But the vēdāntin's so called lunacy is the real Truth and the greatest boon to this world.

499. When the world is shining, 'I am I-ing.'

501. When it is seen that diversity springs from Me (the indefinable one), no diversity remains and therefore it cannot affect Me.

517. I am static and dynamic simultaneously. Or better still, I transcend them both.

522. Absorption is the process by which the subject and the object become one in the 'I'-principle.

The real grace of the Absolute is in having endowed us with the two simple instruments of consciousness and happiness, for the specific purpose of absorbing everything into ourselves by knowledge and love.

524. Since the world proves you, the world may well be said to be a witness.

526. You have a physical life and a mental life, but you rarely know you have a Self life or an ātmic life.

529. A statement of mine helps you not when you take it but when you leave it.

531. Orders of the Guru, as originating from the ultimate Reality itself, are imperative commands and have to be obeyed literally.

536. The establishment of the disciple in the ultimate Truth is the greatest, the fittest and the only dakṣhiṇa (offering) one can humbly place at the feet of one's Guru for the invaluable services rendered by him.

540. There was no violence in Lord Kṛiṣhṇa's advice to Arjuna to fight; because Arjuna was already deprived of his sense of enjoyership and doership, which alone make action binding.

544. I am the world not by my becoming the world, but by the world becoming myself.

546. Truth is transmitted neither through language nor through samādhi [meditative absorption]. Both of them only destroy variety and point to the Truth. Between the two, language is preferable by far, because it retains the power of initiative and discrimination which are lost to the one in samādhi. Discrimination alone can lead you beyond.

556. The one thought which is the permanent background of all thoughts is: 'I am.' Usually this background thought is forgotten, and immediately a plurality of thoughts come in. This plurality is what is called 'time'.

557. The effect is the cause of the cause.

561. When anything other than consciousness is added on to the real 'I'-principle, you become the personal or jīva.

562. Visualization by mere thought is possible only with regard to Ātmā, the Reality. With regard to nothing else is it possible.

567. The non-existence of the non-existent is existence itself. The existence of the non-existent disproves non-existence.

569. Self-forgetfulness is the cause of the creation of the world, and self-remembrance or withdrawal to the Self is the destruction of the world.

571. All paradoxes are dissolved in the Sage.

576. When you are asked what you are, if the answer comes spontaneously to your mind 'I am pure Consciousness', you may be said to have reached the natural state.

577. Religions teach you to love others at the physical and mental levels. But Vēdānta teaches you to become that love, pure and impersonal, beyond the mind's level.

580. Let the one who has the complaint come forward. Why should you voice forth others' complaints and worry about it?

If you want to know anything subjective, you must never refer to anything in the objective world.

582. You had been enamoured of the pot. The Guru has been showing you that it is nothing but earth, without doing the least violence to the pot.

583. A jīvan-mukta who is established in the Absolute does not seek to be conspicuous in any phase of his apparent life. Jīvan-muktas of the traditional path even dread such recognition.

584. We see harmony in this world only on rare occasions and that only superficially. But the Sage sees the same harmony always and everywhere, nay even in apparent misery and discord.

590. Memory merges the past into the present; and the present, when examined minutely, disappears altogether.

591. It is not you who see the world. It is the illusion of the apparent 'I' seeing the illusion of the world. What does it matter to you?

593. Misery depends upon diversity or objects for its very existence, and very often it bursts out into vociferous violence.

599. *Sleep involuntarily* and you will be taken to the ignorant man's deep sleep. *Sleep voluntarily* and you will be taken to nirvikalpa samādhi. *Sleep knowingly* and you will be taken right to your real nature (your natural state) beyond all samādhi.

604. Be unqualified and you are free.

605. What is not conceivable, not knowable and about which you are deeply convinced, that is the Reality. That you are.

612. The shifting of emphasis, from the objective to the subjective part of your activities, is alone necessary to establish you in the Reality.

622. Tears of soft divine emotion are the panacea for all yōgic ills.

629. Admitting that shāstras came from jnyāna [knowledge] and not the other way about, the shāstras can well be dispensed with, if a personification of jnyāna as a Kāraṇa-guru is available to lead you.

638. You need not and cannot know the Guru. If you know the Guru or if you do not know the Guru, in either case you cannot become a disciple. So you had better accept him when you feel you must.

640. Sense objects tie you down to the world. But when you come into 'contact' with a Sage, you get tied down to the Ultimate. You can be relieved from the former bondage; but there is no escape from the latter.

641. Looking at the Guru's body is like trying to catch the figure on a silver screen. All your preconceived standards and expectations regarding it fail.

643. Memory is the last link in the life of an individual, binding him to the world.

If you have seen, you cannot remember; because the rememberer is different from the see-er.

645. When personality comes into the impersonal it is bondage. When personality merges in the impersonal it is liberation.

648. Time is the fourth dimension, according to the vēdāntin.

650. In the world, every question only multiplies diversity.

653. Time strives hard in this world not to connect events, but to disintegrate them and to establish diversity.

654. Knowledge uninterrupted is Consciousness, and Happiness uninterrupted is Peace. Happiness is the first ebullition or sensation of Peace.

655. Liberation is not an escape from bondage. Both are expressions of the real freedom, the former discovering and the latter covering your real nature.

657. It is only the expressed in the expression that makes you covet the expression.

658. Neither the question nor the answer really enriches you. But the level at which both of them emerge is beyond the relative. Be there and you are free.

661. True religion is that which binds you to the background, the Reality. 'Re' = background, and 'lega' = binds.

664. Suicide is prompted by misery and desperation, along with your want of boldness to face and overcome them.

665. 'A sincere atheist is much nearer the Truth than a superstitious and indifferent bhakta [devotee].'

669. Let the mind be asleep to the whole world and wakeful to the real 'I'.

671. The personal in man usurping what really belongs to the impersonal is called 'spiritual larceny'.

674. 'That which spoke to you will always be there to help you, and that which spoke to you should always be loved.'

679. Spirituality is not the monopoly of any nation or country. In my opinion, Shakespeare was a 'realized soul' (in the language of the West), or a 'jīvan-mukta' (in the language of India).

687. Sages as well as sādhakas of all types radiate around them the flavour of their experiences.

690. The result can be perfect only if the Perfect is engaged in it.

691. The impersonal is not connected with the personal; but the personal is connected with the impersonal.

692. The path to the Ultimate lies from the changing, through the changeless, to the beyond.

697. You become a true disciple only at the highest level, when your personality vanishes and you stand as the impersonal Truth. Then there is no duality of any kind, like the Guru or disciple or relationship.

When you say, see or think that you are a disciple, you are a witness to the discipleship and not a disciple.

699. Your slavery to the body, senses and mind is dissolved only in the alchemy of your love for the free – the Guru.

Freedom is the surrender of slavery at the feet of the Guru – the Absolute.

705. The easiest way to understand the Sage is to direct your mind to your deep sleep. The Sage is there.

The Sage is deep sleep as it is rightly understood.

713. So far as the disciple is concerned the Guru is the light that first lights up even the Reality.

714. You realize not by renouncing the world, nor by allowing the world to be; but by taking note of the fact that you are always standing as that Truth.

717. Liberation is complete only when you are liberated from liberation as well.

721. The only clue given to us by the unseen, to understand one's own real nature, is the 'deep sleep state'. That alone is ours in fact.

738. Human effort consists in creating bondage for oneself, clinging fast to it, and wanting to become free without giving up bondage itself.

745. In talking about the Truth, you (the ego) must cease to talk, and allow Truth (the real Self) to talk or express itself in its own language.

752. Deep sleep is the most important part of your life; and it saves you from going mad.

756. Knowledge without object is wisdom.

761. To the individual soul (the ego), everything is outside. To God, everything is inside. To the Sage or Jnyānin, there is neither inside nor outside. He is beyond both.

765. The intellect is given to man only to measure the variety in the world.

766. 'I am Peace; because my Guru has said so', says Shrī Shankara.

778. If happiness assumes the form of riches, it gives rise to bondage.

If riches assume the form of happiness, it results in liberation.

781. You may delightfully say anything, but not take delight in saying anything.

788. Your revilers are your real friends and your flatterers your enemies.

796. Everything other than your real nature, the Self, is a dream,

800. Real sannyāsa [renunciation] is the surrender of your sense of separateness from the Reality, to that Reality itself.

803. Work is a hindrance to spirituality if the ego is present, and a help if the ego is absent.

805. By standing as the witness, you establish yourself in the unity in diversity.

806. See to it that both ends of your sleep are saturated with the thought of your real nature, your native home.

815. The mind and intellect only cleanse the road and pave the way for the royal procession of the heart to the Ultimate.

816. The mind is the father of all illusion.

817. When a Sage remembers, the memory is non-responsible and purely objective, while in the case of the ordinary man it is all subjective.

818. Law deals with logic. So one who takes to law has a good chance of rising to higher logic, leading to the Truth. The Truth is sublime logic or higher reason itself.

820. Death is liberation, provided it is the ultimate death, even of the samskāras [personal conditionings].

Real death is a shift of your centre from the ego to the witness.

821. Attributing reality to the body is the most meaningless of all acts, and the conception of society is only an offshoot of this error. Take your stand in the ultimate subject before examining any object.

822. Liberation is not merely going beyond birth and death, but it is going beyond the delusion of birth and death.

823. When I am there as the object, I am not here in the body.

830. It is the 'living-ness' you transmit to an instrument that really makes it work.

832. Words speak in a child; ideas speak in a man; and Truth speaks in a Sage.

833. It is not happiness from objects or happiness in passivity that is to be shunned, but it is only the wrong notion about one's own real nature that is to be really shunned and destroyed.

The enjoyership does not die even in samādhi.

834. Learning is darkness, and knowledge is light. Learning, pertaining only to objects of ignorance, of course sharpens the intellect and accumulates information; but you do not get a ray of light from all that.

In the light of knowledge, all learning disappears as illusion.

837. When you stand as body, you are a jīva [a personal ego]. When you stand as mind, you are God. When you stand as Truth, beyond both body and mind, you are a jīvan-mukta (the Absolute).

You throw away the body by simply becoming aware of it.

838. Saṃskāras [conditioned habits] are the only impediments to spirituality. Arguments are used only to expel saṃskāras. Otherwise the saṃskāras safely lurk at the back and create havoc.

839. The root cause of all misunderstanding is the misuse of the generic name for the particular.

841. Purity is getting away from all that is extraneous to your real nature.

842. Unless you see inwardly, you cannot see outwardly either. The one is a corollary of the other.

844. Association with objects makes one bad. Association with the 'I'-principle makes one good.

845. Realization is becoming alive to the fact that one is free.

849. Consciousness illumines objects at a distance. It destroys objects on contact.

853. Duality is the parent of fear; and the witness thought is the surest panacea for all ills.

865. The ego never sees the light, though he always uses light. The Sage sees that light alone (the most vital part) in every perception.

No human being has ever reached the Ultimate.

866. Art is an attempt to express the inner harmony of the ultimate Reality, through the outer harmony created by the senses and the mind.

868. The goal of all activity is to make you lonely.

There is fear only when there is duality.

874. Samskāras are habit-channels of thought, or dormant tendencies.

877. You begin to love your Guru only when that which was given by the Guru is accepted wholly by you.

879. Not seeing the Reality, or forgetting the Self, is sleep. Seeing the Reality, or visualizing the Self, is real waking. To be really awake is not to be awake with sense organs and mind, but with Consciousness. The present waking state is verily a sleep or a dream.

881. The mind becomes pure only by its own death. The attempt to purify the mind by any amount of other effort is futile.

882. The sahaja state is the state where you maintain that certainty or deep-rooted conviction that you never leave your real nature of Consciousness and Peace.

884. Knowing, becoming and being the Reality are the three distinct stages in the course of progress to the Ultimate.

886. The purpose of life is to know the Truth and to be it. You can never be happy; you can only be happiness.

888. The Sage is the principle upon which all opposites and paradoxes appear and disappear.

889. If you really love another, you lose yourself in the other.

895. Your life-eternal is ego's death – eternal. True life begins when the ego dies and Consciousness dawns.

896. Things, both by their presence and by their absence, affect you and hide the Truth from you.

902. A means, which is an illusion, is first adopted from the relative sphere which is all illusion. But reaching the goal when you look back you find that the 'world illusion' has disappeared and the 'means-illusion' along with it, leaving you all alone in your own glory.

904. Recognition is an acceptance of the fact of Truth. Repetition of it makes recognition deeper and deeper.

Recognition, remembrance and hope are the three props that maintain the continuity of individual life.

906. It is not the witness as such that matters, but it is only that which appeared as the witness that really matters.

907. You see diversity, because you are diversity yourself.

909. You are given a name to show that you yourself are a changeless principle.

913. You are in the right line of thinking if it takes you to the witness direct.

The real test of the right line of thinking is whether it takes you to the witness.

914. The ignorant man does not experience anything other than the body and is blissfully ignorant of the 'I'-principle. The Sage does not experience anything other than the 'I'-principle and knows the body to be only an illusion.

The ordinary man does not experience anything except as a body, and the Sage does not experience anything except as the 'I'-principle.

917. The vanishing of subject-object relationship is the experience of love.

'Love all' is a glorious ideal accepted by the world and the vēdāntin alike; but their implementations differ. The humanitarian worker emphasizes the 'all', and misses the happiness. But the vēdāntin emphasizes love (happiness) – his own nature – and misses the 'all', which is but an empty word and an illusion.

918. The thought that certain things are obstacles to spirituality is itself the first obstacle.

922. All rules of conduct on the spiritual path lead you to the Sage (Truth), and automatically get dissolved in his presence. So rules humbly follow the Sage and never dare to overtake him.

931. Time is the arch-deceiver of all. You rely upon him to establish the world and its religions.

932. By 'liberation', you seek your own individuality, which is that changeless principle in you.

933. The 'I'-principle has no activity, because it has neither organs nor mind. But it is not dead either. It is ever-present and it is from it that everything else gets light.

935. The witness perceives only the material part of the activity, and never its consciousness part.

936. Your search for the Truth should always be a descent from Ātmā to the world.

937. If the ego does not come in to interfere, indolence is the Reality itself.

940. Desire for liberation or Truth is not the function of the ego, but is the expression of the 'being' in you.

If one says sincerely that he takes a delight in being bound, surely he is liberated.

944. The word of the Guru is the highest proof to a disciple. 'I am not the jīva. By the word of my Guru, I am Peace ultimate.' (Shrī Shankara)

946. If deep sleep loses its sense of objectivity and becomes subjective, you are free.

948. A percept is that which is perceived. If you emphasize the 'that' part of it, the percept becomes 'that' and ceases to be a percept.

952. Aristotle says that man is a social animal and abhors solitude. But I say: 'Man is always in solitude and can never be otherwise.'

Witnessing is disinterested perception.

955. Your real nature is renunciation itself.

Real renunciation is the renunciation of doership and enjoyership from all your activities.

962. Reality is that principle which denies everything else, but cannot deny existence to itself.

963. The jīvan-mukta is a living commentary of the Truth you have visualized.

964. Nobody worships the idol, and nobody worships without an idol.

967. Variety is madness. See the unity (witness) behind the variety and you transcend madness. Be the knower and you are sane and free.

971. It is said that a devotee goes *into* samādhi with tears in his eyes and that a Jnyānin comes *out of* samādhi with tears in his eyes. But I say that this is not yet the whole truth. One can very well both go into and come out of samādhi with tears in his eyes. This is definitely higher than the former experiences.

972. It is only the ignorant man, who had not the good fortune to be blessed by a living Sage (Guru), that usually takes to the shāstras somewhat helplessly.

The ultimate purpose of all shāstras is only to give an indirect idea about the Truth, and above all to impress upon the aspirant the supreme necessity of the help of a Kāraṇa-guru for the attainment of the Truth.

979. Pleasure is a sigh of relief after a course of pain, and is a prelude to the state of Peace. But it is often mistaken for Peace itself.

980. The body is the cell in which both the Sage and the ignorant man seem to rest – one feeling free, and the other bound.

991. You know yourself when there is neither something nor nothing to be known.

996. Worldly knowledge expires in enjoyment; enjoyment expires in becoming; and becoming expires in being.

1004. Ahankāra [ego] is the sense of one's separateness from everything else.

1009. In all phenomenal teaching, it is the 'his' that is transmitted and that only in parts. But in spiritual teaching it is always the 'he' that is transmitted in full.

The Guru's form is the only object in the world which, if deeply contemplated upon, takes you directly to the real subject – the Reality.

1017. The higher reason comes into play when you want to know something beyond the experience of body, senses and mind.

1020. Phenomenal knowledge is the inherent 'knowingness' within you, coming out occasionally through the mind or senses.

1027. The light in the mentation knowledge is itself the witness.

1029. Of course the witness, as such, has a small taint which is neither detrimental nor instrumental to the visualization of the Truth. But the Reality can easily be visualized through the method of the witness.

1032. The world of forms is never the cause of bondage. It is the world of names alone that binds you.

1037. The only moment I really live is when I direct my attention to my real nature, the right Absolute.

1042. Consciousness is in greater evidence in the absence of the object than in the presence of the same.

1053. The higher reason is a supra-rational instrument of thought, and its function cannot rightly be called thinking.

1056. 'I am realizing myself in all of you, when I am talking to you about the Truth; and you are realizing yourself in me, when you are understanding what I say.'

1058. When the heart is full, the tongue refuses to speak.

Beyond subject-object relationship, *to know is to be.*

1059. That alone is the real sādhana which removes the ills of all the three states.

1061. The Guru is addressing the Guru in the disciple. But you should never contemplate oneness with the Guru, in any manner.

Truth, feeling that it is not the Truth (the disciple), is taught by the Truth which knows that it is the Truth (the Guru).

1069. To forget oneself completely, in knowing the Truth, is to know it with one's whole being.

1071. Any knowledge apparently limited, if understood without reference to the object, is knowledge absolute (Truth itself).

1076. If you want to remove the suffering alone and retain the sufferer, it is never possible; because the suffering and the sufferer always appear and disappear simultaneously.

1080. There cannot be degrees in Reality.

1090. Surrender is no surrender, in the strict sense of the term, if you happen even to remember the fact that you have surrendered.

1093. The state of complete identity with non-dual Ātmā, as a result of discrimination and negation of phenomena, is the vēdāntic concept of samādhi.

1099. Vidyā-vṛitti [higher reason] is the fire that burns the forest of illusions (ignorance).

1103. When you come to real poetry, it transcends imagination and all ideation. That is the Reality.

1108. A life of placid enjoyment is inimical to you, if you are given to serious thinking on any serious subject, and much more so when that thinking is spiritual.

1110. 'The exercise of discrimination and reason alone can destroy your samskāras [conditioned tendencies] and take you to the Truth. But the method of using them is to be obtained from the Guru.' [Shrī Gauḍapāda]

The exercise of the higher reason alone can destroy one's innate tendencies and lead one to the Goal.

1114. An ornament is an ornament only by convention; but actually it is only gold.

The object of Vēdānta is not to help you 'not to perceive the appearance'; but to help you to see the essence, even when perceiving the appearance through the senses.

1119. Vēdānta is the unfoldment of one's own real nature (the Truth), from the lowest level to the highest.

Reality is positive in form but negative in meaning. When I say, 'It is existence', I mean only that it is not non-existence.

1120. Higher reason is that supra-intellectual organon present in all human beings, which begins to function only when the aspirant tries to understand something beyond the mind.

1121. The devotee of the Guru should never forget that objects or persons of whatever relationship to the Guru should be utilized only to draw his attention to the Guru. Otherwise, they should be dismissed summarily.

1127. Truth is the text; and the world, senses and mind are the commentaries thereof.

1128. If I claim to be anything, that must be with me wherever I go.

1131. The teacher and the disciple both stand depersonalized when the Truth is expounded by the teacher and understood by the disciple.

1134. The world ties you down by its presence here. The world ties you down by its non-existence or absence in samādhi. You must transcend both in order to reach the Truth.

1135. The teacher shows the disciple that he too is perfect, and there the teaching ends.

1139. The only sādhana that the higher jnyāna shāstras ask the earnest aspirant to undertake is: 'Listen, listen, listen to the words of the Guru, and contemplate nothing.'

1142. Realization is seeing things in the right perspective, knowing yourself first.

1144. Ferrier, the French Philosopher, has said: 'Apprehension of the perception of matter is the subject of metaphysics.' But I say it is not the subject, but only the beginning of metaphysics.

1147. The states [of waking, dream and deep sleep] are the key to the Reality, as expounded by Vēdānta.

1152. Causality as a law has the advantage of taking you from diversity to unity, but not beyond.

1153. The certitude that you are that changeless, self-luminous principle is liberation; and that conviction that you are bound is bondage.

1158. There is no perception either in deep ignorance or in pure Consciousness, either in darkness or in dazzling light. In dim light alone, objects seem to appear.

1159. If you achieve that degree of identification with the light of knowledge as you had with body in the waking state, there is nothing more to be achieved.

1167. The 'is'-ness goes beyond life and death and lights up both. It is from this 'is'-ness that all life flows.

1169. You must give up freedom in order to be really free.

1170. The 'is' is nearer the Truth than that which is.

1172. Sleep is neither an action nor non-action. There is no ego in sleeping, and there can never be a sleeper.

1176. It is often a sweet recreation and delight for an established Sage to expatiate upon Truth with arguments and illustrations, or to talk with tears about devotees and their personal gods.

1177. The disciples, from their own standpoint, have a Guru. But the Guru, from his own standpoint, has no disciples. He is beyond duality and unity.

1179. It may generally be said that one gets enlightened through the head, and gets established in the Truth through the heart.

1183. That by which you consider deep sleep to be a state of unconsciousness, while Consciousness reigns in all its purity there, is avaraṇa [obscuring].

1184. Waking is reality to both the ignorant man and a Sage. To the ignorant man, waking means waking to the gross world; and to the Sage, waking is waking to his own real nature.

1190. You are thought or feeling, devoid of the characteristics of thought or feeling.

1196. If you can bring something from the deep sleep to bear upon the waking state, certainly the pains of the waking state will be relieved considerably here itself.

1209. It is not the vital experience itself that really enlightens one, but it is the correct understanding of its significance.

A wrong and an objective interpretation, even of nirvikalpa samādhi, after the event, posits the ego there retrospectively.

1225. Appearance can never merge in anything else. The non-existent snake can never be said to merge in the rope. [Shrī Gauḍapāda]

1230. All religions serve human tastes and ignorantly multiply differences. But Vēdānta alone serves the changeless Truth and reconciles all differences, without exception.

Where no two religions, mystics, yōgins, scientists or philosophers agree in their own spheres, no two Sages have ever disagreed about the nature of the ultimate Truth.

1231. Awareness cognizes ideas and co-ordinates the states.

1235. There is no bridge between the relative world and the Absolute; because they are in two distinct and separate planes or levels. (But still, the disciple of a Kāraṇa-guru can never deny his own experience that the apparent person of the Guru serves as the safest and the surest bridge to the Truth.)

1244. Rely upon your own higher reason (discrimination) in the light of changelessness and self-luminosity to establish the ultimate Truth. (Shrī Gauḍapāda and Shrī Shankara both assert that it is a 'slave mentality' to rely upon any scripture or other authority for the purpose.)

1245. It is best to see the pot to be nothing but earth, even when the pot remains as pot. It can also be seen to be only earth by destroying the pot as such. But the second method is rather crude and childish.

1251. A jīvan-mukta does not destroy the states, but only illumines them and understands them to be nothing other than the real Self.

1259. To the intellectual the Guru is always an 'enigma'.

1261. One goes to a Guru to get beyond the 'why', and then the question disappears.

1263. Man is both the spectator and the actor in the drama of life. The spectator is real, but the actor is unreal.

1264. The so-called unconditionedness is also a limitation and this is called 'samādhi'. Truth is still beyond.

1265. Knowing and loving come in as a result of your not wanting to be separated from the 'thing'.

1266. With the change of state, the field of reference changes completely.

1267. It is appearance that goes into the make of disappearance. So disappearance appears.

1268. Ordinary illusions have at least a momentary existence in the mental level. But the ego has not even that.

You stray away from knowledge, to the object known; and that is the ego.

1271. Truth is of the nature of differencelessness, and is only one and self-luminous.

1276. If the ego takes leave of you in the course of an activity, it takes you straight to pure love.

1277. 'Being' is being and is independent of its opposite, non-being. Non-being can exist only on being. But being can exist all alone.

1281. Vicāra-mārga (the direct path) is removal of untruth by arguments, leaving over the Truth absolute as the real Self.

1282. You are not a man, when you know that you are a man.

It is wrong to say that you know pain.

1285. In the relative level, the ego loses itself in the object; but in the absolute level, you make the object lose itself in you.

1286. The deep sleep state is always in the past.

1287. Indeterminate ignorance is also the Reality.

1288. It is thought and speech alone that obscure the Reality.

Do not try to objectify Reality. The yōgin tries to objectify what refuses to be objectified.

1289. The knowing act is the last act or link in the chain of any activity. There is nothing else to know it.

The last knowing act, without itself being known, is non-empirical and is the ultimate Reality.

1290. In deep sleep, the concept of general ignorance is destroyed, in order to show your real nature.

Ignorant knowledge is giving reality to objects, forgetting its essence – knowledge.

Here, in the waking state, your ignorant knowledge is destroyed by the Guru, to show that you are the transcendental.

1291. The 'all' (in all-knowingness) is only one object, just like any other object.

1295. The right form of Guru-thought is that 'The Guru is in me.' By this thought, the Ultimate will gradually devour the 'me' and leave one as the ultimate Truth.

The wrong form is that 'I am the Guru.' This thought is strictly forbidden; because, by that, the Ultimate is lost sight of and the apparent 'I' (the ego) gains in strength.

1297. You separate yourself from thought or feeling, and that is life.

Whenever the mind functions, you are spatializing the Absolute.

1300. The very mention of one's age proves that one is changeless, at that period of time. Therefore one is changeless through all time.

That which appears on 'Me' is life.

That which gets separated from 'Me' is death.

Looked at from a deeper level, even death forms part of life.

1301. Every mentation is egoless, at the moment it occurs.

1302. 'If you but open your mouth, advaita [non-duality] is gone.'

1303. Memory is past, and memory is about the past.

1304. You need only to allow Truth to come in uncalled, whenever you happen to forget Truth in the midst of activities.

1306. Objectivity, in any form, is the only obstacle to Truth.

The object is an object on account of you.

1307. A real Sage disowns everything, while most great men own some things if not many.

1310. God is only a concept, though the highest the human mind can make. But *you* are not a concept.

1311. Beware of promises, pleasures and powers achieved or anticipated. All these seduce you from the Truth.

1313. It is only the snake [illusion] that gets transformed into the rope [reality], and not the other way round.

1316. One can be said to be perfectly healthy in body and mind only if no part of the body or mind makes itself felt. You know that you have a head only when it aches.

When you really know a thing, you stand identified with that thing. But when you *say* you know, actually you do not know.

1319. The 'I'-principle or Awareness is the real revelation – the revelation of the three states.

The subject is constitutive of the object.

The moment you perceive and know the object, the object abolishes itself (disappears by self-sacrifice) and reveals the Awareness.

The very word 'appears' signifies Awareness and that Awareness is my real nature.

To become aware of the fact that I am birthless and deathless is real liberation.

To get established in that certitude is jīvan-mukti.

1322. Religion, scholasticism, yōga, devotion etc. can never by themselves take you to the Truth.

The totality of one's experiences consists in the three states, together with the most important factor – 'Awareness' – standing out of the states.

The Awareness is the witness or knower of the appearance and disappearance of the states and also of the content of each state.

1323. *Theory* is speculative thought or mere supposition existing only in the realm of the mind, in order to explain something in the phenomenal.

Practice is that which brings thoughts to the body level. Truth is beyond theory and practice.

If you begin to theorize or practise Truth, it ceases to be the Truth as such. Is 'I am' a theory?

Even thinking or meditation distances the 'I' from you. So you are asked only to repeat what you are, and not to think or meditate.

The knowledge of the 'I'-principle is experiential knowledge, and even 'Consciousness' may be called theory.

1324. Without the 'I' (aham) being there, there can never be the 'this' (idam).

So the 'this' is nothing other than the Truth (the svarūpa of the 'I').

The 'I' is known only in identity.

The generic of anything is neither space-limited nor time-limited.

The known, when it is known, ceases to be known, abolishing itself as known.

1325. The Sage elevates his disciples not through tattvōpadēsha alone, but by a variety of activities and inactivity.

1327. The last of a series of acts, without itself being known, is the subject.

1328. Even in the so-called phenomenal knowledge, it is knowledge in identity that obtains.

1333. Knowledge unites, in being or in identity.

Thinking separates, in subject-object relationship.

1335. Satisfaction is personal or private, and creates the many.

Truth is impersonal or public, and destroys diversity.

1336. Dispense with memory, and you are at once beyond all states and in Truth.

1337. The yōgin's artificial states are all great obstacles to the smooth visualization of Truth.

1341. Truth cannot be understood from anything other than Truth. Everything other than the Truth is untruth. So also is a book an untruth.

1342. The ordinary man's life is a swing between a tear and a smile.

1343. The lesson of deep sleep is that I get to my real nature of Peace and Consciousness when I transcend body, senses and mind.

The lesson of dream and waking states is that it is the one Consciousness – my real nature – that divides itself into the subject series and object series, and that I am witness to all mentations.

1344. Bondage is identification with body, senses and mind. Liberation is the giving up of that identification, by visualizing what you are.

1351. 'Seeing' is the verb form of 'form', and 'consciousness' is the noun form of 'seeing'.

1358. The 'I' and the 'this' are the only two asylums for anyone.

1360. 'Happiness can never be unintelligent.'

1361. Vicāra is a relentless enquiry into the Truth of the Self and the world, utilizing only higher reason and right discrimination.

1367. If Awareness is directed to anything apparently different, that other thing becomes Awareness at once.

1369. Vēdāntic reason is tri-basic in character, having sway over the experiences of all the three states [waking, dream and sleep].

Intellectual reason is only mono-basic in character, being applicable only to the experiences of the waking state.

1383. The Sage cannot stoop to split himself into the helper and the helped, in order to serve humanity with doles.

1391. The ignorant man and the Sage both face the world, apparently in the same manner. The ignorant man understands everything, including knowledge, in terms of object experiencing object alone. But the Sage understands everything in terms of knowledge, his own real nature.

1394. Consciousness by itself never illumines ideas or objects, but only kills them.

1399. Art is that which tends to merge the other into yourself. The mundane is that which separates the other from you.

1401. Misery, as such, is purely man-made, and is born and maintained in duality alone. Happiness is advaita [non-duality], and is natural to man.

1403. Of all that was then and there, Consciousness alone is now and here. Therefore memory is not.

1435. The ego always runs after things adventitious to it, and never turns to its native soil.

1447. Indeterminateness is Reality, and determinateness is unreality.

1450. Desire you may, but only don't forget the goal.

Further statements (numbered with preceding asterisk)

*1. Possessorship is the only sentiment that binds man to the world of objects.

*2. If the existent becomes non-existent, or if the non-existent becomes existent, in either case bondage results.

If the non-existent becomes non-existent, or if the existent becomes existent, in either case liberation results.

*3. In the word 'impersonal', the 'personal' lurks. So you are beyond both.

*4. Vēdānta deals with the movement of states, or in other words the movement of life.

Science and philosophy deal with the movement of objects, and the movement of the thoughts of objects.

*5. Truth is realized only when the Awareness is equated with the 'I'-principle.

*6. The objective world is always changing. Changes can be perceived only by something changeless and self-luminous. That principle is the one indubitable Reality, the Self.

*7. You, as the ego, are the basic lie.

*8. There is ignorance only when you stand in ignorance.

*9. Lower reason is only the measure of variety.

Higher reason is the destroyer of variety, and it helps one to visualize the ultimate Truth.

*10. Language is the language of duality alone. Non-duality has no language of its own.

*11. The many can never be made into one, either in time or in space.

*12. All lower shāstras take advantage of and exploit the common human weakness based on wrong knowledge and wrong habits of the waking state.

*13. Higher reason destroys diversity and establishes Reality, while lower reason multiplies diversity still more.

*14. The most effective of sanctions for the moral progress of man all over the world had been religion. But the bloodiest of wars and the cruellest of tortures and inhumanity have also been perpetrated, all in the name of God and religion.

*15. In every perception of an object, the permanence, continuity and reality belong to your own Self.

*16. Mind must work, and cease to work when Truth dawns.

*17. So long as one thinks that he enjoyed happiness in deep sleep or in nirvikalpa samādhi, he is not enriched at all, and still remains a jīva.

*18. The measure is always in the subject, and not in the object.

*19. We are space-ridden, time-ridden and ego-ridden beings. So the best way to liberation is to retreat and retreat beyond all these to the real 'I'.

*20. 'Brahman' [the all-including] is the self of God, and 'kūṭastha' [the true individuality] is the self of jīva [the seeming person], in the shāstraic sense.

*21. Be a man and nothing more. Then you are free.

*22. I do not want to possess anything, and so am the possessor of all. The ego possesses nothing, and so wants to possess all.

*23. There is absolutely nothing in the mind to help you, except your own samskāras [conditioned tendencies].

*24. It is wrong to say that Consciousness limits itself and appears as the world; but it is you who limit Consciousness to form the world.

*25. If the '-ness' is eliminated from all your mental experiences, your stand is in your real nature.

*26. Remembering is the only 'sin'; and that alone has to be destroyed.

*27. Truth has no standpoint of its own.

*28. Whatever is upādhi (medium) to the jīva [personal ego] becomes upādhi to the witness in the jīvan-mukta.

*29. You have to reverse the order of language, if you want to express Truth as it is.

*30. You may utilize objects to rise to the witness, but never utilize the witness to establish objects.

*31. If at the end of a single activity you go to peace, where else could you go at the end of all activity (death)?

*32. You must be living the Truth, and not merely thinking or contemplating it.

*33. Fasting the body, senses and mind and directing your attention to the Guru is a spiritual feast.

*34. After realization, see your parents as Ātmā itself.

*35. When consigned to the past and reduced to mere ideas, the waking and dream experiences become one, and are cognized by Awareness.

*36. 'Be in Consciousness without knowing that you are in Consciousness.' (This was the last of Shrī Ātmānanda's spiritual messages to his disciples.)

Life sketch of Shrī Kṛiṣhṇa Mēnōn (Shrī Ātmānanda)

Birth and parentage

Shrī Ātmānanda came of an illustrious matriarchal Nair family by name Cherukulam in the village of Peringara in Tiruvalla Tālūk in Central Travancore. He was born in the closing hours of Friday the 23rd of Kārttika in the year 1059 M.E. (corresponding to Saturday the 8th December 1883 – the day is counted from sunrise in India, not from midnight as abroad), his natal star being Pūruruttāti.

His father was Brahmashrī Gōvindan Nambūdiri, a vēdic Brahmin of the influential Mūviḍattu Maṭham and a descendant of the late 'Pattillam' Brahmin oligarchy of Tiruvalla. The father was engaged in teaching the Vedas to the Brahmin children of the locality. Shrī Kṛiṣhṇa Mēnōn had several uncles, a brother and two sisters who were all poets and scholars. His infancy and childhood were quiet and happy.

He evinced however, even from his childhood, instinctive symptoms of deep religiousness and indrawingness. He had a peculiar aversion for food, till he was about ten years of age. At the age of ten, a great and reputed sannyāsin who visited Tiruvalla happened to meet him in his house, and gave him a mantrōpadēsha by way of preliminary initiation.

He was put to school at a very early age, and by the time he was twelve he reached the high school. His parents, elders, neighbours and teachers all noted the boy's capacity for studies, his exemplary honesty and fearlessness. He started writing poetry at the age of fourteen and soon outshone his uncles and brother. He grew up to be an athlete of unusual prowess and some of his physical feats have surprised even the professional circus troupes of his time. Swimming was a favourite recreation for him.

Once when he was in his teens, he was the only survivor in a country boat disaster in a thunderstorm at midnight in the dangerous backwaters of Quilon, just above their junction with the sea. The other eleven passengers were drowned. Providence seems to have been very particular in sparing him for the mission he was to fulfil later in life.

Education

His educational career was exemplary. He stood first in his class in all subjects and was loved both by his teachers and by his companions. Very often he served as a tutor to many of his classmates, particularly in Malayalam in which he was already a poet and a litterateur. Clarity, precision and conciseness were the qualities in which he excelled, even from his boyhood. He finished answering his examination papers long before the time set and still did very well.

The reader will be surprised to learn that such a brilliant student was declared to have failed at the matriculation examination for which he appeared at the age of 14. He was granted special permission to appear for the examination, even though he was underaged, at the instance of his teachers who loved him no less than his own parents. Strangely enough, he had failed in Malayalam, in which he usually excelled. He accepted his fate calmly.

But a month later, he received a telegram from the Registrar of Madras University, informing him that he had really passed and that he was placed in the first class. Simultaneous orders were also issued to the college authorities to grant him all concessions in attendance and the like, with retrospective effect from the date of reopening of the college. The humour of the incident is in the fact that a simple zero was unfortunately omitted in the university mark list, so instead of 90 percent his marks were entered as 9 percent in the Malayalam paper and no wonder he failed. The mistake was detected only a month later. He made frequent references to this simple incident in his spiritual talks, to prove the unreasonableness of causality.

Marriage and graduation

After passing the matriculation examination, he was anxious to continue higher studies at the university. It was the bane of the matriarchal system that the maternal uncles, who were the legitimate guardians of the family, were not sufficiently interested in the education of their nephews. So Shrī Ātmānanda did not get from them the financial help he needed to prosecute further studies. Therefore he worked as a school teacher in a private school, and saved some money from his meagre income. With that money, he joined a college and passed his first examination in Arts. Again he took up his work as a teacher in schools; and with the money he could save, he appeared for the B.A. as a private candidate and secured a creditable pass.

Before graduation, he was married in the year 1910 to Saubhāgyavati Pārukkuṭṭi Amma, who belonged to the distinguished and aristocratic Nair family of Kollaka Bungalow at Karuṇāgappaḷḷi. Since the age of sixteen, his former religious enthusiasm had subsided and a spirit of atheism had taken possession of him. At this stage, he was responsible for shaking the blind religious faith of many of his well-meaning neighbours and friends. But in spite of all this, he continued to observe, at least nominally but regularly, the simple instructions given him by the sannyāsin.

Government appointment and spiritual thirst

After graduation, he accepted an appointment in the High Court at Trivandrum. At the same time, he joined the Law College. In the meanwhile, in spite of the fact that he was physically smaller than the police standard, something in him so favourably impressed the Commissioner of Police that he was recruited to the department as a Senior Inspector. He left the Law course and served as Inspector of Police, in various places. Riding horses was a pleasant hobby for him during this period. While thus in service, he took some months' study leave to complete the law course and took his degree in Law (B.L.) with distinction. He was immediately appointed prosecuting Inspector.

The atheistic tendencies which began to appear at the age of sixteen continued their sway over him till about the time he came as prosecuting Inspector to Padmanābhapuram, the former capital of Travancore. Then, spiritual questions began to engage his serious attention once again. He sought answers through books. This was the only avenue open to him, but nothing satisfied him. As a result of his efforts, however, he was deeply convinced that a Kārana-guru (a

Sage who is prepared to lead an aspirant to the goal) could alone take him to the Truth.

He also knew that he was incompetent to choose the right Guru. Therefore he took the safe course of praying to the personal God to bless him with the right Guru. This prayer went deeper and deeper day by day, and he spent several sleepless nights all drenched in tears. His mental agony was intolerable. His official duties, however, were carried on as before.

In that state, one day at Padmanābhapuram, he met a naked avadhūta sannyāsin by the road side. The sannyāsin was bruised all over with stones pelted by mischievous urchins on the street; yet he only smiled. Immediately, Shrī Kṛishṇa Mēnōn recognized in the avadhūta the old sannyāsin whom he had met at the age of ten. The svāmi embraced him and consoled him and told him that a great and real Mahātma would shortly meet him, to guide him to his spiritual goal. This consoled him, but only for a little while. The old mental agony reappeared after some days, and he began to pray again with redoubled earnestness for a real Guru.

Attainment of Sat-guru

Shrī Kṛishṇa Mēnōn had developed a natural aversion towards sannyāsins as a class, as he had found from his frequent discussions with them that their grasp of the Truth was feeble. At last, one evening in the year 1919, he happened to meet, by the roadside not far from the Police Station at Takkalai, a sannyāsin – visibly great – wearing flowing ochre robes and a big Bengali turban. The sannyāsin looked at him with an enchanting smile. The svāmijī, seated on a culvert, beckoned him to his side and spoke to him in clear and exquisite English, as though he had long known him. Indeed he had, and the sannyāsin alone knew it. He was attracted by the sannyāsin from the first sight of him, and was fascinated by his charming manners, gait and talk. Being invited by him for a short walk, Shrī Kṛishṇa Mēnōn could no longer resist the temptation to accompany him. So they walked together silently, for about a mile, till they reached an old, unoccupied house at the western gate of Padmanābhapuram Fort.

Vehement opposition and ultimate surrender

The sun had set, but darkness did not shroud the earth as usual, since the bright moon had already risen. In that cool and gentle moonlight, they entered the house and sat in the front room. A frank and lively conversation on spiritual topics was started. Shrī Kṛiṣhṇa Mēnōn, as every sincere aspirant is expected to do, asked many shrewd and taxing questions, which under any other circumstances would have seemed to offend against ordinary politeness. But the svāmijī – overflowing with love and inwardly enjoying the earnestness, sincerity and shrewdness of the aspirant – answered the questions most satisfactorily, gently and unostentatiously – covering even those in the mind of the aspirant to which he had not yet given expression.

Much more than the unassailable logic and applicability of the answers, it was the extreme humility of the great svāmijī that captivated the heart of the aspirant and enslaved him at last. The ego being thus paralysed, Shrī Kṛiṣhṇa Mēnōn immediately prostrated at the feet of the svāmijī, literally washing his feet with his tears. After some moments when he could barely speak, he got up and prayed for instructions to enable him to reach the Ultimate, if he was considered worthy. The svāmijī, who was only waiting for that moment of genuine surrender, replied with a smile of love and joy: 'It is for that and that alone that I have come all the way from Calcutta. I have no other interest in Travancore. I knew of your yearnings even from that distance.'

(*Note:* A word of caution may not be out of place here, about this and other such incidents. Please do not stoop to examine, from a purely mental plane, the possibility or reasonableness of this and other instances that might follow in the course of this sketch. Suffice it to say that they are quite possible, perfectly reasonable and definitely more real than the mental experiences of the waking state. They appear in a state or plane which virtually governs the waking state of one who had the good fortune to reach such a state.)

Initiation, and departure of the Guru

They talked in that room the whole night through. Before daybreak, all instruction needed for the whole of the disciple's spiritual career had been imparted by the svāmijī and imbibed by the disciple. The instructions covered the path of devotion to the personal God Kṛiṣhṇa (as Ātma-mūrti and not as Bhāgavata Kṛiṣhṇa), and also different paths of yōga like raja-yōga, Shiva-rāja-yōga, praṇava-yōga, etc. They ended with the path of jnyāna (following the direct perception method – strict vicāra-mārga – adopting the separation process, as distinguished from the method of meditation adopting the absorption process).

The svāmijī shrewdly discovered a lack of enthusiasm on the part of his disciple to take to the paths of devotion and yōga as directed. So the svāmijī said gently: 'I appreciate your reluctance to take to the preliminary courses of devotion and yōga, and I admit you are quite right. For mere realization of the ultimate Truth, the last course – namely the jnyāna path – is alone necessary. But I want you to be something more, which you will understand only later on. Therefore, please undertake them first. It won't take you long to finish them both. Evidently, the svāmijī had already decided to crown him as an Ācārya; and to be an ideal Ācārya, one has to be familiar with all the intricate experiences along all the different paths.

Before sunrise, the svāmijī got up, satisfied with the fulfilment of his mission. It was only then that Shrī Kṛiṣhṇa Mēnōn thought of the impending departure of his Guru. The day had not dawned, and his home was somewhat far away. It was not possible for him to offer his Guru the hospitality of his household or even a conventional 'dakṣhiṇa'. The svāmijī at once discerned his thoughts and feelings and said with a smile: 'There is no obligation in spirituality, there being no personality involved. Follow my instructions faithfully and you shall attain perfection soon. That alone, and nothing else, is the real dakṣhiṇa to the Guru. Therefore don't worry.' So saying, the svāmijī took his leave and returned straight to Calcutta via Nagercoil.

This was the first and the last meeting, in flesh and blood, between the Guru and the disciple.

A note about Guru-svāmi

The svāmijī was no ordinary sannyāsin. He was a great yōgin and a jnyānin, by name Yōgānanda, the like of whom the world has rarely seen. He was a great scholar and had mastery over many languages including English. He came of a princely family in Rājaputāna. He became a sannyāsin at the age of twelve, and became a jnyānin well established in the Absolute in his early teens. From Rājasthān he came to Calcutta, where he lived in a small āshram with four sannyāsin disciples – all of whom lived with him.

It was in the year 1919 that Shrī Kṛiṣhṇa Mēnōn was pining in Travancore for a real Guru. When his agony was deep, it touched a tender chord in the svāmijī, then resting in Calcutta. The Guru-disciple relationship is believed to be predestined and not accidental. No amount of intellectual reasoning can explain it. The Guru-disciple relationship is outside the ken of human understanding. Otherwise, how could we explain the experience of Shrī Ātmānanda himself? The spiritual pangs of an earnest aspirant in Travancore were transmitted over a thousand miles straight to Calcutta. They were received there by that great sannyāsin alone, while they missed the notice of all other sages and yōgins then living all over India, both far and near.

As soon as the svāmijī heard the call, he said to his chief sannyāsin disciple: 'My child is crying for help in Travancore. I am going there to console him.' So saying, he started by the next train, at his own expense, to Trivandrum and thence to Padmanābhapuram, where he sat on the culvert. He knew full well that Shrī Kṛiṣhṇa Mēnōn would come that way, and so he did.

Shrī Kṛiṣhṇa Mēnōn was the last disciple of Svāmi Yōgānanda. He was also the only gṛihasta (householder) disciple of the svāmijī.

Spiritual sādhana and realization

The very day the svāmijī left him, Shrī Kṛiṣhṇa Mēnōn started an intense practice of his spiritual exercises, beginning with the path of devotion, in strict conformity with the instructions given to him. He rose steadily in the line of devotion till he took up Rādhā-hṛidaya-bhāvana (meditation on the heart of Rādhā), the highest exercise of personal devotion to the iṣhṭa-dēva. Thus he went through all the thrilling and intoxicating experiences of selfless love, culminating in its own samādhi. It did not take him more than six months to cover all this. It was towards the end of this period that he composed his classic work, *Rādha-mādhavam*, of 48 verses in Malayalam.

Next, he went through the hardest grind of yōgic exercises, following the paths of different yōgas in order. In the course of his yōgic exercises once, his body was paralysed. This happens to all yōgins when they transcend a particular ādhāra-cakra (nerve centre). It is only a simple yōgic reaction on the strained human constitution, and it disappears in due course without leaving any adverse effects. But the family of Shrī Kṛiṣhṇa Mēnōn was terribly upset, and so they turned to all kinds of medical treatments which were of no avail.

At last the news reached the ears of a great yōgin and jnyānin called Shrī Caṭṭampi Svāmikaḷ, who was then in his old age, living at Trivandrum. He said that it was no disease, that it would have no adverse results, and that no doctor's medicine would have any effect on his body which was then in a hyper-sensitive state. It was then about a fortnight since the malady had become acute. Anyhow, Shrī Svāmikaḷ took compassion upon the anxious condition of the family of Shrī Kṛiṣhṇa Mēnōn and so prescribed a simple herbal preparation to be applied to the soles of his feet. It was applied at about 5 p.m. that day. In a few minutes, he fell into an unusually long and deep sleep, till 8 a.m. next morning. When he awoke, he was normal. The herbal application was continued for two more days, as directed by the svāmijī.

Some months later, Shrī Kṛiṣhṇa Mēnōn paid Shrī Caṭṭampi Svāmikaḷ a courtesy visit. It was then that the svāmijī revealed to him that it was not at his own instance that he had administered the antidote for the yōgic ailment, but because it was desired by the great Yōgānanda himself, who had requested him through the subtle sphere to do so. He declared that otherwise no spiritual man would ever interfere in the sādhana of a Kāraṇa-guru's disciple and nothing untoward would ever happen to the sādhaka.

A few more months of intense yōgic practices took Shrī Kṛiṣhṇa Mēnōn to the highest experiences in the line of yōga. Long and deep nirvikalpa samādhi he enjoyed often and at will. But it failed to satisfy him, because it was time limited and caused as a result of intense effort. According to him, Truth is uncaused, permanent and self-luminous.

Therefore, he had to seek for the ultimate Truth by other means. Then he took to regular jnyāna-sādhana with great ease and fortitude, and visualized the ultimate Truth in a very short time.

The period of his spiritual practices, covering all the three paths, did not last for more than four years (till about 1923). All necessary instructions were clearly and regularly imparted to him by his Guru, appearing before him in lively vision during his sādhana. He was given the spiritual name Ātmānanda by his own Guru, and he has been known by that name ever since.

Inclination towards sannyāsa and confirmation in gṛihastāshrama (householdership)

Towards the end of his spiritual sādhana, he felt a strong urge to take to sannyāsa and live with his Guru for the rest of his life. With this idea, he made all arrangements to go to Calcutta towards the end of May. A few months' leave was also sanctioned by Government, and he intended to resign his job towards the end of the leave. He chose not to disclose his whole intention, even to his wife, but said only that he desired to be with his Guru for some time. With all her characteristic love and devotion to him she readily agreed to what he so earnestly longed for.

But Guru-svāmi saw through all this plan and found that the new move would thwart his own purpose. He had marked out his only gṛihasta disciple for a great mission. Therefore, towards the end of May, a day before Shrī Ātmānanda was to leave for Calcutta, Guru-svāmi appeared before him in a vision and told him that he should not start as he had planned. He was to continue as a householder for life, guarding the spiritual and phenomenal well-being of his own wife and children and many others yet to come. Continuing, svāmijī said: 'If you start, you shall miss me. I shall have entered into mahāsamādhi on the 1st of June.'

The last part of the information upset Shrī Ātmānanda completely. The slightest hint or suggestion from the Guru was a peremptory order for him. Immediately, he cancelled his leave and waited, hoping against Truth that the latter part of the revelation would not be correct. This was how Shrī Ātmānanda was confirmed in his gṛihastāshrama. Exactly as he had been told, the great svāmijī left his mortal coil and entered into mahāsamādhi precisely at 9 a.m. on the 1st of June.

Services of his devoted wife

Shrīmati Pārukkuṭṭi Amma, the wife of Shrī Mēnōn, was extremely loving and devoted to him. She was the ideal of Indian womanhood in all respects. During the four long years of his spiritual sādhana, she devoted herself to her own rigorous sādhana, which was to serve her husband in every way and make it possible for him to devote all his time and energy for his spiritual pursuit.

His sādhana was intense, one pointed and continuous. Hers was also intense, but multifarious and disconnected. She had taken upon herself the responsibility of the entire household. They were blessed already with three children, the youngest one being only an infant. She looked after her husband's physical needs with clock-like regularity and devotion. That had the first priority over all her domestic duties. He had rarely to ask her for anything he needed. She successfully anticipated all his needs. Very often, she had to bathe him and feed him with her own hands, as if he were a child, during those periods when he was in the transcendental plane and had very little body consciousness left. Even during the four short hours of rest that Shrī Ātmānanda took in the middle of the night, she could not always sleep; because her domestic labours were not always finished before his retirement at night. She had to start again before he woke at 3 a.m. for the next day's sādhana.

Her sleepless service and devotion to him for years remind us of the mythological services of Shrī Lakṣhmaṇa to Shrī Rāma for fourteen years in the forest without sleep or rest. It also reminds us that the age old ideal of Indian womanhood is not yet extinct. The marriage mantra of the Hindus enjoins: 'Thou shalt not part even after death'. This is no exaggeration, but the simple truth. It suggests that both the husband and wife stand as that principle which survives even death. It can never be the body, senses or mind which we see disintegrating here in front of us. It can only be that permanent, self-luminous, non-dual principle in man, transcending body, senses and mind. That is Ātmā, the ultimate Truth which knows no death. The married couple is asked to stand as that. What greater upadēsha does one need?

The practical implementation of this noble ideal was worked out by the great women of ancient India, by their unrivalled observance of the ideal of pati-vratya. Mythology abounds in instances of the most wonderful powers resulting from the sweet practice of this wonderful 'devotional yōga'. The woman, though apparently ignorant, considers her husband as her God incarnate and as such gives him all her love and devotion. Phenomenal love is only an expression of the knowledge of oneness, and the goal of love is that oneness itself.

That oneness was gradually experienced by such women as a result of their simple but sincere tapasya. This experience bestowed on them the mysterious powers of Īshvara-bhāva, in varying degrees, even without their knowing or desiring them. The powers danced before them as their slaves. Even when the husbands had not reached any high spiritual level, their wives by such sincere tapasya were able to acquire many such powers. But when a woman gets the rare privilege of doing such tapasya towards the husband who is well established in the ultimate Truth, she is indeed enviable. That feeling of oneness or identification with the husband at all levels makes her a rightful partner in all his attainments.

So it was with Shrī Ātmānanda's devoted wife Shrīmati Pārukkuṭṭi Amma – Swarūpānanda being her spiritual name.

First disciples

Of the five disciples of Swami Yōgānanda, Shrī Ātmānanda (the only householder disciple) was alone permitted to take the role of a Kārana-guru to accept disciples and guide them. Accordingly, he accepted his first few disciples during the period 1923-24. He was Prosecuting Inspector of Police at Padmanābhapuram throughout the period of his spiritual sādhana and for some years more. Though he could not spare much time for his official preparations at home, his official work never suffered in any way on that account. Government proceedings gave him glowing tributes for his masterly prosecution of cases even during the period of his sādhana. This has proved to the reasonable observer that legitimate phenomenal duties are never a hindrance to an earnest spiritual aspirant.

Police department and spirituality

Many years later (in 1949), Sir S. Rādhākṛishṇan interviewed Shrī Ātmānanda, at the latter's residence, Pārvati Vilāsam, in Trivandrum.

During this interview, Sir Rādhākṛiṣhṇan asked out of curiosity: 'Well Sir, is it a fact that you had all your spiritual sādhana while serving in the Police Department?'

Shrī Ātmānanda replied firmly: 'Yes, it is perfectly true. And I am quite serious when I say that if anybody sought my advice regarding the vocation or profession most helpful towards spiritual advancement, I would always recommend either the police or the military. Because they offer the maximum obstacles and temptations. Success obtained under such conditions is final and irrevocable.'

His service and government appreciation

From Padmanābhapuram, he was transferred in succession to Trivandrum, Kottayam, Nagercoil, Chengannur, Alwaye, and again to Kottayam, Trivandrum and Quilon – as Prosecuting Inspector, Station Inspector, Assistant Superintendent of Police and District Superintendent of Police. For over a year, he was deputed on special duty to codify and prepare the long neglected Police Manual of the state. He retired from service in 1939, while serving as District Superintendent of Police at Quilon.

He was the terror of advocates who opposed him, because of his mastery over the law. Several heads of the Government under whom he served have recorded their high appreciation of his integrity, resourcefulness, intelligence, deep respect for the law and above all his unquestionable efficiency. In service as well as in phenomenal life, he always upheld established law, high moral standards and humane justice. He fought stubbornly against his own superiors in service and even against Government, for principle and justice. His retirement a few months before superannuation was precipitated by such a fight against Government for principle and justice. He neither let down his erring subordinates, nor gave them up to the mercy of his superiors. He always punished them himself leniently and they in return loved him unreservedly and obeyed him, to the envy of even his superiors. He never made use of the services of his official subordinates except for strictly official purposes.

He had around him always a host of disciples waiting to do any service of love, unasked. He loved to have them around him and he enjoyed their services more than those of his official subordinates. A constable was very rarely seen in his house, except when he brought some urgent message from Government. He was in his element and freedom when surrounded by his disciples. Even during long tours on foot over hills and forests for days together, he was followed by dozens of his devoted disciples.

Of course when he went on any official business, he was formally escorted by the police force.

Need of a Guru (and danger of more than one)

He asserted most emphatically that no aspirant, however great, could ever attain liberation without the help of a Kāraṇa-guru *in person*.

Accepting more than one guru at a time is even more dangerous than having none at all. It will keep the aspirant pinned to the phenomenal and in bondage. This assertion is expressed by him in the most unambiguous terms, in a letter in his own hand in Malayalam dated 11-10-1104 M.E. (May 1929 A.D.) from Kottayam, sent to one of his earliest lady disciples, Nityānanda (Ponnu, as he used to call her). She was then but a girl of 13, and already doing sādhana (devotion to her personal God Kṛiṣhṇa as Ātma-mūrti). A photostat of the letter is given at the beginning of this book with an English translation facing it. [The photostat is omitted in this second edition – the translation is the same as below.] Since she was in the infancy of her spiritual career, the letter is most skilfully clothed in language designed to appeal to her sentiments at that age and yet not deviating in the least from the path to the ultimate Truth. The letter may be of help to some seekers as it has already been to many others. It runs thus:

Kottayam, 11-10-1104
(24th May 1929)

To Ponnu

Peace thou be,

Letter received. The *unconditioned love towards one's own Guru* is the only ladder to the goal of Truth. That prēma-bhakti is *not something which could be shared*. No other kind of love or devotion should be capable of bearing comparison to it. A disciple should never bow allegiance to two Gurus at the same time.

May the Lord Bhagavān who is the embodiment of sat-cit-ānanda abide in Ponnu for ever.

With love and blessings
(*signed)*
P. Kṛiṣhṇa Mēnōn

He held that liberation is a change of perspective: from the basic error of 'knowledge by subject-object relationship', to 'the experiential Truth or knowledge in identity'. The latter is neither a result nor an evolution of the former. The former has to die, in order that the latter might dawn. At the point of the death of the former perspective, there must be some agency transcending the phenomenal, to direct the aspirant's attention to his own being or real nature. This agency is the Guru. He is the ultimate Truth itself, though he appears as a person to the naked eye. This Kāraṇa-guru in person is indispensable for Self-realization, though in some very mature cases of uttamādhikāris the contact might be only for a few seconds, by a word or a touch or even a look.

Wider spiritual activities and the increase of Indian disciples

When he was transferred to Kottayam in the year 1927, he had only a handful of Malayali disciples. At Kottayam, the clarity, simplicity and directness of his approach to the Truth, sweetened by his temperament of deep devotion to Truth without form or with form, attracted the admiration of a large number of persons, many of whom gradually sought and accepted his discipleship. Their numbers began to swell; and in the course of about seven years there were about three hundred, many of them being women. Among them were graduates, lawyers, teachers, officers high and low, landlords, feudal chiefs and men of diverse professions. The disciples in those days used to visit him periodically and stay around him for days and weeks, listening to his discourse.

Once in the year 1934, late at night, he was talking in chaste and simple Malayalam about the significance of the concept of 'Atma-mūrti'. Some of us – then in the prime of our youth – felt drowsy and began to yawn. He noted this and at the end of the talk said: 'After a few years, streams of foreign disciples from far off continents will flock to hear me, and then you will long to hear me talk in Malayalam. Therefore beware. Don't waste your opportunity now.' Our experience of later years proved this warning to be literally true.

He did not need more than three hours a day to dispose of his official papers most satisfactorily. He needed less than five hours for his night's rest. The rest of his day was devoted to discoursing with the disciples on spiritual matters in Malayalam, expatiating mostly on real bhakti and jnyāna.

Though he was himself a great yōgin, he did not choose to guide any of his disciples through the path of yōga. He had, however, two disciples who came to him as yōgins and who under his direction through the jnyāna path became perfect jnyānins. One of them, a centenarian avadhūta sage [Kumaḷi-svāmi, described in the next section], is still living in the high ranges of Travancore. The other was a schoolmaster at Eraniel called Narayana Pillai. After listening for some months to Shrī Ātmānanda during the year 1922(?), Mr. Narayana Pillai one day succeeded in securing a mantrōpadēsha from him. Immediately, he resigned his job, took the sannyāsin's robe which he got sanctified by placing it in front of Shrī Ātmānanda's photograph, and went straight off to the Himalayas. There at the foot of the Himalayas he began his sādhana with all earnestness and sincerity, guided by the mantrōpadēsha alone. Complete directions from his Guru were available in the subtle sphere, whenever he needed them. In the course of a few years, he became a great jnyānin, revered and worshipped by the sannyāsins of Haridvār and Hṛiṣhikēsh. In the year 1948, he appeared before his Guru Shrī Ātmānanda at Trivandrum in the subtle sphere, took his permission to leave his mortal coil and immediately entered into mahāsamādhi at Hṛiṣhikēsh.

The enlightening of Kumaḷi-svāmi

One morning in 1932 at Kottayam, where Shrī Ātmānanda was then the Assistant Superintendent of Police, he felt an unusual urge to go to the eastern hills of Kumaḷi in the High Ranges. Immediately, he started on a surprise inspection tour of the police hill stations around

Kumaḷi. He was already in a semi-transcendental mood. Alighting at the Police Station, he found the Inspector was out on his usual round. Sending word to him to come up soon, Shrī Ātmānanda, without an escort of any kind, began to climb the hill on the left, in response to the urge which was getting stronger within him as he proceeded.

There, at the top of the hill, he met an old avadhūta yōgin, stark naked. He was evidently waiting for him. On coming closer, he recognized in the avadhūta the old sannyāsin who had given him a mantra in his tenth year in his own home and whom he had met later on two occasions. The yōgin had reached the highest state of yōgic development and was habitually immersed in long and deep nirvikalpa samādhi for days together. There were very brief intervals when he woke out of this state. Fortunately, that was a time when he was awake.

In the waking state, this yōgin had his own doubts that he had not reached the ultimate Truth. Shrī Ātmānanda, who was also of the same opinion, wished to give him a lift. They talked frankly and openly about the actual state of the yōgin in his samādhi. His mind was so pure and sāttvic that Shrī Ātmānanda had no difficulty in convincing him of the basic error which he had not yet transcended. In the next few minutes the ultimate Truth of his own real nature was clearly expounded to him, in very few words. The great yōgin visualized the ultimate Truth then and there, and fell down in a deep nirvikalpa samādhi. This time it was not his usual nirvikalpa samādhi, where he was accustomed to stand as the witness of the samādhi. But now he transcended even the witnesshood, and stood as one with the ultimate Reality itself. This is Self-realization, pure and simple.

He had to be brought back to body consciousness by some effort on the part of Shrī Ātmānanda himself, because he could not be left in that state. If he were, he might continue indefinitely. Shrī Ātmānanda's official duty was waiting for him at the Police Station. Thus forced back to the waking state after two hours, the great yōgin got up and prostrated before Shrī Ātmānanda, as a regular disciple. This was Shrī Ātmānanda's second yōgin disciple. We call him from that day the Kumaḷi-svāmi, since no other name of his is known to us.

He had known for several years that Shrī Ātmānanda was to be his Kāraṇa-guru and was waiting anxiously for that long desired opportunity. Ever since 1930, he used his yōgic powers to go to Shrī Ātmānanda's house at Kottayam in subtle form and kept in touch with the activities there. Through this form of contact, the svāmi had studied by heart many of the verses and songs composed by Shrī Ātmānanda and which were frequently sung at his house. Some of these verses were, incidentally, repeated by the svāmi to Shrī Ātmānanda, during their meeting at the hill top.

They parted soon after the svāmi woke up, and met only once again in the gross plane. But the svāmi occasionally met his Guru and paid his respects in the subtle sphere. This was more frequent just before Shrī Ātmānanda's passing away. Of course the svāmi had sensed the disaster as soon as Shrī Ātmānanda had made his last decision. Kumaḷi-svāmi is now a hundred years old and is living deep in the Kumaḷi forests. His avadhūta samskāras were so deep-rooted in him that it was impossible for him to gather enough body consciousness to lead a restricted life in society.

Enlightening his own household

It has to be mentioned that Shrī Ātmānanda imparted regular tattvōpadēsha to his own wife and children, to his own mother, sister, uncle and father-in-law, absorbing them into him the Ultimate, along with his other disciples.

The advent of European disciples

The influx of his European disciples, though predicted by him as early as 1934, began to take effect only about 1937. It was in 1937 that Mr. Thompson – a young English writer and poet from London, with very strong spiritual samskāras – happened to meet him. He had been for some time with Shrī Ramaṇa Maharṣhi. After a few day's lively discussion with Shrī Ātmānanda, he begged to be accepted as a regular disciple and to be initiated into the ultimate Truth. But Shrī Ātmānanda replied, with his usual courtesy, that he must first get the formal permission of the Maharṣhi himself for that purpose. So Mr. Thompson went straight to Ramaṇāshramam, got the glad permission and blessings of the Maharṣhi, and came back to Quilon. But Shrī

Ātmānanda had already known of this in the subtle sphere; and so, without even asking Mr. Thompson any more about it, accepted him as a regular disciple and continued the discussions. It was only many days later that Mr. Thompson himself gave an account of his last visit to the Maharṣhi. Mr. Thompson was the first of Shrī Ātmānanda's European disciples.

He was followed in 1941 by Miss Ella Maillart, a well-known journalist and explorer from Switzerland, and Mr. John Levy from London, a wealthy aristocrat, composer, musician and architect, deeply interested in the enquiry after Truth.

Though a Jew by birth, Mr. John Levy had pushed his enquiry through different faiths. Being dissatisfied with all of them, he roamed all over India, meeting various spiritual leaders of repute.

At last Miss Ella Maillart, followed by Mr. John Levy, came to Shrī Ātmānanda. Shrī Ātmānanda's rational and non-technical approach to the ultimate Truth, and the simple logic which he pursued in his discussions, appealed to them immensely. They listened to the discourses for only a few days and then they found that their questions were all exhausted and that they were intellectually satisfied. They also begged Shrī Ātmānanda to show them the way to the ultimate Truth, and were accepted as his disciples.

They were followed in course of time by many others. To mention only a few: Messrs. M. Arnold Mayer and M. Robert Ceresole from Switzerland, Dr. Roger Godel and Alice Godel from France, His Excellency Moyine Al Arab from Cairo, Mr. Kamal D. Joumblatte the leader of Lebanon, Mr. Max Yergan and Dr. Leena Yergan from USA, and Mr. Freddy Guthmann and Mr. Leon Michel from Argentina.

As time passed, disciples and pilgrims, some of them notable figures, came in larger and larger numbers from these and many other countries as well. It is indeed pleasing to note that nearly half of them were ladies. The biggest complement of foreign disciples came from Argentina in South America and the rest from France, United States of America, Switzerland and England, and a few also came from Egypt, Lebanon, Italy, Greece, Germany, Netherlands, Israel, Latin America, etc. Many came from different parts of India, chiefly from Bombay and Hyderabad, and a small number from Ceylon. Most of these disciples used to come from their homes in distant continents to meet him periodically and to be near him, listening to his discourses as long as their time and resources would permit.

Those of the disciples who were chosen by him were given the final course of regular tattvōpadēsha, when the whole Truth was expounded by him in a connected manner. Each time, it was particularly addressed to a few disciples, who were thus enabled by unassailable logic and argument to direct their attention wholly to the real being in them, beyond body, senses and mind. At this point, in spite of all their resistance, a mysterious force (the force of Truth) emanated from the Guru and encompassed each of them in a sense of oneness with the Guru. This enabled them to stand consciously as that ultimate principle whose characteristics were already expounded in unambiguous language.

This non-dual experience of one's own real nature is called 'realization' or 'visualization' of the Truth, then and there. They [the disciples] were then asked simply to cling on to that experience, and to make themselves more and more familiar with it, by trying to transcend body, senses and mind as often as possible, automatically experiencing the ultimate Truth every time. This they did and gradually got themselves established in the ultimate Truth, in response to their own earnestness, sincerity and effort.

In March 1959, the number of his disciples, from India and abroad, amounted to several hundreds. Many more had received substantial spiritual help from him, though not in the form of direct Guru-disciple relationship. He has often said: 'Don't think that all those who move around me most of the time are my disciples. I accept only those in whom I find the proper attitude of surrender or true devotion to Truth.' Of course, the others also have certainly profited by the contact, though not to the extent of ultimate liberation.

Other spiritual activities and aversion to publicity

Besides the usual discourse, he used to grant interviews to numerous spiritual seekers from all parts of India and abroad. Dr. and Mrs. Julian Huxley, Sir S. Rādhākṛiṣhṇan, Dr. Mukerjee, Raymond Mortimer, the famous English critic, were a few amongst them. Mr.

Paul Brunton, who was with Shrī Ramaṇa Maharṣhi for a long time, was allowed to listen to Shrī Ātmānanda's discourses as an observer for a period of three months in the year 1952, on the understanding that nothing direct or indirect about the topics (as discussed by Shrī Ātmānanda) would be published by him, without the previous approval of Shrī Ātmānanda himself. This was only a precaution against possible misrepresentation, since a mind – however pure and well intentioned – is incapable of imbibing the ultimate Truth.

Shrī Ātmānanda was by nature averse to publicity of any kind, and he avoided publicists and journalists as far as possible; because he asserted that even the rudiments of spirituality and Truth could be imparted only by personal contact and never through any other medium. In obedience to his desire, we have with great difficulty refrained from publishing anything regarding his life and activities. This was indeed unusual. Very often persons of international repute stayed in Trivandrum for weeks and months, listening to his daily discourses. Naturally, press men came to us for information regarding such persons and their activities. But we could reveal to them no more than the personal identity of the visitors and the general purpose of their stay.

Retirement from service and his sojourns abroad

After retirement from Government service in 1939, he began to devote all his time to his disciples. He fixed his residence with his family at his old country house, Ānandawāḍi, at Mālakkara, near Chengannur, on the left bank of the sacred river Pampa. But from the year 1943, his wife's health began to deteriorate and therefore he shifted his residence to Trivandrum, for convenience of medical aid.

In the year 1945, the then ruling Prince, Raja Rameswara Rao of Vanaparti, who was one of his disciples, invited him with family and retinue for a visit to his state. So he went with his family and some disciples and stayed at the royal palace at Vanaparti and later at Hyderabad for some weeks as his highness's guest.

At the request of his European disciples, headed by Mr. John Levy of London, he flew to Europe in June 1950, through Bombay and Cairo. He spent a fortnight in Paris, another fortnight in Switzerland

and about ten days in Egypt, giving spiritual discourses almost every day to groups of his disciples and select persons in each place.

He discussed the Truth with visitors following different paths, in terms of the path followed by each. He did not discredit any particular path, but only pointed out the wrong emphasis in the application of instructions, if there were any, and advised each to follow his own chosen path with right discrimination and deep earnestness. Many yōgins and bhaktas from different parts of India, and some even from abroad, who had been victims of various ailments and disorders as a result of slips in their instructions or wrong emphasis in their exercises, came often to seek his help. He listened to them compassionately and helped most of them by proper explanation, interpretation or correction.

He always insisted that the ground should never be cut off from under the feet of a spiritual sādhaka, without giving him something better instead.

His view of social obligations

He was very particular about following strictly all healthy customs and conventions, religious as well as social. He held that they played a very important part in moulding character and maintaining the healthy life of an aspirant. Simply because we do not grasp the real purpose and significance of social restrictions introduced by wiser persons, it is foolish and sometimes even disastrous to ignore or discard them, allowing ourselves at the same time to continue as social beings.

In the course of Shrī Ātmānanda's more casual remarks recorded herein, he has thrown light upon several such customs which are unfortunately being discarded by the younger generation. It might be interesting to note in this connection the manner in which he himself acted.

In the year 1932, his own mother passed away in a most dynamic manner without any ailment whatsoever, roaring out at the last breath: 'I am sat-cit-ānanda. Sat-cit-ānanda am I.' After her demise, Shrī Ātmānanda (though established in the ultimate Truth) burned camphor before the dead body of the mother and prostrated before it in tears, like a devoted son. Further, he performed all the rites, rituals and ceremonials under the instructions of the village priest, in strict conformity with existing social customs and conventions.

Again, when his own wife passed away in 1953, he advised his own children to perform the rituals likewise, and he enjoined them to follow the same course when he would leave his body some years hence. Of course they did everything as ordered. He asserted that all this was phenomenal, and had therefore to be guided by phenomenal laws and customs.

His own indisposition, the passing away of Mother and after

On the first of January 1952, we had startling news of faint premonitions of some impending catastrophe to him. Shrī Ātmānanda suddenly developed an occasional inner weakness and indrawingness. There was no physical ailment whatsoever. This weakness grew so alarming, before the 3rd of January 1952, that it puzzled the doctors and we almost feared we had lost him. He recovered suddenly and completely on the evening of the 3rd of January, but with a clear premonition that it would recur after two months. Thanks to the premonition, much was done by the disciples, including his wife and children, to ward off the impending calamity two months hence. Exactly as was foreboded, the trouble reappeared on the 1st of March, with more serious developments. But fortunately, on the 4th of March, he was again kindly spared to us.

In the meanwhile, his wife's health began to worsen. She was in bed for a whole year, under his personal supervision and nursing. She peacefully left her mortal coil on the 4th of March 1953, under the soothing hand of Shrī Ātmānanda, her Guru and husband, and in the presence of most of her children and many of Shrī Ātmānanda's devoted disciples. Her body was cremated in the characteristic Hindu style, with plenty of sandalwood, camphor and incense, on the grounds of his country house at Mālakkara. The rites, rituals and ceremonials were conducted in strict conformity with the local social practice.

Immediately on the conclusion of all the ceremonial rites, which lasted for 12 days, Shrī Ātmānanda returned to his residence at Trivandrum. After a stay of three weeks in Trivandrum, carrying out a heavy spiritual programme, he returned to Mālakkara in the second week of April. On the 41st day after the passing away of Swarūp-ānandāmba, a beautiful samādhi monument in black granite was installed in the heart of Ānandawāḍi in the presence of Shrī Ātmānanda himself, and her mortal remains deposited with due ceremonial rites in a vault inside it. After the ceremony, he told his children and disciples gathered around him to construct a similar structure close to the south of it, to preserve his own mortal remains when he passed away – probably six years hence.

How he faced her passing away

It might be interesting to record the way in which Shrī Ātmānanda faced the passing away of his own wife, and the manner in which he assisted at the after rites. The depth of their mutual love and regard when they lived was classical and proverbial. A minute scrutiny of his conduct during the few days before and after her demise will disclose both the man and the sage in him. He was sleeplessly awake to her physical needs and calls, tending her day and night, ever since the 4th of March 1952, and his own health suffered severely on that account. He knew quite well that she was passing away, and had hinted to those nearest him to be there positively on the 4th morning [of March 1953]. But some of the unfortunate few still missed being present at the last moment.

When she was about to pass away, he sat close by, and passing his hand along with her ascending prāṇa helped her to be tranquil and conscious of her real nature – the Truth. At the last moment, when the life principle was about to leave her body, in the right yōgic fashion, he pressed his forehead against hers and helped her life principle to merge in Him – the Ultimate. Immediately he got up, and in less than five seconds came out of the room, collected and composed, and announced her passing away in one word to the European and Indian disciples anxiously waiting: 'Finished.' How sharp, short and significant this announcement was, need not be commented upon.

Left alone as the head of the family, he had to make all the arrangements for cremation and after rites. Of course, he had to follow the body to Mālakkara and stay there for about a fortnight. We were surprised to see him personally making all the necessary arrangements. He packed his own suitcase as though nothing had happened, and without a tear or a gloom. Some of the European lady disciples, who happened to be present on the occasion, remarked that it was because he was a Sage he was so unconcerned about phenomenal incidents.

The cremation was over at night and the rituals of the next morning were completed before 9 a.m. Then Shrī Ātmānanda was resting on his cot surrounded by his children and disciples, and talking about our departed 'Mother' (as we used to call her). Then he talked to us with visible emotion about her genuine nobility and recounted to us innumerable incidents of love and self-sacrifice during her life. He then wept and shed tears in torrents. The disciples and relatives also wept profusely. Shrī Ātmānanda's weeping did not abate, and we began to be frightened over the turn it might take next.

Restraint of and indulgence in emotions

At this moment Shrī Kallor Narayana Pillai – an old friend and classmate of Shrī Ātmānanda – came to offer his condolences, and a disciple took the message to him. In less than a minute, Shrī Ātmānanda stopped weeping, wiped his eyes, washed his face and went into the drawing room. There the old friends met and exchanged a few preliminary words about the disease and departure of the wife. It is to be remembered that both of them were writers and poets from their boyhood. In a few minutes the conversation drifted to literature and poetry. A verse composed by the visitor more than forty years ago happened to be quoted by the author himself, but he could not remember the latter half. At once Shrī Ātmānanda repeated it from his own memory which was even then so crystal clear, and they laughed and made themselves merry over it, as if they had forgotten that this was a condolence visit.

After talking for about three quarters of an hour, the friend left, and Shrī Ātmānanda returned to the disciples and relatives inside, who had with difficulty just composed themselves. He took up the trend where he had left it and began to talk of our departed Mother again. Then he began to weep and shed tears in profusion, as before. This conduct surprised us all the more, but we did not dare to ask him anything about it just then. After some days we asked him the meaning of it all.

Then he calmly replied: 'It is the yōgin in one that restrains the feelings and keeps oneself composed, by dint of effort. It is the bhakta in one that indulges in soft emotions profusely, and that also by dint of effort. Both these are only mental expressions, and therefore artificial. The one who restrains cannot indulge, and the one who indulges cannot restrain feelings as he chooses. It is the real Sage alone that can do both as he chooses.

'He does so, not by effort, but spontaneously. Feelings never come to him uninvited. If he thinks that it is the time to act with discretion, feelings respectfully keep at a distance. But the moment he invites them, they rush in like torrents. Again, the moment he puts on the brake, by a mere thought, they disappear. This was what you were witnessing in me in those days.

'It is wrong to attribute either composure or indulgence to the Sage. He is the conscious background of both. The human element as man will be clear on the surface of all his activities; but the ātmic element will be even more clear to the discerning few, behind the apparent activities of the Sage.'

Visits to health resorts in the hot months

After the conclusion of the ceremony on the 41st day, our first concern was to see that he recouped his already shattered health. With this object in view, we prevailed upon him to take a change of air to some health resort. Therefore we took him to Cape Commorin, escorted by some of the closest disciples and a few servants. In a fortnight's time his health had improved considerably, and encouraged by this we stayed on for another fortnight. He delighted in the daily dip in the open sea and in the traditionally sāttvic atmosphere of Cape Commorin.

Thereafter, every year during the hot season, he went for a pleasant change with chosen disciples and servants, sometimes accompanied by some relatives, to health resorts like Bangalore, Varkalai and Kodaikanal, besides Cape Commorin. Of all these places, he liked Cape Commorin the most and chose to go there for three alternate summers since 1953, the last being in April 1959.

His domestic life

This was indeed ideal, in all respects. From their marriage in 1910 till Mother's passing away in 1953, there was not even a single instance of their having done or said anything against the wish of either. The wonderful secret of it all was the fact that he had no individual wish of his own in any phenomenal matter, and in spiritual matters she knew her place and would never interfere. There was no necessity for him to advise his disciples how they should conduct themselves in their own homes; because his own domestic life was always a glowing example before them.

How he utilized music

He loved music, and was a musician himself. According to him, spiritual realization was a harmonious blending of the head and the heart in Peace. He asserted that music was a 'mōkṣha-kalā' which, if utilized with right discrimination, would take one smoothly to the ultimate Truth.

One of his closest lady disciples, Nityānanda, who came to him in 1927 at the age of twelve and who became a musician of repute in her youth, was guided by Shrī Ātmānanda through music in the latter stages of her spiritual course. She began by singing songs extolling Lord Kṛiṣhṇa – her personal God. She grew along with her God and her music to the ultimate Truth. She now spends her days completely engrossed in singing the glories of the Guru – the ultimate Truth.

The singing of devotional songs which spoke of the ultimate Truth aroused in him soft and sāttvic emotions of a high order. This was the one thing which he always enjoyed and appreciated. Nityānanda, who had dedicated her life to the Guru (the Ultimate), had the envious privilege of singing in his presence for over thirty years; and for the last fifteen years of his life, she did this every day. This was the real sādhana she did for herself. He enjoyed these songs so much that they often threw him into deep moods for hours together. He used to say that it was only his own spiritual talks and the few hours of listening to the spiritual songs that really sustained his life.

His own proficiency in music is evident from the fact that he had himself taught her several rare rāgas like Duhkha-khanḍāra, Dvijavanti, Gōpikavasant etc. (some of them not much current in modern Karnatic music). He had not made a formal study of music. But in the days of his saguṇa sādhana, there was a period when for days and weeks together he was drowned in divine music from within himself, as though from the flute of Lord Kṛiṣhṇa, throughout the waking state. Many of his friends and eminent musicians during that period had the pleasure of enjoying it and forgetting themselves for the time being, by putting their ears close to Shrī Ātmānanda's. This flood of divine music had left in him such an indelible samskāra as to enable him to give lessons in music to Nityānanda.

His hobbies (kathakaḷi and chess)

The peculiar art of kathakaḷi is a harmonious mixture of classical poetry, exquisite rhythmic dancing with emphasis on the display of emotions, and classical Indian music particularly adapted to Kerala (and called the sōpānam path of music). It was the one art he used to enjoy throughout his life. So much so that he used to have the kathakaḷi dance dramas enacted in his own home very often. Of course, he himself would select the stories, which would be of high spiritual, devotional and literary excellence. He deplored the fact that the professional kathakaḷi singers had, many of them, become prosaic and unemotional in their usual performances. This was because of over-exertion and under-payment. It may be mentioned that kathakaḷi had been accepted as a permanent feature of his birthday celebrations from 1954 onwards.

In the year 1955, Shrī Ātmānanda ordered Nityānanda to make up for the deficiency in music by herself singing to the dancers on the kathakaḷi stage during the important scenes. Though kathakaḷi music on the stage was considered an exclusively masculine job, she gladly undertook the task. It must be remembered in this context that the singer has always the first place of honour on the kathakaḷi stage. She was conscious of her own incompetency. It had been her supreme experience, how a 'mere word' from her Guru had in a moment dashed her across the invincible ocean of samsāra 'worldliness' and landed her safely in permanent Peace in which she was still resting contented. But here it was much more. It was not a 'mere word' as before It was his sacred wish and peremptory order. She had only to start and stop not. She did so on the birthday, leading the best dancers of Kerala on the kathakaḷi stage, with her Guru reclining in front of her, freeing her of all her diffidence. She did her job wonderfully well, to the highest approbation of the dancers and the audience, and her Guru blessed her profusely. Shrī Ātmānanda enjoyed the performance so much that he desired its continuance in succeeding years. She obeyed and led the kathakaḷi with her songs on the three succeeding years, with increasing success every year, till the last birthday on the 20th November 1958.

One other recreation in which he evinced great interest throughout life was the game of chess, in which he was the champion of his days. He used to play chess very often with two of his disciples, till his indisposition towards the end of April 1959. He has often stated that he utilized even the game of chess to speed up the spiritual progress of those who played with him.

His habits and daily life

Even though he had been an athlete in his youth, he took no physical exercise during the last thirty years of his life. The purity of his system (kāya-shuddhi) obtained by his intense yōgic sādhana had made him immune in many ways. His control over breath was so perfect that by a mere thought he could use this control in such a manner that it served the same purpose as physical exercise would.

He was brought up in pure sāttvic brahmanic samskāras, and was a strict vegetarian throughout his life. He would wake up regularly before 4 a.m. and finish all his ablutions and bath before daybreak. His food was the usual Kerala brahmin vegetarian food – composed of rice, vegetables, milk and milk products. The quantity he consumed every day was incredibly small. Considering that he talked incessantly for anything from 6 to 12 hours a day and considering the deficiency of calories in his usual food, it was a puzzle to the doctors how he managed to live.

He chewed fresh Jaffna tobacco of the strongest variety available, to the extent of about four to five pounds a month. He would stop doing so completely, sometimes for days, perhaps to show that he was not enslaved either by this or any other habit. He took to smoking sweet and mildly flavoured cigarettes when he went to Europe in 1950 and gave up the habit completely in September 1958.

He insisted vehemently that no trace should ever be left behind after any activity, and observed it to the very letter all through his life. He held that any trace left behind by an activity was the pernicious seed of its samskāra. Procrastination was unknown to him. Whenever he decided upon any specific programme he was obstinate like a child and did not rest until it was completed. He proved by practice and precept alike his cherished ideal that everyone should live by the sweat of his brow. He held that the slavery of the body was but a prelude to the slavery of the soul.

His independence and his integrity

Ever since his wife passed away in 1953, though he continued to live in the house, Pārvati Vilāsam, which was given in partition to his only daughter, he was looked after exclusively by his devoted disciples – of course at his own expense. He detested being under any obligation, financial or otherwise, to anybody, including his children and relatives.

On different occasions, the disciples – and the children as disciples – used to offer presents at his feet, of different kinds. Of course he accepted them all with pleasure. But whenever anything was offered to him in any capacity other than that of a genuine disciple, he managed to reciprocate in kind with princely generosity and absolved himself from all obligations. There was no question of any obligation to disciples who did everything only to make themselves happy by making him comfortable; they had already surrendered themselves to him.

He was always the custodian of his privy purse. His wife always looked after the financial side of the household, till she passed away. After that, he took one of his devoted disciples into confidence, to help him in keeping house. Nobody else had any insight into his financial affairs, except from what was casually announced by Shrī Ātmānanda himself with regard to his occasional plans and suggestions.

His strict punctuality

Though he stood for the absolute Truth beyond time, he was strict and punctual to the minute, in all his activities. One day, having previously decided to go with his family at 8 a.m. to participate in a domestic ceremony elsewhere, he got into the car precisely at 8 and waited for five minutes for his wife. She had not completed her domestic arrangements and wanted a few minutes more. This was mercilessly denied and she had to start forthwith, leaving her arrangements incomplete. Ever since then, she was always ready at least some minutes before him.

Once a guest of the ruling Mahārāja of the State had fixed an appointment to interview Shrī Ātmānanda at 4.30 p.m. The guest, because of some delay in the palace, could not turn up in time. Shrī Ātmānanda waited patiently till 5 p.m., then cancelled the engagement and informed the palace office about it. In the meanwhile, the guest had started and reached Pārvati Vilāsam only at 5.10 p.m. He was politely informed that the engagement was cancelled after half an hour's waiting and that a fresh appointment had to be fixed for another day, if the guest wanted to see him. The guest returned to the palace sorely disappointed. Many little men around were frightened that His Highness might get terribly cross with Shrī Ātmānanda. When the guest returned to the palace disappointed, his highness sympathized with him in his misfortune, and applauded the manner in which Shrī Ātmānanda upheld the dignity of the ultimate Truth, of Vēdānta and of the state, by his simple conduct.

His love of beauty and his hospitality

Scenes of natural beauty, majesty and grandeur – like beautiful landscapes, majestic rivers, grand waterfalls, great mountains and the raging sea – threw him into long and deep moods – often beyond the mental level.

His heart was tender out of all proportion, and in charity and hospitality he was princely. Devotees and sannyāsins were always welcome to partake of his hospitality. His wife and he took pleasure in standing and watching dozens of children below the age of twelve being sumptuously fed at his home on frequent festive occasions.

His family

The matriarchal system of family and inheritance still prevails in Kerala State. Shrī Ātmānanda's maternal family has become extinct with his generation, as though nature has responded to a standing tradition that the family of a sage shall terminate with him.

Shrī Ātmānanda has three children, the eldest son being a graduate and landlord. The second one, the only daughter, was married to a well known doctor and a professor of the Trivandrum Medical College. She passed away in her 48th year in March 1962, leaving an only daughter. The last son is a business man. They have all been married, blessed with children and well provided for in life. They have also been given regular instructions for spiritual progress.

His ban on institutionalization in spirituality

He enjoined his disciples, including his children, to continue to live like a homogeneous family, never forgetting the fact that the spiritual relationship of each one is directly with his or her Guru alone. He forbade them in the clearest terms from converting their sacred spiritual household into an institution in any manner and therefore he openly declared his refusal to nominate any successor to himself, in spite of requests from different quarters.

He was against institutions of any kind for Vēdānta, and has discussed his views at length in the course of his talks recorded in this book.

His correspondence and personal activities

With the steady increase in the number of his foreign disciples, his correspondence also swelled proportionately. From the year 1949, the author [of this book] was personally ordered by Shrī Ātmānanda himself to officiate as his private secretary – to attend to his correspondence, official as well as domestic, run errands and make engagements. After the demise of his wife in 1953, the author was entrusted with the additional responsibility of attending more closely upon his person and personal affairs.

His last days and mahāsamādhi

Shrī Ātmānanda's 75th birthday was celebrated by his disciples on an unprecedented and magnificent scale at Pārvati Vilāsam on the 20th November 1958. For the next three months, he was busy with frequent spiritual talks and two regular courses of tattvōpadēsha. By the end of February 1959, the city of Trivandrum grew sultry and a change to some health resort became inevitable. Shrī Ātmānanda preferred to go to Cape Commorin.

Therefore we started on the 7th of April 1959, with a few of his servants and the closest disciples who used to attend upon his person. We reached the Cape the same evening, and he started his bath in the open sea immediately. Many dozens of his devoted disciples, including his eldest son, accompanied him and established themselves independently, in separate quarters very near where he stayed. He recouped much of his lost health and vigour in the course of the week. It was a regular spiritual feast for all the disciples, for more than twelve hours every day, in the form of incessant discourses, spiritual songs and interviews. This continued unabated till the end of the third week of April.

On the 22nd of April 1959 (the star day of Mother's demise), the occasional fits of weakness he once had now reappeared, and he began to lose appetite by slow degrees. Medical aid did not have the desired effect. Therefore we took him back to Trivandrum on the 2nd of May. At Trivandrum, he was given all available medical aid by expert doctors. The weakness only grew deeper. Still, he did not give up his daily bath or break his routine till the twelfth evening. We could see that he was drawing more and more inward, and that his outward activities were all mechanical. His physical condition seemed to get still worse on the morning of the 13th of May. By the evening of that day, we lost all hope in any further medical aid.

During the night of the 13th, Nityānanda, who was always attending by his side, sang in despair, with the utmost force of her voice and devotion, some of the songs and verses he always used to enjoy. His immediate response was clear and agreeable. His face, which was apparently fading, began to blush and bloom. The whole body got ruddy, even the few wrinkles disappeared, and his expression showed an emphatic and loving response to the songs sung.

Precisely at ten minutes past seven o'clock in the morning of Thursday the fourteenth May 1959, he peacefully left his mortal coil, in the presence of his grieving family, disciples and relatives. But the bloom and the radiance the body had assumed the night before never left him.

Thus he left us physically and entered into mahāsamadhi as he had himself decided and arranged. He had given us innumerable hints regarding the intended mahāsamādhi; but we failed to take them with the gravity and seriousness they demanded. He had given us all instructions regarding the disposal of his mortal remains once he entered into mahāsamādhi. Some days before mother passed away in March 1953, he had promised us, in her presence, that he would continue in his body for six years more. He kept the promise literally and left us in 1959. Nature had skilfully. arranged all the environment needed to make his leaving his own body appear natural. He made use of the opportunity in time, and passed away normally.

As directed by himself when he was living, his body was taken to his country house, Ānandawāḍi, at Mālakkara in Chengannūr, on the banks of the sacred river Pampa. After all the usual rites and rituals prescribed by society, his body was lifted jointly by his children and his disciples, and placed over the decorated funeral pyre. The sacred body was thus cremated in piles of sandalwood, camphor and incense sticks, together with the customary mango wood. All the after rites, ceremonials and conventions of society were strictly observed. The mortal remains, religiously and devoutly collected from the sacred ashes, were carefully preserved for a year, with solemn rites and austere observances.

On the first anniversary day (the 3rd of May 1960), the mortal remains were devoutly deposited inside a vault, in a beautiful granite monument, constructed beside that of his own wife, on the spot pointed out by him in 1953. The two samādhi monuments are now covered by a combined roof; and they are preserved, revered and worshipped by his devoted disciples, both in India and abroad. Many of them meet there on the anniversary day every year, and solemnly observe the memory of their revered Guru. The local public co-operate with zeal in all these ceremonials, considering it as much their own concern as of the sons and disciples of Shrī Ātmānanda.

Perpetuation of the samādhi installations

The children and disciples of Gurunāthan [Shrī Ātmānanda] were anxious to perpetuate the sacred samādhis in a manner fitting a Sage. Therefore, with the unstinted help and co-operation of the devout disciples, both far and near, his children were able to clear the ground of all its encumbrances; so as to ensure, for the whole family of disciples, full and free opportunity of worship at the samādhis, for all time.

The eldest son, who is in possession of the whole estate, is devoutly looking after the routine and maintenance of the samādhis, on behalf of the family and all the disciples. Further, the foundation stone has also been laid most auspiciously, at 8:30 a.m. on the 26th November 1963 (being the eightieth birthday of Shrī Ātmānanda), for a magnificent superstructure housing the two samādhis, beaming their full sāttvic radiance and bestowing spiritual consolation, for all posterity.

Bibliography

Shrī Ātmānanda was in the habit of writing books even from his early youth. Of his earlier writings, the only book that happened to be published was a novel in Malayalam, called *Tārāvati* (reprinted in 1958). The manuscripts of another long novel and a book in verse form were lost. They were stolen by pretentious and deceitful friends. The book in verse has appeared subsequently in print, in a mutilated form.

His writings of a strictly spiritual nature begin with *Rādhā-mādhavam*. These are written in simple and elegant Malayalam verse. They have all been published and preserved intact. His spiritual books are an index of a clear, continuous and progressive development of an ideal aspirant – from devotion, which appears only on the surface to be in the plane of duality, to the realization of and establishment in the ultimate Truth.

1. The first of the series was the classical and devotional treatise called *Rādhā-mādhavam*, already mentioned above. It was composed in the year 1919, describing the personal experiences of the author on the path of devotion to his personal God, Lord Kṛiṣhṇa, without losing sight of the real nature of God himself. The text was circulated in manuscript form for many years and consequently was much mutilated. It was finally corrected and approved by the author himself, and published by me in 1958

through S.R. Press, Trivandrum. It is a small book, of only 48 verses, of very high poetic musical and literary excellence.

Each verse, without exception, was the spontaneous outcome of an experience in samādhi. The divine harmony (gross as well as subtle) overflowing from it has earned for the book a sacred place in thousands of Hindu and even non-Hindu homes, as the favourite text for bhajana and chanting in the mornings and evenings. Having flowed out of samādhi, where the expression of the divine harmony was perfect, each verse has all the potentialities of a virtual mantra. (Several tāntrics have already discovered this secret and are successfully utilizing many of its verses for the purpose of exorcizing ghosts and spirits.)

The depth of sublime emotion that it arouses takes the earnest singer to the very brink of the phenomenal. This work is of immense service to persons who have taken to devotional exercises with the ultimate Reality as their goal.

2. The next book called *Atmārāmam* ('The flower garden of Ātmā', published in 1935 by the author from Shrī Rama Vilasom Press, Quilon) is a continuation of *Rādhā-mādhavam* in the ladder of spiritual progress. It consists of only 69 verses, and though small is more serious and concise. It does not have a continuous theme, but is a collection of individual verses or groups of verses composed at different times for different purposes, all pointing to the ultimate Truth from varying standpoints. Some of these compositions do not represent his own chosen path of direct approach to the ultimate Truth. They were composed for the benefit of different persons following different paths in different orders and yet pointing to the right Absolute.

3. The next and the most important book is the first half of *Ātmānandōpaniṣhad* – separately called *Ātma-darshanam* – in Malayalam, published by the author in 1945 through Reddiar Press, Trivandrum, and the second edition published in 1958 by Vedanta Publishers, Trivandrum through the same press.

   In this volume, he expounds the ultimate Truth in the simplest language, using only direct discrimination and reason, and relying upon nothing other than the Self, the inmost core of one's being, which is the only thing that can never be denied or even thought of to be unreal. He expounds the Truth from various standpoints, in the course of twenty distinct chapters of only 155 verses in all, most of them being in the briefest metre in the language.

A close study of this book, even by an ordinary aspirant, enables him to have an indirect knowledge of Ātmā, the Self. This indirect knowledge of the Truth in turn intensifies his earnestness and sincerity to know the Truth directly, and thus transforms him into a genuine jijnyāsu or a true aspirant, thereby guaranteeing the attainment of a Kāraṇa-guru and liberation.

An English rendering of the book by the author himself, in prose, under the same name *Atma-Darshan* (translated as 'At the Ultimate'), was published in 1946 by the disciples through the Shrī Vidya Samiti, Tiruvannamalai, and offered to Shrī Ātmānanda on his birthday on the 2nd of December, 1946.

4. The next and the last of his books is the second half of *Ātmānandōpaniṣhad*, separately called *Ātma-nirvṛiti*. It was published in Malayalam in 1951 by the author direct through the Reddiar Press, Trivandrum. The English rendering by the author himself, in prose, under the same name *Atma-Nirvṛiti* (translated as 'Freedom and felicity in the Self') was published in 1952 by the Vedanta Publishers, Trivandrum, through the Government Central Press, Trivandrum.

   In the course of the twenty-three short chapters of this book, comprising in all of only 122 simple verses, he expounds the same Truth from different angles of vision. The author himself says about the book: 'In many places the book goes beyond "Atma Darshan" and expounds the Truth from a higher level. A study of this book will be of considerable help to those who have gained Knowledge of the Truth from "Atma Darshan", to make that Knowledge steady and thereby obtain lasting peace.'

   Besides these verses, there are three short articles added at the end of this book, on the two vital problems of man and their solution. These articles are by themselves of immense help to the new aspirant; because in them his need, the goal and the means to be adopted for his spiritual enquiry are properly analysed and clarified. This is the first prerequisite for any successful enquiry.

A Sanskrit translation by Shrī Ravi Varma Thampan, of the two books *Ātma-darshanam* and *Ātma-nirvṛiti*, has also been published by the Vedanta Publishers, Trivandrum, in the year 1955.

The true monument

A word about the future to my dear co-disciples seems indispensable, merely as a presentation of my humble views to them, for what they are worth. A craze for monuments and memorials has seized the society. As soon as some great personality passes away, institutions and mute structures spring up, all over the world. In view of the extraordinary services of self-sacrifice performed in the phenomenal sphere by such heroes and the noble ideals and principles they stood for, such monuments and memorials, being also phenomenal, have a significance and attract the emulation of the younger generation to similar fields of worldly activity. Nothing phenomenal is ever perfect, and therefore progress is towards an ideal and effort is always a necessity.

But in the case of a Sage like Shrī Ātmānanda, who is the ultimate Truth itself and ever perfect and not a personality which is never perfect, the conditions and terms of reference are quite different. No phenomenal monument or memorial can successfully represent the Truth he was and the Truth he lived. But there is only one way out. That is to create living monuments to perpetuate his memory.

He has often repeated to us: 'I am Atma the indivisible. I am there in the heart of everyone of you, in my fullness. You have only to recognize it, and never to forget it.' We do recognize it, no doubt. But unfortunately, we often forget it, in moments of weakness. This has to be overcome by strenuous effort on our part, to remember as often as we can that Truth we already recognize, and thus get established in the ultimate Reality, the Guru. Thus we ourselves become perfect.

The perfect alone can be a monument to the perfect. So let each of the true disciples of Shrī Ātmānanda become a living monument of the Guru as Shrī Ātmānanda was of Shrī Yōgānanda and as Shrī Vivēkānanda was of Shrī Rāmakṛiṣhṇa.

By this I do not mean that everything else about him may be forgotten. No, not in the least. He has left a sacred heritage to humanity in the form of his books and his discourses enshrining the

Truth he stood for and advocated. Both these have to be preserved, in all their pristine purity and grandeur. Ways and means may wisely be designed to achieve this purpose.

Added to this, if at least one or more of his devout disciples succeed in establishing themselves in the ultimate Truth, and are able to live the Truth as shown by Shrī Ātmānanda himself in his life, nothing else can be a more fitting monument to the great Shrī Ātmānanda Guru.

Nitya Tṛipta

Glossary

PRELIMINARY

Ātmika (spiritual). Whatever directs one's attention to, or brings one nearer to Ātmā, the impersonal Self within, is alone spiritual.

Ātmā, 'I'-principle, consciousness, awareness, peace, Truth, Reality, experience, advaita, svarūpa, rasa, anubhava, the being, the Absolute, the Ultimate, the changeless, the self-luminous, ultimate subject, ultimate background, ultimate knowledge, ultimate love, ultimate knower, ultimate perceiver, etc. are all synonyms.

Vidyā-vṛitti, functioning consciousness, higher reason, higher logic, mahā-buddhi, shuddha sattva, etc. are also another set of synonyms.

Truth, in its essence, is absolute and unconditioned, its essential characteristics being changelessness, self-luminosity and peace. It is in this sense that 'Truth' is discussed here. Truth can only be experienced and can never be expressed in words, language being designed for worldly traffic alone. At the most, language can only direct one's attention to the Truth and remove some of the impediments.

Gradation of spiritual advancement:

A *disciple* is a person who longs with sincerity and earnestness to know his own real nature, the ultimate Truth, and thus surrenders his ego unconditionally to a Kāraṇa-guru and takes instructions from him.

A *jīvan-mukta* is the mature disciple who listens to the Truth from the lips of the Guru and visualizes the ultimate Truth then and there.

A *Sage* is a jīvan-mukta who has by continued effort established himself in the ultimate Truth.

A *Guru* is a Sage who, out of compassion for the ignorant, voluntarily undertakes to guide the earnest and sincere aspirants who come to him to the ultimate Truth. He does it as easily and effortlessly as holding a stolen bull by the horn and showing it to the owner for identification or recognition. Such a one is alone said to be a Kāraṇa-guru.

An *Ācārya* is such of the Kāraṇa-gurus who is proficient in all the paths of devotion, yōga and jnyāna, and who has the highest experiences in all the three paths. All these Gurus are usually addressed as Guru-nātha, Guru-dēva, Guru-svāmi and by many other such names showing the highest veneration and endearment.

ALPHABETICAL LIST

Ācārya is the highest class of Kāraṇa-gurus (ultimate teachers), proficient in all the paths of devotion, yōga and jnyāna. [See note 565.]

Ādhāra-cakras are the vital nerve-centres along the spinal chord, chosen for the purpose of yōgic concentration. [See note 1387.]

Adhikāris: Spiritual aspirants of different grades of understanding.

Aham is the 'I'-principle.

Ahankāra [ego] is the sense of one's separateness from everything else. It is also the identification with body, senses and mind. [See note 1004.]

Ahimsa: In the worldly sense, it means 'non-injury'. Spiritually, it means not prompted by anything of the lower self. [See note 545.]

Ajāta-vāda is the vēdāntic perspective emphasizing that nothing other than the real Self (Consciousness) was ever born, ever is, or ever shall be. [See note 1392.]

Ajnyāna: Wrong knowledge.

Anasūyā was the wife of the renowned Sage Atṛi, and an established pati-vratā herself. [See note 507.]

Anātmā: Everything other than Ātmā.

Aphorism (mahāvākya) is usually a short and pointed expression emphasizing the identity of jīva, the life principle, with the Reality. It is intended for the contemplation of the spiritual aspirants under instructions from their Guru. [See note 560.]

Arjuna was the third of the Pāṇḍavas and the greatest archer of the Mahābhārata.

Asambhāvana is the firm belief that an ultimate principle called 'Ātmā' is non-existent.

Asvabhāva is the opposite of one's own real nature. [See note 24.]

Ātmā: The real Self.

Ātma-mūrti is the form of any personal God conceived by the mind, on the background of Ātmā itself.

Ātma-tattva: The truth of the 'I'-principle.

Avadhūtas are a class of spiritual aspirants who practice self-mortification and cultivate aversion to the body, acquiring some yōgic powers on the way. [See note 409.]

Avidyā: Wrong knowledge.

Bhāgavatam is the story of Lord Kṛiṣhṇa's life, graphically described by Shrī Veda-vyāsa.

Bhagavad-gītā is one leg of the tripod of Indian philosophy. It expounds Karma-yōga in particular. It is supposed to be the instructions of Lord Kṛiṣhṇa to his friend and disciple Arjuna on the battlefield.

Bhakta is the aspirant who follows the path of devotion to a personal God.

Bhāva is one's own real nature.

Bhīṣhma was a great prince, who in his boyhood renounced the rights to his kingdom for the sake of his father, and took to the spiritual quest. He became a great yōgin, respected by all alike.

Buddhi: Intellect.

Buddhi-vivēka: Discrimination functioning through the phenomenal intellect. [See note 1449.]

Caitanya was a reputed devotional saint of North India.

Cārvaka was a great intellectual genius of ancient India, who held that there was nothing beyond the apparent world. He was honoured as a ṛiṣhi (saint) for his stubborn earnestness and sincerity in his enquiry. [See note 1253.]

Dakṣhiṇa: Something of phenomenal value placed as a mark of respect and devotion at the feet of the Guru, usually at the termination of a course of study.

Darshana: (1) Ultimate experiences of the Truth recorded by Sages and accepted as vēdāntic authority, like the Upaniṣhads, both ancient and modern. (2) Any objective vision of a personal God (in the mental level).

'Dēshikōktya': 'By the word of my Guru.'

Dharma: Quality [literally, that which is held or supported].

Dharmi: The qualified [the holder or supporter of qualities, which is itself unaffected by the qualities that depend on its support].

Dhyāna: Meditation upon any model or ideal.

Disciple: A spiritual aspirant striving to visualize the ultimate Truth, under instructions from a Kāraṇa-guru.

Dṛishya: That which is perceived.

Gāṇḍīva is the divine bow presented by the God of fire to Arjuna.

Gauḍapāda was a great Sage, who was Shrī Shankara's Guru's Guru.

Jijnyāsu: A true aspirant.

Himsa, in the phenomenal sense, means causing injury or pain to another jīva [living creature]. According to Vēdānta, it means any action prompted by the interest of the lower self.

Hṛidaya-vivēka: Discrimination functioning through the heart. [See note 1449.]

Ignorance: Wrong notion.

Iṣhṭa-dēva: A personal God adopted for the purpose of cultivating devotion.

Īshvara [God], as it existed before creation, is the ultimate Truth itself. But after creation, it is the supposed creator, preserver and destroyer of the universe.

Īshvara-bhāva: The powers of Īshvara, or God in parts.

Jīvan-mukta: A spiritual aspirant who is liberated from bondage during his life itself, by visualizing the ultimate Truth under instructions from a Kāraṇa-guru.

Kailāsa is supposed to be the abode of Lord Shiva on the heights of the Himalayas.

Kāraṇa-brahman: The ultimate Reality viewed as the ultimate cause of the world.

Kāraṇa-guru: A Sage who is established in the ultimate Truth and undertakes to guide spiritual aspirants to the same goal.

Karma: Action of any kind by the body, senses or mind. *Akarma* is actionlessness. [See note 574.]

Karma-sannyāsa is the perfection of the passive principle in man, usually through the path of renunciation and sannyāsa.

Karma-yōga: Doing action disinterestedly. It is the perfection of the active principle in man, and is the theme of the *Bhagavad-gītā*.

Karmattha(?) is one who believes that liberation can be achieved only by the performance of karmas (actions) strictly as ordained in the scriptures.

Kārya-brahman: The impersonal conceived with name and form for any purpose (iṣhṭa-dēva).

Kārya-guru is a teacher who, having not reached the Ultimate, guides students in the study of anything below the ultimate Truth.

Kūṭastha is the witness of the individual jīva or life principle.

Kṣhaṇika-vijnyāni is one of a class who believe that knowledge is momentary or time-limited.

Kuṇḍalinī is the vital energy located at the lower end of the spinal chord. [See note 1387.]

Lakṣhaṇa: Pointer.

Līla: Play.

Mahābhārata: One of the great epics of the Hindus, describing the story of the rivalry between the Pāṇḍavas and the Kauravas – the rival claimants to the same kingdom.

Mahākāsha is the unconditioned space.

Māṇḍūkya-kārikā is a commentary of the *Māṇḍūkyōpaniṣhad* by Shrī Gauḍapāda.

Mantra is a harmonious sound or group of sounds, capable of creating or applying some definite and potential energy, if properly uttered. [See note 379.]

Mantra-dēvata is the deity created by the energy generated by the proper chanting of a mantra.

Mārgas (paths): (1) The *cosmological* path is an objective enquiry into the source of the world and the individual, finally striking an identity between the backgrounds of both. (2) The *direct* path is a subjective enquiry into the changeless principle in the individual, on reaching which you find the world only an appearance on that principle.

Māyā is the illusion which shows the ultimate Reality as the manifested universe.

Mōkṣha-kalā: An art that is conducive to liberation.

Mūla-prakṛiti is the cause and source of the apparent universe.

Nalla-taṅṅaḷ is an old drama full of deep pathos from start to finish.

Nārada is the famous mythological Sage supposed to be traversing the world incessantly in his subtle body, rendering spiritual help to the godly-minded devotees in distress.

Nirguṇa-brahman: The attributeless Reality, which is the background of the individual as well as of the cosmos.

Nirvikalpa-samādhi is the state in which the mind becomes merged in consciousness for a while and there is deep Peace, so long as the state lasts.

Nivṛitti: Liberation.

Padmapāda was one of the devoted disciples of Shrī Shankara.

Pāncālī (Draupadī) was the wife of the Pāṇḍavas and the daughter of the king of Pancāla.

Pāṇḍavas were the five sons of King Pāṇḍu, who were sāttvic devotees of Lord Kṛiṣhṇa. They came out victorious in the battle of the *Mahābhārata*.

Parōkṣha is indirect or formal.

Pati-vratās were the celebrated ladies of ancient India who, by the practice of simple pati-vratya (husband worship), acquired wonderful yōgic powers and purity of heart, to vie even with the great Gods of the supreme trinity.

Pati-vratya was a process of sweet devotional yōga, through which the ideal housewife of ancient India practised chastity and devotion to her husband, considering him as her visible God.

Pauruṣha: The quality of being a puruṣha, the inmost core of one's Self. [See note 281.]

Pitṛis are the subtle thought-forms of departed souls which are supposed to linger in their subtle bodies, awaiting another physical body on rebirth.

Prakaraṇa: Original and independent expression of one's own views regarding the ultimate Truth and its visualization.

Prakṛiti is the active principle in man [as opposed to puruṣha, the passive principle].

Prakriyā is any regular process of analysing the individual or the cosmos and eliminating the changing aspects from the changeless.

Praṇava is the harmonious group of sounds 'a', 'u' and 'mm…' merging into the inaudible, thus representing the ultimate Reality.

Praṇava-yōga is a process of yōgic concentration on the sound 'aum', merging in the inaudible and thus representing its goal, the ultimate Reality.

Prārabdha-karmas are the mature karmas [chains of action] for the fulfilment of which this body and life have been particularly designed.

Prasthānatraya is the tripod of Indian philosophy, comprising of (1) the *Brahma-sūtra*s, (2) the *Dashōpaniṣhads*, and (3) the *Bhagavad-gītā*.

Pratyakṣha (aparōkṣha) literally means perceivable by the sense organs. Spiritually, it means direct or subject to the ultimate experience, and that is the real 'I'-principle.

Puruṣha is the passive principle in man [as opposed to prakṛiti, the active principle].

Rādha-mādhavam is the story of the divine love of Rādhā for Lord Kṛiṣhṇa, and the progress of this love through different stages.

Rāga is the attraction born out of desire for phenomenal pleasure.

Rākṣhasa: A wicked-minded person of very great powers, harassing the sāttvic and the virtuous ones.

Rāma is supposed to be an incarnation of Lord Viṣhṇu. He was the king of Ayōdhya and was the hero of the *Rāmāyaṇa* epic.

Rāvaṇa was the mythological demon king of Lanka, who was killed by Rāma in battle.

Ṛiṣhi is an extremely holy person – in particular, the composer of a sacred mantra, the one who first visualized its deity.

Sādhaka is one who is undergoing any course of regular training.

Sādhana is the process of such training.

Sage is one who has visualized the ultimate Truth and is firmly established in it.

Saguṇa-brahman (the same as kārya-brahman) is usually the form of one's Iṣhṭa-dēva, visualized on the background of the impersonal for the mere convenience of doing devotion to it.

Sahaja state: The natural state.

Sākṣhāt-kāraṇa: The ultimate cause. [See note 1237.]

Samādhi is the pleasurable experience either on the vision of a personal God or during the state of stillness of mind obtained by effort after prolonged yōgic exercises.

Samsāra: The phenomenal experiences of the mind within the circle of birth and death.

Samskāras are the tendencies of past experiences.

Sankalpa: A thought about the future, with or without using the will-power.

Sānkhya philosophy was first founded by Shrī Kapilācārya. It was later on perfected into the Advaita philosophy by other Sages.

Sārasāyana(?): The bed of arrows on which Shrī Bhīṣhma rested, awaiting the auspicious day for leaving his mortal coil.

Sarva-jnyatva is knowing for certain that the essence of everything is one's own real self – the Ātmā. [See note 1389.]

Sāttvika-dēva is the iṣhṭa-deva visualized by an aspirant whose goal is ultimate liberation. [See note 348.]

Sāyujya is the state of temporary merger in and complete identification with one's iṣhṭa-dēva. [See note 1137.]

Shravaṇa: Listening to the Truth from the lips of the Guru. [See note 1237.]

Siddha-dēva is the iṣhṭa-dēva visualized by an aspirant whose goal is any thing short of ultimate liberation. [See note 348.]

Siddhis are powers acquired by the mind as a result of devotion, yōga or jnyāna – the former two being temporary and the latter permanent.

Sphuraṇa is the subjective, self-luminous manifestation of 'I am', without any specific object.

Svabhāva: One's own real nature.

Svadharma: A profession one is accustomed to, either hereditarily or by long practice.

Svarūpa: Real nature.

Svarūpānanda, means one who takes delight in one's own real nature. (It is also one of the many spiritual names given to a disciple on his visualization of the Truth.)

Sva-sthiti: Natural state.

Shyāmantapancaka is a sacred bathing ghat where Lord Kṛiṣhṇa went on a holy pilgrimage, together with the Gōpīs, Gōpas, the Pāṇḍavas and his own family. It was there that the Gōpīs, the chosen disciples of Lord Kṛiṣhṇa, were given the final tattvōpadēsha.

Taoism: A religious system founded by the ancient Chinese philosopher Lao Tsu in the seventh century BC. Their philosophy comes close to Advaita.

Tapas: Austere penance and practice of meditation and such other exercises.

Tattvarāyar was a jīvan-mukta of Tamilnāḍ who was deeply samādhi-minded. Samādhi was an obstacle for him in getting established in the ultimate Truth. So his Guru, Shrī Svarūpānanda, had to apply something like a spiritual shock treatment, to wean him away from his samādhi mania to deep discrimination.

Tattvas: Different aspects of the Truth.

*Tattvōpadēsh*a is the final expounding of the ultimate Truth in the regular order, to the disciple, by the Guru in person.

Tila-havana: Offering of gingelly [sesame] seeds to the holy fire, in propitiation of the pitṛis (thought-forms) of the departed souls.

Triguṇas: The fundamental qualities of (1) *tamas* (inclination to sloth, sleep and sluggishness), (2) *rajas* (inclination to activity and emotions), and (3) *sattva* (balancing the former two, leading the way to peace and Truth).

Trimūrtis: The three broad concepts of Hinduism, namely Brahma as the creator, Viṣhṇu as the preserver, and Shiva as the destroyer of the world.

Tripuṭī: Perceiver, perception and the perceived in every activity.

Turīya is the state of pleasurable stillness of the mind attained by a long course of yōgic exercises and intense effort.

Upādhis: Mediums.

Upaniṣhads, also called shrutis, are recordings of the spiritual experiences of the great Sages of India, both ancient and modern, and recognized as authorities on the ultimate Truth.

Upāsana: Practice of regular devotional exercises to a personal God (iṣhṭa-dēva).

Uttara Rāma Caritam is the story of Shrī Rama after his coronation as king of Ayōdhya.

Vaikuṇṭha: The world and the seat of Lord Viṣhṇu.

Vairāgya is dispassion towards objects, primarily towards one's own body, senses and mind.

Vāsanas: Tendencies of past activities.

Vastu-tantra: Outcome of the ultimate Reality alone.

Vaṭivīshvarattamma was an illiterate lady from a village called Vaṭivīshvaram, on the way to Cape Commorin. She became a renowned Sage of great esteem, by her deep devotion alone to her Guru, without taking to any other kind of sādhana whatsoever. She did not even care to listen to her Guru's spiritual talks; because she was engaged in cooking his food and doing other personal services to her Guru, which she rightly considered by far superior to every other sādhana.

Vendee: Buyer.

Vendor: Seller.

Vicāra-mārga is the path of subjective analysis of the Self – eliminating the non-self, and getting established in the real Self.

Vidyā: Right knowledge.

Vikṣhēpa: Restlessness of the mind.

Viparīta-bhāvana is the thought that you are anything other than Ātmā, the ultimate Reality.

Virāṭ is an all-comprehensive vision of the whole manifested universe.

Vishiṣhṭādvaita: Qualified non-dualism.

Vishva-rūpa: Same as 'virāṭ' above.

Vivēka is discrimination, which may function either through the intellect (buddhi) or through the heart (hṛidaya).

Vṛindāvana is the grazing meadow where Lord Kṛiṣhṇa spent his childhood and boyhood, grazing the cows and playing his divine līlas with the Gōpas and Gōpīs of the village.

Yōga: Any process by which the mind is sought to be controlled or expanded.

Yōga-samādhi is the samādhi (state of stillness of the mind) acquired by dint of long yōgic practices, or by its deep samskāra inherited from previous life.

Yōga-vāsiṣhṭha is the text describing the discourses of Sage Vasiṣhṭha (the Guru) to Shrī Rāma (his disciple) for eighteen days, expounding the ultimate Truth from different standpoints. Here, yōga means jnyāna-yōga.

Terms in Groups of Three or Four

Bhakta, yōgin and *jnyānin* are the three important types of spiritual personalities. The former two are only striving to purify or expand their minds to qualify themselves to take to jnyāna sādhana and to become jnyānins.

Dvaita, Vishiṣhṭādvaita, and *Advaita* are the three recognized approaches to the ultimate Truth. The former two are only preparation courses, to be crowned with Self-realization through Advaita alone.

Shruti, yukti and *anubhava* are the three regular stages through which one rises to the visualization of the ultimate Truth. [See note 1199.]

Shravaṇa, manana and *nididhyāsana:* According to the traditional or cosmological method, these are the three progressive stages of understanding the Truth. [See note 1019.]

Sṛiṣhṭi-dṛiṣhṭi, dṛiṣhṭi-sṛiṣhṭi and *ajāta-vāda* are the three distinct methods of explaining the world from three different levels of understanding, namely from the standpoints of variety, unity and non-duality respectively. [See note 1392.]

Shruti, Smṛiti, Purāṇa and *Itihāsa:* Shrutis (Upaniṣhads) are the authorities on the ultimate Truth and its realization. The latter three classes are subsequent periodical commentaries and explanations in different forms, justifying the assertions of the shrutis.

Index

(To all 3 volumes. References here are to note numbers, not page numbers)

Happiness 101, 141, **148**, **465**, **628**, 836, 1209, 1325, **1360**, **1396**, 1445, *see also* pleasure… *and* enjoyment

Happiness and Peace 178, 322, **333**, **740**, 979

harmony 280, 435, 584, **924-926**, **986**

heart 156, **207**, 253, **282**, **374**, 401, 583, 734, 900, **1179**, 1449

himsa and ahimsa 545

'I'-ness and 'this'-ness 350, 1045, 1373

'I'-principle 3, **6**, **20-22**, 24, **81**, 139, 149, 245, 250, 255, 260, 352, 366, **390**, 394, **436**, 447, **499**, 593, 594, 712, 754, 810, 933, 973, 1007, 1045, **1085**, **1128**, **1224**, 1255, 1358, *see also* Ātmā (Self)

ideas **286**, 297, **399**, 694, 1223, **1284**, 1394, *see also* thought…

identification **144**, 156, 256, **284**, **307**, 309, 404, **1380**, *see also* apparent 'I'…

ignorance **722**, 731, 1095, **1183**, 1287, 1308, **1447**, *see also* causal… *and* deep sleep and…

illusion **247**, **339**, **359**, 513, 735, 785, 816, 1185

illustration and analogy 566, **592**, **748**, 785, 846, 939, 1072, **1245**, 1317

improving the world 108, 439, **770**, **819**, 897

indifference 1046

individuality 192, 438, **814**, 932, **1036**, **1157**

infinite 381

inside and outside 761, 1256, 1378

institutions 223

instruments **60**, **73**, 358, 608, 830

interval (between mentations, perceptions or actions) **5**, 65, 334, **902**, 992, **1010**, 1013, 1086

'It' 291, **981**, **1026**, 1063

jīva *see* apparent 'I'…

jīvan-mukta **54**, **532**, 679, 1116, 1211, 1235, 1251, 1266, **1340**, *see also* Sage…

jnyāna path 161, 685, 1275, 1392

karma and samskāra 498, **574**, 575, 663, **1110**, **1124**

karma-yōga 67, 170, 244, **292**, **538-541**, 678, **1062**, *see also* work

knower *see* witness

knowledge **26**, 101, 233, 384, **411**, 468, **1082**, 1083, 1105-1106, 1130, 1376, **1440**

knowledge and functioning **82**, 145, **175**, 462, 620

knowledge and learning 107, 756, **834**, 1020, 1382

598, 613, 704, **705**, 720, **725**, 727, 746, 763, **771**, **835**, 858, 865, 898-899, 914, 922, 944, 970, 982, 987, **1123**, 1181, 1319, **1390**, 1400, *see also* sahaja… *and* jīvan-mukta

sahaja or natural state **23**, **243**, **464**, 576, 630, 677, 795, 817, **882**

saints and mystics 388, 1104, 1178, **1181**

samādhi 14, 171, 198, **203**, 311, 324, 406, 630, 634, 795, 817, 828, 833, 923, 927, 928, 941, 971, 1052, **1068**, **1109**, **1115**, 1134, **1182**, **1209**, **1231**, 1337, **1364**, 1381

samskāras *see* karma and…

sat-cit-ānanda 27, **192**, 318, 345, 346, 831, 1036, 1192, **1239**, **1272**, 1434

satisfaction 759, **1240**, 1271

sattva, rajas and tamas 170, **538**-540, 937

science 103, **114**, **226**, 861, **1087**, 1147, 1217, 1223

scriptures *see* shāstras…

secrecy **50**, 254

security 1358, 1362

seeing *see* perception… *and* form and…

self *see* Ātmā… *and* 'I'-principle *and* apparent 'I'…

self-luminosity 112, **294**, 392, **410**, 786, 1395

Shakespeare 679

Shankara, Shrī 129, 443, 473, **1205**

shāstras (scriptures) 44, 177, 236, **238**, 240, 254, 442, **547**, 629, 829, 893, 972, **1099**, 1236, 1244, 1302

Shivōham 1092

siddhis or powers 332, **905**, 943, 1146

sincerity and earnestness 194, 282, 632

sleep knowingly 1, **39**, 112, 597, **599**, **669**, **879**, *see also* deep sleep

social service 108, 271, 458, 684, 746, 760, 762, 897, 987, **1078**, **1112**, 1113, 1383, 1413

Socrates 732

solipsism 1011

sound *see* music *and* language

space and time **121**, 164, **323**, 469, 648, **1002**, 1355, **1409**

spiritual name 787, 909

spiritual progress 485, 519, 726, **884**, **1074**, 1162

spirituality 28, 57, 134, **135**, 361, **363**, 407, 760, 918, **1076**, **1093**, 1108, 1216, 1302, **1420**

spontaneity 1096

static and dynamic 480, 517, 783

subjective correction 17, **151**, 167, **439**, 670

subject-object relationship 371, **757**, 917, 1187, **1294**, 1326, 1327, **1367**, **1448**

suicide 664, 709, 961, 1260

superimposition 318, 566

surrender 316, 798, 1090

svadharma 485

talking about Truth **50**, **85**, 254, 546, **745**, **857**, 870, 908, 911, 970, 1015, 1135, **1388**

tamas *see* sattva…

tears 622, 971

Tennyson 39

texts *see* shāstras… *and* books

theoretical and practical 122, 491, 1021, **1080**, 1323, 1438

thing in itself **16**, 47, 176, 786, **978**, **1432**, *see also* Reality

thought **267**, 313, **389**, 400, 491, **504**, 562, **610**, 615, 618, **791**, 801, **864**, 903, 913, 1047, **1173**, 1180, 1226, **1333-1334**, 1350, *see also* ideas

thoughts and feelings **104**, 179, **285**, 375, 885, **1190**

time 275, 362, **556**, 653, **718**, 902, **931**, 1141, *see also* space and…

translation 354

transmigration *see* rebirth

tripuṭī 425, **446**, 642, 954, **968**, 1029

Truth 345, 415, 428, 544, 764, 769, **779**, 936, **975**, 1031, 1046, **1186**, 1222, **1257**, 1261, **1331-1332**, 1374, **1423**, 1441, 1443, *see also* talking about… *and* recognizing…

unconscious *see* ignorance *and* causal ignorance *and* deep sleep

understanding 338-339, 450, **607**, 682, 839, **847**, **1009**, **1188**, 1217, 1391

unity and diversity **76**, 103, 343, 344, 368, **486**, **496**, 608, 609, 827, 907, **1022**, 1084, *see also* connection *and* change…

universal **440**, 886, 916, 1078

values 1271

variety *see* unity…

Vēdānta *see* Advaita…

vicāra-mārga *see* paths to Truth – the direct method

vidyā-vṛitti (higher reason) **111**, 132, 330, 856, 867, 1017, 1053, **1107**, 1120, **1125**, **1201**, 1356, **1449**, *see also* reason

virtue 673, *see also* morality

visions **195**, 235, 349, 950, 1296, 1377

visualization and establishment 15, 30-31, 36, 208, 214, **298**, 319, 370, **562**, **618**, 711, 934, 990, 1018, **1050**, 1065, **1075**, **1122**, 1124, **1153-1154**, 1160, **1175**, 1232, 1431, 1443, *see also* realization

69338190R00166

Made in the USA
San Bernardino, CA
14 February 2018